# Latin American
# **Spanish**
## phrase book

PERIPLUS

Published by Periplus Editions (HK) Ltd. with editorial offices at
364 Innovation Drive, North Clarendon, Vermont 05759 U.S.A.
and 130 Joo Seng Road #06-01, Singapore 368357.

LCC Card No.: 99-066978
ISBN-13: 978-962-59 3-805-9
ISBN-10: 962-593-805-2

Distributed by:

*Asia Pacific*
**Berkeley Books Pte. Ltd.**
130 Joo Seng Road #06-01
Singapore 368357
Tel: (65) 6280-1330   Fax: (65) 6280-6290
inquiries@periplus.com.sg
www.periplus.com

*North America, Latin America & Europe*
**Tuttle Publishing**
364 Innovation Drive
North Clarendon, VT 05759-9436 U.S.A.
Tel: 1 (802) 773-8930
Fax: 1 (802) 773-6993
info@tuttlepublishing.com
www.tuttlepublishing.com

*Japan*
**Tuttle Publishing**
Yaekari Building, 3rd Floor
5-4-12 Osaki
Shinagawa-ku
Tokyo 141-0032
Tel: (81) 3 5437-0171
Fax: (81) 3 5437-0755
tuttle-sales@gol.com

*Indonesia*
**PT Java Books Indonesia**
Kawasan Industri Pulogadung
Jl. Rawa Gelam IV No. 9
Jakarta 13930
Tel: (62) 21 4682-1088
Fax: (62) 21 461-0206
cs@javabooks.co.id

11 10 09 08 07    10 9 8 7 6 5

Printed in Singapore

# Contents

# Introduction

● **Welcome to the Periplus Essential Phrase Books series, covering the world's most popular languages and containing everything you'd expect from a comprehensive language series. They're concise, accessible, and easy to understand, and you'll find them indispensable on your trip abroad.**

Each guide is divided into 15 themed sections and starts with a pronunciation table that explains the phonetic pronunciation for all the words and phrases you'll need to know for your trip. At the back of the book is an extensive word list and grammar guide that will help you construct basic sentences in your chosen language.

Throughout the book you'll come across colored boxes with a ⬤ beside them. These are designed to help you if you can't understand what your listeners are saying to you. Hand the book over to them and encourage them to point to the appropriate answer to the question you are asking.

Other colored boxes in the book—this time without the symbol—give alphabetical listings of themed words with their English translations beside them.

For extra clarity, we have put all English words and phrases in **black**, foreign language terms in red, and their phonetic pronunciation in *italic*.

This phrase book covers all subjects you are likely to come across during the course of your visit, from reserving a room for the night to ordering food and drink at a restaurant and what to do if your car breaks down or you lose your traveler's checks and money. With over 2,000 commonly used words and essential phrases at your fingertips, you can rest assured that you will be able to get by in all situations, so let the Essential Phrase Book become your passport to a secure and enjoyable trip!

# Pronunciation table

The pronunciation provided should be read as if it were English, bearing in mind the following main points:

## Vowels

Vowels in Spanish are very open

| a | is like **a** in ope**r**a, | *ah* | as in **casa** | *kahsah* |
|---|---|---|---|---|
| e | is like **e** in egg, | *eh* | as in **esta** | *ehstah* |
| i | is like **ee** in seen, | *ee* | as in **isla** | *eeslah* |
| o | is like **o** in over, | *oh* | as in **hotel** | *ohtehl* |
| u | is like **oo** in room, | *oo* | as in **uno** | *oonoh* |
| y | is like **ee** in seen, | *ee* | as in **y** | *ee* |

the diphthong **ay** is pronounced as in aisle or eye

| | | as in **hay** | *eye* |
|---|---|---|---|

## Consonants

Consonants are as in English, pronounced less clearly, except

| b/v | are pronounced roughly the same | | |
|---|---|---|---|
| | | as in **vamos** | *bahmohs* |
| c | before e and i is pronounced **s** | | |
| | | as in **la acera** | *lah ahsehrah* |
| | before a,o and u is hard | | |
| | | as in **cosa** | *kohsah* |
| cu | before another vowel is pronounced like **cw** | | |
| | | as in **la cuenta** | *lah kwehntah* |
| d | is like **th** in **the** | | |
| | | as in **donde** | *thawnthay* |
| g | before e and i is soft and is like the Scottish **ch** as in lo**ch**, | | |
| | | as in **la gente** | *lah hehnteh* |
| | before a, o and u is hard | | |
| | | as in **gato** | *gahtoh* |
| gu | before e and i is pronounced as hard **g** | | |
| | | as in **la guía** | *geeah* |
| | before a, o and u is pronounced like **gw** | | |
| | | as in **guapo** | *gwahpoh* |
| gü | before e and i is pronounced like **gw** | | |
| | | as in **lingüística** | *leengwees-teekah* |
| h | is silent | | |
| j | is like the soft **g** | as in **jarra** | *hahrrah* |
| ll | is like **lli** in billion | as in **llave** | *lyahbeh* |
| ñ | is like **ni** in onion | as in **año** | *ahnyoh* |
| r | is rolled; **rr** is a longer roll | | |
| z | is pronounced **s** | as in **taza** | *tahsah* |

The stress normally falls on the last syllable of the word (**hotel**), except that words ending in a vowel (not including **y**) or in n or s (**casa, casas**) are stressed on the next to the last syllable. All exceptions are indicated by a written acute accent (**Córdoba**, kohrdohbah). Note: Unlike Spain, soft **c** and **z** are pronounced **s** in all Latin-American countries.

# Useful lists

# **U**seful lists

## **1** .1 **T**oday or tomorrow?

| | |
|---|---|
| What day is it today? _____ | ¿Qué día es hoy? |
| | *keh deeah ehs oy?* |
| Today's Monday _____ | Hoy es lunes |
| | *oy ehs loonehs* |
| – Tuesday _____ | Hoy es martes |
| | *oy ehs mahrtehs* |
| – Wednesday _____ | Hoy es miércoles |
| | *oy ehs myehrkohlehs* |
| – Thursday _____ | Hoy es jueves |
| | *oy ehs <u>h</u>ooehbehs* |
| – Friday _____ | Hoy es viernes |
| | *oy ehs byehrnehs* |
| – Saturday _____ | Hoy es sábado |
| | *oy ehs sahbahdoh* |
| – Sunday _____ | Hoy es domingo |
| | *oy ehs dohmeengoh* |
| in January _____ | en enero |
| | *ehn ehnehroh* |
| since February _____ | desde febrero |
| | *dehsdeh fehbrehroh* |
| in spring _____ | en primavera |
| | *ehn preemahbehrah* |
| in summer _____ | en verano |
| | *ehn behrahnoh* |
| in autumn _____ | en otoño |
| | *ehn ohtohnyoh* |
| in winter _____ | en invierno |
| | *ehn eenbyehrno* |
| 1999 _____ | mil novecientos noventa y nueve |
| | *meel nohbehsyentohs nohbehntah ee* |
| | *nwehbeh* |
| the twentieth century _____ | el siglo XX (veinte) |
| | *ehl seegloh beheenteh* |
| What's the date today? ____ | ¿Qué día es hoy? |
| | *keh deeah ehs oy?* |
| Today's the 24th _____ | Hoy es 24 (veinticuatro) |
| | *oy ehs beheenteekwahtroh* |
| Monday 3 November _____ 1999 | lunes 3 (tres) de noviembre de 1999 (mil novecientos noventa y nueve) |
| | *loonehs trehs deh nohbyehmbreh deh meel nohbehthyehntohs nohbehntah ee nwehbeh* |
| in the morning _____ | por la mañana |
| | *pohr lah mahnyahnah* |
| in the afternoon _____ | por la tarde |
| | *pohr lah tahrdeh* |
| in the evening _____ | por la noche |
| | *pohr lah nohcheh* |
| at night _____ | por la noche |
| | *pohr lah nohcheh* |
| this morning _____ | esta mañana |
| | *ehstah mahnyahnah* |

8

| this afternoon | esta tarde |
| | *ehstah tahrdeh* |
| this evening | esta noche |
| | *ehstah nohcheh* |
| tonight | esta noche |
| | *ehstah nohcheh* |
| last night | anoche |
| | *ahnohcheh* |
| this week | esta semana |
| | *ehstah sehmahnah* |
| next month | el mes próximo |
| | *ehl mehs prohxeemoh* |
| last year | el año pasado |
| | *ehl ahnyo pahsahdoh* |
| next... | el/la... próximo/a |
| | *ehl/lah... prohxeemoh/ah* |
| in...days/weeks/ | dentro de...días/semanas/meses/años |
| months/years | *dehntroh deh...* |
| | *deeahs/sehmahnahs/mehsehs/ahnyohs* |
| ...weeks ago | hace...semanas |
| | *ahse...sehmahnahs* |
| day off | día libre |
| | *deeah leebreh* |

## .2 Legal Holidays

● **Some common public holidays are listed.** You should consult a guide book for dates which may vary between countries and from year to year.

| New Year's Day (January 1) | Año nuevo |
| Maundy Thursday | Jueves Santo |
| Good Friday | Viernes Santo |
| Holy Saturday | Sabado de Gloria |
| Labour Day (May 1) | Día del Trabajo |
| Independence Day | Día de la Independencia |
| Day of the Americas (October 12) | Día de las Américas |
| Revolution Day | Día de la Revolución |
| Christmas Day (December 25) | Navidad |

## .3 What time is it?

| What time is it? | ¿Qué hora es? |
| | *keh ohrah ehs?* |
| It's nine o'clock | Son las nueve |
| | *sohn lahs nwehbeh* |
| – five past ten | Son las diez y cinco |
| | *sohn lahs dyes ee seenkoh* |
| – a quarter past eleven | Son las once y cuarto |
| | *sohn lahs ohnseh ee kwahrtoh* |
| – twenty past twelve | Son las doce y veinte |
| | *sohn lahs dohse ee beheenteh* |
| – half past one | Es la una y media |
| | *ehs lah oonah ee mehdyah* |
| – twenty–five to three | Son veinticinco para las tres |
| | *sohn beheenteeseenkoh para lahs trehs* |

Useful lists

| | | |
|---|---|---|
| – a quarter to four | Son cuarto para las cuatro | *sohn kwahrtoh pahrah lahs kwahtroh* |
| – ten to five | Son diez para las cinco | *sohn dyehs pahrah lahs seenkoh* |
| – twelve noon | Son las doce del mediodía | *sohn lahs dohseh dehl mehdyohdeeah* |
| – midnight | Son las doce de la noche | *sohn lahs dohseh deh lah nohcheh* |
| half an hour | media hora | *mehdyah ohrah* |
| What time? | ¿A qué hora? | *ah keh ohrah?* |
| What time can I come round? | ¿A qué hora puedo pasar? | *ah keh ohrah pwehdoh pahsahr?* |
| At... | A las... | *ah lahs...* |
| After... | Después de las... | *dehspwehs deh lahs...* |
| Before... | Antes de las... | *ahntehs deh lahs...* |
| Between...and... | Entre las...y las... | *ehntreh lahs...ee lahs...* |
| From...to... | De las...a las... | *deh lahs...ah lahs...* |
| In...minutes | Dentro de...minutos | *dehntroh deh...meenootohs* |
| – an hour | Dentro de una hora | *dehntroh deh oonah ohrah* |
| – ...hours | Dentro de...horas | *dehntroh deh...ohrahs* |
| – a quarter of an hour | Dentro de un cuarto de hora | *dehntroh deh oon kwahrtoh deh ohrah* |
| – three quarters of an hour | Dentro de tres cuartos de hora | *dehntroh deh trehs kwahrtohs deh ohrah* |
| early/late | muy temprano/tarde | *mwee tehmprahnoh/tahrdeh* |
| on time | a tiempo | *ah tyehmpoh* |
| summer opening hours | horario de verano | *ohrahryoh deh behrahnoh* |
| winter opening hours | horario de invierno | *ohrahryoh deh eenbyehrnoh* |

## **1** .4 One, two, three...

| | | |
|---|---|---|
| 0 | cero | *sehroh* |
| 1 | uno | *oonoh* |
| 2 | dos | *dohs* |
| 3 | tres | *trehs* |
| 4 | cuatro | *kwahtroh* |
| 5 | cinco | *seenkoh* |
| 6 | seis | *sehees* |
| 7 | siete | *syehteh* |
| 8 | ocho | *ohchoh* |
| 9 | nueve | *nwehbeh* |
| 10 | diez | *dyes* |
| 11 | once | *ohnseh* |

| | | |
|---|---|---|
| 12 _____ | doce | *dohseh* |
| 13 _____ | trece | *trehseh* |
| 14 _____ | catorce | *kahtohrseh* |
| 15 _____ | quince | *keenseh* |
| 16 _____ | dieciséis | *dyeseesehees* |
| 17 _____ | diecisiete | *dyeseesyehteh* |
| 18 _____ | dieciocho | *dyeseeohchoh* |
| 19 _____ | diecinueve | *dyeseenwehbe* |
| 20 _____ | veinte | *beheenteh* |
| 21 _____ | veintiuno | *beheenteeoonoh* |
| 22 _____ | veintidós | *beheenteheedohs* |
| 30 _____ | treinta | *treheentah* |
| 31 _____ | treinta y uno | *treheentah ee oonoh* |
| 32 _____ | treinta y dos | *treheentah ee dohs* |
| 40 _____ | cuarenta | *kwahrehntah* |
| 50 _____ | cincuenta | *seenkwehntah* |
| 60 _____ | sesenta | *sehsehntah* |
| 70 _____ | setenta | *sehtehntah* |
| 80 _____ | ochenta | *ohchehntah* |
| 90 _____ | noventa | *nohvehntah* |
| 100 _____ | cien | *syehn* |
| 101 _____ | ciento uno | *syehntoh oonoh* |
| 110 _____ | ciento diez | *syehntoh dyes* |
| 120 _____ | ciento veinte | *syehntoh beheenteh* |
| 200 _____ | doscientos | *dohsyehntohs* |
| 300 _____ | trescientos | *trehsyehntohs* |
| 400 _____ | cuatrocientos | *kwahtrohsyehntohs* |
| 500 _____ | quinientos | *keenyehntohs* |
| 600 _____ | seiscientos | *seheesyehntohs* |
| 700 _____ | setecientos | *sehtehsyehntohs* |
| 800 _____ | ochocientos | *ohchohsyehntohs* |
| 900 _____ | novecientos | *nohbehsyentohs* |
| 1000 _____ | mil | *meel* |
| 1100 _____ | mil cien | *meel syehn* |
| 2000 _____ | dos mil | *dohs meel* |
| 10,000 _____ | diez mil | *dyes meel* |
| 100,000 _____ | cien mil | *syehn meel* |
| 1,000,000 _____ | un millón | *oon meelyohn* |
| 1st _____ | primero | *preemehroh* |
| 2nd _____ | segundo | *sehgoondoh* |
| 3rd _____ | tercero | *tehrsehroh* |
| 4th _____ | cuarto | *kwahrtoh* |
| 5th _____ | quinto | *keentoh* |
| 6th _____ | sexto | *sehxtoh* |
| 7th _____ | séptimo | *sehpteemoh* |
| 8th _____ | octavo | *ohktahboh* |
| 9th _____ | noveno | *nohbehnoh* |
| 10th _____ | décimo | *dehseemoh* |
| 11th _____ | undécimo | *oondehseemoh* |
| 12th _____ | duodécimo | *doo-ohdehseemoh* |
| 13th _____ | decimotercero | *dehseemohtehrsehroh* |
| 14th _____ | decimocuarto | *dehseemohkwahrtoh* |
| 15th _____ | decimoquinto | *dehseemohkeentoh* |

| | | |
|---|---|---|
| 16th _____ | decimosexto | *dehseemohsehxtoh* |
| 17th _____ | decimoséptimo | *dehseemosehpteemoh* |
| 18th _____ | decimoctavo | *dehseemohktahboh* |
| 19th _____ | decimonoveno | *dehseemonobenoh* |
| 20th _____ | vigésimo | *beeheseemoh* |
| 21st _____ | vigesimoprimero | *beeheseemohpreemeroh* |
| 22nd _____ | vigesimosegundo | *beeheseemohsegoondoh* |
| 30th _____ | trigésimo | *treeheseemoh* |
| 100th _____ | centésimo | *sentehseemoh* |
| 1,000th _____ | milésimo | *meelehseemoh* |

| | |
|---|---|
| once _____ | una vez |
| | *oonah behs* |
| twice _____ | dos veces |
| | *dos behses* |
| double _____ | el doble |
| | *ehl dohbleh* |
| triple _____ | el triple |
| | *ehl treepleh* |
| half _____ | la mitad |
| | *lah meetath* |
| a quarter _____ | un cuarto |
| | *oon kwartoh* |
| a third _____ | un tercio |
| | *oon tehrsyoh* |
| a couple, a few, some _____ | unos, algunos |
| | *oonohs, algoonohs* |

| | |
|---|---|
| 2 + 4 = 6 _____ | dos más cuatro, seis |
| | *dohs mahs kwahtroh, sehees* |
| 4 – 2 = 2 _____ | cuatro menos dos, dos |
| | *kwahtroh mehnohs dohs, dohs* |
| 2 x 4 = 8 _____ | dos por cuatro, ocho |
| | *dohs pohr kwahtroh, ohchoh* |
| 4 ÷ 2 = 2 _____ | cuatro dividido entre dos, dos |
| | *kwahtroh deebeedeedoh ehntreh dohs, dohs* |

| | |
|---|---|
| odd/even _____ | par/impar |
| | *pahr/eempahr* |
| total _____ | (en) total |
| | *(ehn) tohtahl* |
| 6 x 9 _____ | seis por nueve |
| | *sehees pohr nwehbeh* |

## 1 .5 The weather

| | |
|---|---|
| Is the weather going _____ to be good/bad? | ¿Hará buen/mal tiempo? |
| | *ahrah bwehn/mahl tyehmpoh?* |
| Is it going to get _____ colder/hotter? | ¿Hará más frío/calor? |
| | *ahrah mahs freeoh/kahlohr?* |
| What temperature is it _____ going to be? | ¿Cuántos grados hará? |
| | *kwahntohs grahdohs ahrah?* |
| Is it going to rain? _____ | ¿Va a llover? |
| | *bah ah lyohbehr?* |
| Is there going to be a _____ storm? | ¿Tendremos tormenta? |
| | *tehndrehmohs tohrmehntah?* |

| Is it going to snow? | ¿Va a nevar? |
| | *bah ah nehbahr?* |
| Is it going to freeze? | ¿Va a helar? |
| | *bah ah ehlahr?* |
| Is the thaw setting in? | ¿Comenzará el deshielo? |
| | *kohmehnsahrah ehl dehsyehloh* |
| Is it going to be foggy? | ¿Habrá niebla? |
| | *ahbrah nyehblah?* |
| Is there going to be a thunderstorm? | ¿Habrá tormenta eléctrica? |
| | *ahbrah tohrmehntah ehlehktreekah?* |
| The weather's changing | Va a cambiar el tiempo |
| | *bah ah kahmbyahr ehl tyehmpoh* |
| It's cooling down | Va a refrescar |
| | *bah ah rehfrehskahr* |
| What's the weather going to be like today/tomorrow? | ¿Qué tiempo hará hoy/mañana? |
| | *keh tyehmpoh ahrah oy/mahnyahnah?* |

| | | |
|---|---|---|
| algo nublado/nublado | granizo | ola de calor |
| light/heavy clouds | hail | heat wave |
| bochornoso | ...grados (bajo/sobre cero) | pesado |
| stormy | ...degrees (above/below zero) | muggy |
| bueno | helada | sofocante |
| fine | (black) ice | scorching hot |
| caluroso | húmedo | soleado |
| hot | damp | sunny |
| chubasco | huracán | suave |
| shower | hurricane | mild |
| cielo cubierto | llovizna | tormenta eléctrica |
| overcast | drizzle | thunderstorm |
| desapacible | lluvia | vendaval |
| bleak | rain | gale |
| despejado | lluvioso | ventoso |
| clear | wet | windy |
| escarcha | niebla | viento |
| frost | fog | wind |
| fresco | nieve | viento leve /moderado/ fuerte |
| chilly | snow | light/moderate/ strong wind |
| frío | nublado | tempestad |
| cold | cloudy | squall |

## .6 Here, there...

*See also 5.1 Asking for directions*

| here/there | aquí/allá |
| | *ahkee/ahlyah* |
| somewhere/nowhere | en alguna/ninguna parte |
| | *ehn algoonah/neengoonah pahrteh* |
| everywhere | en todas partes |
| | *ehn tohdahs pahrtehs* |
| far away/nearby | lejos/cerca |
| | *lehhos/sehrkah* |
| right/left | a la derecha/izquierda |
| | *ah lah dehrehchah/eeskyehrdah* |

**Useful lists**

|  |  |
|---|---|
| to the right/left of _____ | a la derecha/izquierda de |
| | *ah lah dehrehchah/eeskyehrdah deh* |
| straight ahead _____ | todo recto |
| | *tohdoh rehktoh* |
| via _____ | pasando por |
| | *pahsahndoh pohr* |
| in _____ | en |
| | *ehn* |
| on _____ | sobre |
| | *sohbreh* |
| under _____ | debajo de |
| | *dehbahhoh deh* |
| against _____ | contra |
| | *kohntrah* |
| opposite _____ | frente a |
| | *frehnteh ah* |
| next to _____ | al lado de |
| | *ahl lahdoh deh* |
| near _____ | junto a |
| | *hoontoh ah* |
| in front of _____ | delante de |
| | *dehlahnteh deh* |
| in the center _____ | en el medio |
| | *ehn ehl mehdyoh* |
| forward _____ | hacia adelante |
| | *ahsyah ahdehlanteh* |
| down _____ | (hacia) abajo |
| | *(ahsyah) ahbahhoh* |
| up _____ | (hacia) arriba |
| | *(ahsya) ahrreebah* |
| inside _____ | (hacia) adentro |
| | *(ahsya) ahdehntroh* |
| outside _____ | (hacia) afuera |
| | *(ahsya) ahfwehrah* |
| behind _____ | (hacia) atrás |
| | *(ahsya) ahtrahs* |
| at the front _____ | delante |
| | *dehlahnteh* |
| at the back _____ | detrás |
| | *dehtrahs* |
| in the north _____ | en el norte |
| | *ehn ehl nohrteh* |
| to the south _____ | hacia el sur |
| | *ahsya ehl soor* |
| from the west _____ | del oeste |
| | *dehl ohehsteh* |
| from the east _____ | del este |
| | *dehl ehsteh* |
| ...of _____ | al...de |
| | *ahl...deh* |

### .7 What does that sign say?

*See 5.4 Traffic signs*

---

| | | |
|---|---|---|
| abierto/cerrado<br>**open/closed** | horario (de apertura)<br>**opening hours** | prohibido pisar el<br>césped<br>**keep off the grass** |
| agua no potable<br>**not drinking water** | información<br>**information** | información<br>**inquiries** |
| alta tensión<br>**high voltage** | liquidación (por<br>cese)<br>**close-out sale** | rebajas<br>**clearance** |
| elevador<br>**elevator** | no funciona<br>**out of order** | recepción<br>**reception** |
| caballeros<br>**gents/gentlemen** | no tocar<br>**please do not touch** | recién pintado<br>**wet paint** |
| caja<br>**cashier** | peligro<br>**danger** | reservado<br>**reserved** |
| completo<br>**full** | peligro de incendio<br>**fire hazard** | saldos<br>**sale** |
| propiedad privada<br>**private (property)** | ...piso<br>**...floor** | salida<br>**exit** |
| cuidado con el perro<br>**beware of the dog** | primeros auxilios<br>**first aid** | salida de<br>emergencia/salida<br>de socorro |
| cuidado, escalón<br>**watch your step** | prohibido el paso<br>**no entry** | **emergency exit** |
| entrada<br>**entrance** | prohibido fotografiar<br>**no photographs** | se alquila<br>**for hire** |
| entrada libre<br>**free admission** | prohibido fumar<br>**no smoking** | se ruega no molestar<br>**do not disturb** |
| escalera<br>**stairs** | prohibido hacer<br>fuego<br>**no open fires** | se vende<br>**for sale** |
| escalera de<br>incendios<br>**fire escape** | prohibido para<br>animales<br>**no pets allowed** | damas<br>**ladies** |
| escalera mecánica<br>**escalator** | | baños<br>**bathrooms** |
| freno de emergencia<br>**emergency brake** | | empujar/jalar (tirar)<br>**push/pull** |

###  .8 Telephone alphabet

Pronouncing the alphabet, e.g. A as in Ana

| | | | |
|---|---|---|---|
| a | *ah* | de Ana | *deh ahnah* |
| b | *beh* | de bueno | *deh bwehnoh* |
| c | *seh* | de Carlos | *deh kahrlohs* |
| ch | *cheh* | de chocolate | *deh choh kohlahteh* |
| d | *deh* | de dedo | *deh dehdoh* |
| e | *eh* | de Eduardo | *deh ehdwahrdoh* |
| f | *hefeh* | de Francia | *deh frahnthyah* |
| g | *heh* | de gato | *deh gahtoh* |
| h | *ahcheh* | de historia | *de eestohryah* |
| I | *ee* | de Inés | *deh eenehs* |
| j | *hohtah* | de José | *deh hohseh* |
| k | *kah* | de Kilo | *deh keeloh* |

15

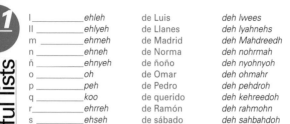

| | | | |
|---|---|---|---|
| l | _ehleh_ | de Luis | _deh lwees_ |
| ll | _ehlyeh_ | de Llanes | _deh lyahnehs_ |
| m | _ehmeh_ | de Madrid | _deh Mahdreedh_ |
| n | _ehneh_ | de Norma | _deh nohrmah_ |
| ñ | _ehnyeh_ | de ñoño | _deh nyohnyoh_ |
| o | _oh_ | de Omar | _deh ohmahr_ |
| p | _peh_ | de Pedro | _deh pehdroh_ |
| q | _koo_ | de querido | _deh kehreedoh_ |
| r | _ehrreh_ | de Ramón | _deh rahmohn_ |
| s | _ehseh_ | de sábado | _deh sahbahdoh_ |
| t | _teh_ | de Teresa | _deh tehrehsah_ |
| u | _oo_ | de Ulises | _deh ooleesehs_ |
| v | _beh_ | de Victor | _deh beektohr_ |
| w | _dohblehbeh_ | de Washington | _deh washeengtohn_ |
| x | _ehkees_ | de Xiquena | _deh <u>h</u>eekehnah_ |
| y | _ee_ | griega | _gryehgah_ |
| z | _saytah_ | de Zaragoza | _deh sahragosah_ |

## **1** .9 **P**ersonal details

| | |
|---|---|
| surname | apellido<br>_ahpehlyeedoh_ |
| christian/given name(s) | nombre<br>_nohmbreh_ |
| initials | iniciales<br>_eeneeyahlehs_ |
| address (street/number) | dirección (calle/número)<br>_deerehksyohn (kahlyeh/noomehroh)_ |
| post code/town | código postal/población<br>_cohdeegoh pohstahl/pohblahsyon_ |
| sex (male/female) | sexo (v = varón, m = mujer)<br>_sehksoh (v = bahrohn, m = moo<u>h</u>ehr)_ |
| nationality | nacionalidad<br>_nahsyohnahleedah_ |
| date of birth | fecha de nacimiento<br>_fehchah deh nahseemyehntoh_ |
| place of birth | lugar de nacimiento<br>_loogahr deh naseemyehntoh_ |
| occupation | profesión<br>_profehsyohn_ |
| married/single/divorced | casado, casada/soltero, soltera/<br>divorciado, divorciada<br>_kahsahdoh, kahsahdah/sohltehroh,<br>sohltehrah/deebohrsyahdoh,<br>deebohrsyahdah_ |
| widowed | viuda/viudo<br>_byoodah/byoodoh_ |
| (number of) children | (número de) hijos<br>_(noomehroh deh) ee<u>h</u>ohs_ |
| passport/identity<br>card/driving license/<br>number, place and date<br>of issue | pasaporte/carnet de identidad/permiso de<br>conducir/número, lugar y fecha de<br>expedición<br>_pahsahpohrteh/kahrneh deh<br>eedehnteedahdh/pehrmeesoh deh<br>kohndooseer/noomehroh, loogahr ee fehchah<br>deh ehkspehdeesyohn_ |

# Courtesies

17

## **C**ourtesies

● **Always** use the formal **Usted** (you) in preference to the informal **tu** (you). The misuse of **tu** can be, at best, rude and, at worst, insulting.

### .1 **G**reetings

| | |
|---|---|
| Hello _____ | Hola, buenos días |
| | *ohlah, bwehnohs deeahs* |
| Hello, Peter _____ | Hola, Pedro |
| | *ohlah, pehdroh* |
| Hi, Helen _____ | Qué tal, Elena |
| | *keh tahl, ehlehnah* |
| Good morning, madam____ | Buenos días, señora (before midday) |
| | *bwehnohs deeahs, sehnyohrah* |
| Good afternoon, sir_____ | Buenas tardes, señor (after midday) |
| | *bwehnahs tahrdehs, sehnyohr* |
| Good evening_____ | Buenas tardes (before 7pm), buenas noches (after 7pm) |
| | *bwehnahs tahrdehs, bwehnahs nohchehs* |
| How are you? _____ | ¿Qué tal? |
| | *keh tahl?* |
| Fine, thank you, and you?__ | Muy bien, ¿y usted? |
| | *mwee byehn, ee oostehdh?* |
| Very well _____ | Estupendo |
| | *ehstoopehndoh* |
| Not very well _____ | Regular |
| | *rehgoolahr* |
| Not too bad_____ | Tirando |
| | *teerando* |
| I'd better be going _____ | Bueno, me voy |
| | *bwehnoh, meh boy* |
| I have to be going. _____ Someone's waiting for me | Tengo que irme. Me están esperando |
| | *tehngoh keh eermeh, meh ehstahn ehspehrahndoh* |
| Bye!_____ | ¡Adiós! |
| | *ahdyohs!* |
| Good-bye_____ | Hasta luego |
| | *ahstah lwehgoh* |
| See you soon _____ | Hasta pronto |
| | *ahstah prohntoh* |
| See you later _____ | Hasta luego |
| | *ahstah lwehgoh* |
| See you in a little while ____ | Hasta ahora |
| | *ahstah ahohrah* |
| Sleep well _____ | Que descanse |
| | *keh dehskahnseh* |
| Good night _____ | Buenas noches |
| | *bwehnahs nohchehs* |
| All the best _____ | Que le vaya bien |
| | *keh leh bahyah byehn* |
| Have fun_____ | Que se divierta, que lo pase bien |
| | *keh seh deebyehrtah, keh loh pahseh byehn* |
| Good luck_____ | Mucha suerte |
| | *moochah swehrteh* |

|  |  |  |
|---|---|---|
| Have a nice vacation _____ | Felices vacaciones | *fehleesehs bahkahsyohnehs* |
| Have a good trip _____ | Buen viaje | *bwehn byahheh* |
| Thank you, you too _____ | Gracias, igualmente | *grahsyahs, eegwahlmehnteh* |
| Say hello to...for me _____ | Saludos a... | *sahloodohs ah...* |
| Who? _____ | ¿Quién? | *kyehn?* |

 **.2 How to ask a question**

|  |  |  |
|---|---|---|
| Who's that? _____ | ¿Quién es? | *kyehn ehs?* |
| What? _____ | ¿Qué? | *keh?* |
| What's there to see here? _____ | ¿Qué se puede visitar aquí? | *keh seh pwehdeh beeseetahr ahkee?* |
| What kind of hotel is that? _____ | ¿Qué clase de hotel es? | *keh klahseh deh ohtehl ehs?* |
| Where? _____ | ¿Dónde? | *dohndeh?* |
| Where's the bathroom? _____ | ¿Dónde están los baños? | *dohndeh ehstahn lohs bahnyohs?* |
| Where are you going? _____ | ¿A dónde va? | *ahdohndeh bah?* |
| Where are you from? _____ | ¿De dónde es usted? | *deh dohndeh ehs oostehdh?* |
| How? _____ | ¿Cómo? | *kohmoh?* |
| How far is that? _____ | ¿A qué distancia queda? | *ah keh deestahnsyah kehdah?* |
| How long does it take? _____ | ¿Cuánto dura? | *kwahntoh doorah?* |
| How long is the trip? _____ | ¿Cuánto dura el viaje? | *kwahntoh doorah ehl byahheh?* |
| How much? _____ | ¿Cuánto? | *kwahntoh?* |
| How much is this? _____ | ¿Cuánto vale? | *kwahntoh bahleh?* |
| What time is it? _____ | ¿Qué hora es? | *keh ohrah ehs?* |
| Which? _____ | ¿Cuál? ¿Cuáles? | *kwahl? kwahlehs?* |
| Which glass is mine? _____ | ¿Cuál es mi copa? | *kwahl ehs mee kohpah?* |
| When? _____ | ¿Cuándo? | *kwahndoh?* |
| When are you leaving? _____ | ¿Cuándo se va? | *kwahndoh seh bah?* |
| Why? _____ | ¿Por qué? | *pohr keh?* |
| Could you...me? _____ | ¿Podría...? | *pohdreeah...?* |
| Could you help me, please? _____ | ¿Podría ayudarme? | *pohdreeah ahyoodahrmeh?* |

| | |
|---|---|
| Could you point that_____ out to me? | ¿Me lo podría indicar? *meh loh pohdreeah eendeekahr?* |
| Could you come _____ with me, please? | ¿Puede acompañarme? *pwehdeh ahkohmpahnyahrmeh?* |
| Could you..._____ | ¿Quiere...?/¿Podría...? *kyehreh...?/pohdreeah...?* |
| Could you reserve some ___ tickets for me, please? | ¿Me podría reservar entradas? *meh pohdreeah rehsehrbahr ehntrahdahs?* |
| Do you know...? _____ | ¿Sabe...? *sahbeh...?* |
| Do you know another_____ hotel, please? | ¿Sabría indicarme otro hotel? *sahbreeah eendeekahrmeh ohtroh ohtehl?* |
| Do you know whether...?___ | ¿Sabe si...? *sahbeh see...?* |
| Do you have a...?_____ | ¿Me podría dar un(a)...? *meh pohdreeah dahr oon(ah)...?* |
| Do you have a _____ vegetarian dish, please? | ¿Tendría comida vegetariana? *tehndreeah kohmeedah behhehtahreeahnah?* |
| I'd like... _____ | Quisiera... *keesyehrah...* |
| I'd like a kilo of apples, ____ please. | Quisiera un kilo de manzanas *keesyehrah oon keeloh deh mahnsahnahs* |
| Can I...?_____ | ¿Puedo...?/¿Se puede...? *pwehdoh...?/seh pwehdeh...?* |
| Can I take this?_____ | ¿Podría llevármelo? *pohdreeah lyehbahrmehloh?* |
| Can I smoke here? _____ | ¿Se puede fumar aquí? *seh pwehdeh foomahr ahkee?* |
| Could I ask you _____ something? | ¿Puedo hacerle una pregunta? *pwehdoh ahsehrleh oonah prehgoontah?* |

## 🧱 .3 How to reply

| | |
|---|---|
| Yes, of course_____ | Sí, claro *see, klahroh* |
| No, I'm sorry_____ | No, disculpe *noh, deeskoolpeh* |
| Yes, what can I do _____ for you? | Sí. ¿En qué puedo servirle? *see, ehn keh pwehdoh sehrbeerleh?* |
| Just a moment, please ____ | Un momento, por favor *oon mohmehntoh, pohr fahbohr* |
| No, I don't have _____ time now | No, ahora no tengo tiempo *noh, aohrah noh tehngoh tyehmpoh* |
| No, that's impossible _____ | No, eso es imposible *noh, ehsoh ehs eempohseebleh* |
| I think so _____ | Creo que sí *krehoh keh see* |
| I agree_____ | Estoy de acuerdo *ehstohee deh ahkwerdo* |
| I hope so too_____ | Yo también lo espero *yoh tahmbyehn loh ehspehroh* |
| No, not at all_____ | No, de ninguna manera *noh, deh neengoonah mahnehrah* |
| No, no one _____ | No, nadie *noh, nahdyeh* |
| No, nothing_____ | No, nada *noh, nahdah* |

| | |
|---|---|
| That's (not) right _____ | (No) es cierto |
| | *(noh) ehs syehrtoh* |
| I (don't) agree _____ | (No) estoy de acuerdo con usted |
| | *(noh) ehstoy deh ahkwehrdoh kohn* |
| | *oostehdh* |
| All right _____ | Está bien |
| | *ehstah byehn* |
| Okay _____ | De acuerdo |
| | *deh ahkwehrdoh* |
| Perhaps _____ | Quizá |
| | *keesah* |
| I don't know _____ | No lo sé |
| | *noh loh seh* |

 **.4 Thank you**

| | |
|---|---|
| Thank you _____ | Gracias |
| | *grahsyahs* |
| You're welcome _____ | De nada |
| | *deh nahdah* |
| Thank you very much _____ | Muchísimas gracias |
| | *moocheeseemahs grahsyahs* |
| Very kind of you _____ | Muy amable (de su parte) |
| | *mwee ahmahbleh (deh soo pahrteh)* |
| I enjoyed it very much _____ | Ha sido un verdadero placer |
| | *ah seedoh oon behrdahdehroh plahsehr* |
| Thank you for your _____ trouble | Gracias por la molestia |
| | *grahsyahs pohr lah mohlehstyah* |
| You shouldn't have _____ | No se hubiera molestado |
| | *noh seh oobyehrah mohlehstahdoh* |
| That's all right _____ | No se preocupe |
| | *noh seh prehohkoopeh* |

 **.5 Sorry**

| | |
|---|---|
| Excuse me _____ | Disculpe |
| | *deeskoolpeh* |
| Sorry! _____ | ¡Perdón! |
| | *pehrdohn!* |
| I'm sorry, I didn't know... _____ | Perdón, no sabía que... |
| | *pehrdohn, noh sahbeeah keh...* |
| I do apologize _____ | Discúlpeme |
| | *deeskoolpehmeh* |
| I'm sorry _____ | Lo siento |
| | *loh syehntoh* |
| I didn't do it on purpose, _____ it was an accident | No lo hice a propósito; fue sin querer |
| | *noh loh eeseh ah prohpohseetoh; fweh seen* |
| | *kehrehr* |
| That's all right _____ | No importa |
| | *noh eempohrtah* |
| Never mind _____ | Déjelo |
| | *dehhehloh* |
| It could've happened to _____ anyone | Le puede pasar a cualquiera |
| | *leh pwehdeh pahsahr ah kwahlkyehrah* |
| Which do you prefer? _____ | ¿Qué prefiere? |
| | *keh prehfyehreh?* |

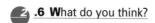

## .6 What do you think?

| | |
|---|---|
| What do you think?_____ | ¿Qué te parece?<br>*keh teh pahrehseh?* |
| Don't you like dancing?____ | ¿No te gusta bailar?<br>*noh teh goostah bahylahr?* |
| I don't mind _____ | Me da igual<br>*meh dah eegwahl* |
| Well done! _____ | ¡Muy bien!<br>*mwee byehn!* |
| Not bad!_____ | ¡No está mal!<br>*noh ehstah mahl!* |
| Great! _____ | ¡Excelente!<br>*ehksehlehnteh!* |
| Wonderful! _____ | ¡Qué delicia!<br>*keh dehleesyah!* |
| It's really nice here! _____ | ¡Qué bien se está aquí!<br>*keh byehn seh ehstah ahkee!* |
| How nice! _____ | ¡Qué lindo/bonito!<br>*keh leendoh/bohneetoh!* |
| How nice for you! _____ | ¡Cuánto me alegro por usted!<br>*kwahntoh meh ahlehgroh pohr oostehdh!* |
| I'm (not) very happy with... | (No) estoy muy contento con...<br>*(noh) ehstoy mwee kohntehntoh kohn...* |
| I'm glad..._____ | Me alegro de que...<br>*meh ahlehgroh deh keh...* |
| I'm having a great time ____ | Me estoy divirtiendo mucho<br>*meh ehstoy deebeertyehndoh moochoh* |
| I'm looking forward to it ___ | Tengo muchas ganas de...<br>*tehngoh moochahs gahnahs deh...* |
| I hope it'll work out_____ | Espero que salga bien<br>*ehspehroh keh sahlgah byehn* |
| That's ridiculous! _____ | ¡Qué ridículo!<br>*keh reedeekooloh!* |
| That's terrible! _____ | ¡Qué horror!<br>*keh ohrrohr!* |
| What a pity! _____ | ¡Qué lástima!<br>*keh lahsteemah!* |
| That's filthy! _____ | ¡Qué asco!<br>*keh ahskoh!* |
| What nonsense!_____ | ¡Qué tontería!<br>*keh tohntehreeah!* |
| I don't like... _____ | No me gusta...<br>*noh meh goostah...* |
| I'm bored to death _____ | Estoy muy aburrido<br>*ehstoy mwee ahboorreedoh* |
| I've had enough _____ | Estoy harto(a)<br>*ehstoy ahrtoh(ah)* |
| This is no good _____ | No puede ser<br>*noh pwehdeh sehr* |
| I was expecting something completely different | Yo había esperado otra cosa<br>*yoh ahbeeah ehspehrahdoh ohtrah kohsah* |

# Conversation

# 3 Conversation

## 3.1 I beg your pardon?

| | |
|---|---|
| I don't speak any/ I speak a little... | No hablo/hablo un poco de... <br> *noh ahbloh/ahbloh oon pohkoh deh...* |
| I'm American | Soy <br> *soy* |
| Do you speak English/French/German? | ¿Habla inglés/francés/alemán? <br> *ahblah eenglehs/frahnsehs/ahlehmahn?* |
| Is there anyone who speaks...? | ¿Hay alguien que hable...? <br> *ay ahlguyehn keh ahbleh...?* |
| I beg your pardon? | ¿Cómo dice? <br> *kohmoh deeseh?* |
| I (don't) understand | (No) entiendo <br> *(noh) ehntyehndoh* |
| Do you understand me? | ¿Me entiende? <br> *meh ehntyehndeh?* |
| Could you repeat that, please? | ¿Me lo podría repetir? <br> *meh loh pohdreeah rehpehteer?* |
| Could you speak more slowly, please? | ¿Podría hablar más despacio? <br> *pohdreeah ahblahr mahs dehspahsyo?* |
| What does that (word) mean? | ¿Qué significa esto/esta palabra? <br> *keh seegneefeekah ehstoh/ehstah pahlahbrah?* |
| Is that similar to/the same as...? | ¿Es (más o menos) lo mismo que...? <br> *ehs mahs oh mehnohs loh meesmoh keh...?* |
| Could you write that down for me, please? | ¿Podría escribírmelo? <br> *pohdreeah eskreebeermehloh?* |
| Could you spell that for me, please? | ¿Podría deletreármelo? <br> *pohdreeah dehlehtrehahrmehloh?* |

*(See 1.8 Telephone alphabet)*

| | |
|---|---|
| Could you point that out in this phrase book, please? | ¿Me lo podría señalar en esta guía? <br> *meh loh pohdreeah sehnyahlahr ehn ehstah geeah?* |
| One moment, please, I have to look it up | Espere que lo busco en la guía <br> *ehspehreh keh loh booskoh ehn lah geeah* |
| I can't find the word/the sentence | No puedo encontrar la palabra/la frase <br> *noh pwehdoh ehnkohntrahr lah pahlahbrah/lah frahseh* |
| How do you say that in...? | ¿Cómo se dice eso en...? <br> *kohmoh seh deeseh ehstoh ehn...?* |
| How do you pronounce that? | ¿Cómo se pronuncia? <br> *kohmoh seh prohnoonsyah?* |

| | |
|---|---|
| May I introduce myself? ___ | Permítame presentarme |
| | *pehrmeetahmeh prehsehntahrmeh* |
| My name's... _____ | Me llamo... |
| | *meh lyahmoh...* |
| I'm... _____ | Soy... |
| | *soy...* |
| What's your name? _____ | ¿Cómo se llama? |
| | *kohmoh seh lyahmah?* |
| May I introduce...? _____ | Permítame presentarle a... |
| | *pehrmeetahmeh prehsehntahrleh ah...* |
| This is my wife/ _____ | Esta es mi esposa/mi hija/mi mamá/mi |
| daughter/mother/ | amiga |
| girlfriend | *ehstah ehs mee ehspohsah/mee eehah* |
| | */mee mahmah/mee ahmeegah* |
| – my husband/son/ _____ | Este es mi marido/mi hijo/mi papá/mi |
| father/boyfriend | amigo |
| | *ehsteh ehs mee mahreedoh/mee* |
| | *eehoh/mee pahpah/mee ahmeegoh* |
| How do you do _____ | Hola, mucho gusto |
| | *ohlah, moochoh goostoh* |
| Pleased to meet you_____ | Encantado(a) (de conocerlo/a) |
| | *ehnkahntahdoh(ah) (deh kohnohsehrloh/ah)* |
| Where are you from? _____ | ¿De dónde es usted? |
| | *deh dohndeh ehs oostehdh?* |
| I'm from _____ | Soy de |
| the United States | *soy day* |
| What city do you live in? __ | ¿En qué ciudad vive? |
| | *ehn keh syoodahdh beebeh?* |
| In..., It's near... _____ | En...Eso está cerca de... |
| | *ehn...ehstah sehrkah deh...* |
| Have you been here _____ | ¿Hace mucho que está aquí? |
| long? | *ahseh moochoh keh ehstah ahkee?* |
| A few days _____ | Unos días |
| | *oonohs deeahs* |
| How long are you _____ | ¿Cuánto tiempo piensa quedarse? |
| staying here? | *kwahntoh tyehmpoh pyehnsah kehdahrseh?* |
| We're (probably) _____ | Nos iremos (probablemente) |
| leaving tomorrow/ | mañana/dentro de dos semanas |
| in two weeks | *nohs eerehmohs (prohbahblehmehnteh)* |
| | *mahnyahnah/dehntroh deh dohs* |
| | *sehmahnahs* |
| Where are you staying?____ | ¿Dónde se aloja? |
| | *dohndeh seh ahlohhah?* |
| In a hotel/an apartment ____ | En un hotel/departamento |
| | *ehn oon ohtehl/dehpahrtahmehntoh* |
| On a camp site_____ | En un camping |
| | *ehn oon kahmpeen* |
| With friends/relatives _____ | En casa de amigos/parientes |
| | *ehn kahsah deh ahmeegohs/pahryehntehs* |
| Are you here on your_____ | ¿Vino solo(a)/con su familia? |
| own/with your family? | *beenoh sohloh(ah)/kohn soo fahmeelyah?* |

**Conversation**

25

**Conversation**

| | |
|---|---|
| I'm on my own _____ | Vine solo(a) |
| | *beeneh sohloh(ah)* |
| I'm with my _____ partner/wife/husband | con mi pareja/esposa/marido |
| | *kohn mee pahrehhhah/ehspohsah/mahreedoh* |
| – with my family _____ | con mi familia |
| | *kohn mee fahmeelyah* |
| – with relatives _____ | con unos parientes |
| | *kohn oonohs pahryehntehs* |
| – with a friend/friends _____ | con un amigo/una amiga/unos amigos |
| | *kohn oon ahmeegoh/oonah ahmeegah/oonohs ahmeegohs* |
| Are you married? _____ | ¿Está casado/casada? |
| | *ehstah kahsahdoh/kahsahdah?* |
| Do you have a steady _____ boyfriend/girlfriend? | ¿Tienes novio/novia? |
| | *tyehnehs nohbyoh/nohbyah?* |
| That's none of your _____ business | ¿Qué le importa? |
| | *keh leh eempohrtah?* |
| I'm married _____ | Soy casado |
| | *soy kahsahdoh* |
| – single _____ | Soy soltero |
| | *soy sohltehroh* |
| – separated _____ | Estoy separado |
| | *ehstoy sehpahrahdoh* |
| – divorced _____ | Estoy divorciado |
| | *ehstoy deebohrsyahdoh* |
| – a widow/widower _____ | Soy viuda/viudo |
| | *soy byoodah/byoodoh* |
| I live alone/with _____ someone | Vivo solo(a)/con otra persona |
| | *beeboh sohloh(ah)/kohn ohtrah pehrsohnah* |
| Do you have any _____ children/grandchildren? | ¿Tiene hijos/nietos? |
| | *tyehneh eehohs/nyehtohs?* |
| How old are you? _____ | ¿Cuántos años tiene? |
| | *kwahntohs ahnyohs tyehneh?* |
| How old is she/he? _____ | ¿Cuántos años tiene? |
| | *kwahntohs ahnyohs tyehneh?* |
| I'm... _____ | Tengo...años |
| | *tehngoh...ahnyohs* |
| She's/he's... _____ | Tiene...años |
| | *tyehneh...ahnyohs* |
| What do you do for a _____ living? | ¿En qué trabaja? |
| | *ehn keh trahbahhhah?* |
| I work in an office _____ | Trabajo en una oficina |
| | *trahbahhhoh ehn oonah ohfeeseenah* |
| I'm a student/ _____ I'm at school | Estudio |
| | *ehstoodyoh* |
| I'm unemployed _____ | No tengo trabajo |
| | *noh tehngoh trahbahhhoh* |
| I'm retired _____ | Soy jubilado |
| | *soy hoobeelahdoh* |
| I'm on a disability _____ pension | Tengo una pensión de invalidez |
| | *tehngoh oonah pehnsyohn deh eenbahleedes* |
| I'm a housewife _____ | Soy ama de casa |
| | *soy ahmah deh kahsah* |

| Do you like your job? _____ | ¿Le gusta su trabajo? |
| | *leh goostah soo trahbahhoh?* |
| Most of the time _____ | Casi siempre |
| | *kahsee syehmpreh* |
| I usually do, but I prefer ___ vacations | Por lo general sí, pero prefiero las vacaciones |
| | *pohr loh hehnehrahl see, pehroh prehfyehroh lahs bahkahsyohnehs* |

## .3 Starting/ending a conversation

| Could I ask you _____ something? | ¿Podría preguntarle una cosa? |
| | *pohdreeah prehgoontahrleh oonah kohsah?* |
| Excuse me | Perdone |
| | *pehrdohneh* |
| Excuse me, could you _____ help me? | ¿Podría ayudarme? |
| | *pohdreeah ahyoodahrmeh?* |
| Yes, what's the problem? __ | Sí, ¿qué pasa? |
| | *see, keh pahsah?* |
| What can I do for you? ____ | ¿En qué puedo servirlo/a? |
| | *ehn keh pwehdoh sehrbeerloh/ah?* |
| Sorry, I don't have time now | Lo siento, ahora no tengo tiempo |
| | *loh syehntoh, ahohrah noh tehngoh tyehmpoh* |
| Do you have a light? _____ | ¿Tiene fuego? |
| | *tyehneh fwehgoh?* |
| May I join you? _____ | ¿Me puedo sentar? |
| | *meh pwehdoh sehntahr?* |
| Could you take a _____ picture of me/us? Press this button | ¿Podría sacarme/sacarnos una foto? Hay que apretar este botón |
| | *pohdreeah sahkahrmeh/sahkahrnohs oonah fohtoh? ay keh ahprehtahr ehsteh bohtohn* |
| Leave me alone _____ | Déjeme en paz |
| | *dehhehmeh ehn pahs* |
| Get lost_____ | Váyase al diablo |
| | *bahyahseh ahl deeahbloh* |
| Go away or I'll scream_____ | Si no se vaya, yo grito |
| | *see noh seh bahyah, yoh greetoh* |

## .4 Congratulations and condolences

| Happy birthday/many_____ happy returns | Feliz cumpleaños/felicidades |
| | *fehlees koomplehahnyohs/fehleeseedahdehs* |
| Please accept my_____ condolences | Lo/a acompaño en el sentimiento |
| | *loh/ah ahkohmpahnyoh ehn ehl sehnteemyehntoh* |
| I'm very sorry for you _____ | ¡Cuánto lo siento por usted! |
| | *kwahntoh loh syehntoh pohr oostehdh!* |

## .5 A chat about the weather

**See also 1.5 The weather**

| It's so hot/cold today!_____ | ¡Qué calor/frío hace hoy! |
| | *keh kahlohr/freeoh ahseh oy!* |
| Nice weather, isn't it?_____ | ¡Qué buen tiempo hace! ¿Verdad? |
| | *keh bwehn tyehmpoh ahseh! behrdadh?* |

**Conversation**

| | |
|---|---|
| What a wind/storm! _____ | ¡Vaya viento/tormenta! |
| | *bahyah byehntoh/tohrmentah!* |
| All that rain/snow! _____ | ¡Cómo llueve/nieva! |
| | *kohmoh lywehbeh/nyehbah!* |
| All that fog! _____ | ¡Cuánta niebla! |
| | *kwahntah nyehblah!* |
| Has the weather been _____ like this for long here? | ¿Hace mucho que hace este tiempo? |
| | *ahseh moochoh keh ahseh ehsteh tyehmpoh?* |
| Is it always this hot/cold ___ here? | ¿Aquí siempre hace tanto calor/frío? |
| | *ahkee syehmpreh ahseh tahntoh kahlohr/freeoh?* |
| Is it always this dry/wet ____ here? | ¿Aquí siempre hace un tiempo tan seco/lluvioso? |
| | *ahkee syehmpreh ahseh oon tyehmpoh tahn sehkoh/lyoobyohsoh?* |

### 3 .6 Hobbies

| | |
|---|---|
| Do you have any _____ hobbies? | ¿Tiene algún hobby? |
| | *tyehneh ahlgoon hohbee?* |
| I like painting/_____ reading/photography | Me gusta pintar/leer/la fotografía/el bricolaje |
| | *meh goostah peentahr/lehehr/lah fohtohgrahfeeah/ehl breekohlahheh* |
| I like music _____ | Me gusta la música |
| | *meh goostah lah mooseekah* |
| I like playing the _____ guitar/piano | Me gusta tocar la guitarra/el piano |
| | *meh goostah tohkahr lah gueetahrrah/ehl pyahnoh* |
| I like going to the movies __ | Me gusta ir al cine |
| | *meh goostah eer ahl seeneh* |
| I like travelling/_____ playing sports/fishing/ walking | Me gusta viajar/hacer deporte/pescar/salir a caminar |
| | *meh goostah byahhahr/ahsehr dehpohrteh/pehskahr/sahleer ah kahmeenahr* |

### 3 .7 Being the host(ess)

*See also 4 Eating out*

| | |
|---|---|
| Can I offer you a drink? ____ | ¿Le gustaría algo de beber? |
| | *leh goostahreeah ahlgoh deh behbehr?* |
| What would you like _____ to drink? | ¿Qué quieres beber? |
| | *keh kyehrehs behbehr?* |
| Something non-alcoholic, __ please | Algo sin alcohol |
| | *ahlgoh seen ahlkohl* |
| Would you like a _____ cigarette? | ¿Quiere un cigarro/un puro? |
| | *kyehreh oon seegahrroh/oon pooroh?* |
| I don't smoke _____ | No fumo |
| | *noh foomoh* |

| | |
|---|---|
| Are you doing anything tonight? | ¿Tiene algo que hacer esta noche? <br> *tyehneh ahlgoh keh ahsehr ehstah nohcheh?* |
| Do you have any plans for today/this afternoon/tonight? | ¿Ya tiene planes para hoy/ esta tarde/esta noche? <br> *yah tyehneh plahnehs pahrah oy/ehstah tahrdeh/ehstah nohcheh?* |
| Would you like to go out with me? | ¿Quieres salir conmigo? <br> *kyehrehs sahleer kohnmeegoh?* |
| Would you like to go dancing with me? | ¿Quieres ir a bailar conmigo? <br> *kyehrehs eer ah baylahr kohnmeegoh?* |
| Would you like to have lunch/dinner with me? | ¿Quieres ir a comer/cenar conmigo? <br> *kyehrehs eer ah kohmehr/sehnahr kohnmeegoh?* |
| Would you like to come to the beach with me? | ¿Quieres ir a la playa conmigo? <br> *kyehrehs eer ah lah plahyah kohnmeegoh?* |
| Would you like to come into town with us? | ¿Quieres ir a la ciudad con nosotros? <br> *kyehrehs eer ah lah thyoodahdh kohn nohsohtrohs?* |
| Would you like to come and see some friends with us? | ¿Quieres ir a casa de unos amigos con nosotros? <br> *kyehrehs eer ah kahsah deh oonohs ahmeegohs kohn nohsohtrohs?* |
| Shall we dance? | ¿Bailamos? <br> *baylahmohs?* |
| – sit at the bar? | ¿Vienes a sentarte conmigo en la barra? <br> *byehnehs ah sehntahrteh kohnmeegoh ehn lah bahrrah?* |
| – get something to drink? | ¿Vamos a beber algo? <br> *bahmohs ah behbehr ahlgoh?* |
| – go for a walk/drive? | ¿Vamos a dar una vuelta? <br> *bahmohs ah dahr oonah bwehltah?* |
| Yes, all right | Sí, vamos <br> *see, bahmohs* |
| Good idea | Buena idea <br> *bwehnah eedehah* |
| No (thank you) | No (gracias) <br> *noh (grahsyahs)* |
| Maybe later | Quizá más tarde <br> *keesah mahs tahrdeh* |
| I don't feel like it | No tengo ganas <br> *noh tehngoh gahnahs* |
| I don't have time | No tengo tiempo <br> *noh tehngoh tyehmpoh* |
| I already have a date | Ya tengo otro compromiso <br> *yah tehngoh ohtroh kohmprohmeesoh* |
| I'm not very good at dancing/volleyball/ swimming | No sé bailar/jugar al vóleibol/nadar <br> *noh seh baylahr/hoogahr ahl vohleheebohl/nahdahr* |

## .9 Paying a compliment

| | |
|---|---|
| You look wonderful! | ¡Te ves muy bien! <br> *teh behs mwee byehn!* |
| I like your car! | ¡Qué bonito coche! <br> *keh bohneetoh kohcheh!* |

| I like your ski outfit! _____ | ¡Qué bonito traje de esquiar! |
| | keh bohneetoh trahhheh deh ehskeeahr! |
| You're a nice boy/girl _____ | Eres muy bueno/buena |
| | ehrehs mwee bwehnoh/bwehnah |
| What a sweet child! _____ | ¡Qué niño tan lindo/niña tan linda! |
| | keh neenyoh tahn leendoh/neenyah tahn |
| | leendah! |
| You're a wonderful _____ dancer! | Bailas muy bien |
| | bahylahs mwee byehn |
| You're a wonderful _____ cook! | Cocinas muy bien |
| | kohseenahs mwee byehn |
| You're a terrific soccer _____ player! | Juegas muy bien al fútbol |
| | hwehgahs mwee byehn ahl footbohl |

## 3 .10 Intimate comments/questions

| I like being with you _____ | Me gusta estar contigo |
| | meh goostah ehstahr kohnteegoh |
| I've missed you so much___ | Te extrañé mucho |
| | teh ehkstrahnyeh moochoh |
| I dreamt about you _____ | Soñé contigo |
| | sohnyeh kohnteegoh |
| I think about you all day ___ | Pienso todo el día en ti |
| | pyehnsoh tohdoh ehl deeah ehn tee |
| You have such a sweet _____ smile | Tienes una sonrisa muy bonita |
| | tyehnehs oonah sohnreesah mwee |
| | bohneetah |
| You have such beautiful ___ eyes | Tienes unos ojos muy bonitos |
| | tyehnehs oonohs ohhohs mwee |
| | bohneetohs |
| I'm in love with you _____ | Estoy enamorado/enamorada de ti |
| | ehstoy ehnahmohrahdoh/ehnahmohrahdah |
| | deh tee |
| I'm in love with you too ___ | Yo también de ti |
| | yoh tahmbyehn deh tee |
| I love you_____ | Te quiero |
| | teh kyehroh |
| I love you too _____ | Yo también a ti |
| | yoh tahmbyehn ah tee |
| I don't feel as strongly _____ about you | Yo no siento lo mismo por ti |
| | yoh noh syehntoh loh meesmoh pohr tee |
| I already have a _____ boyfriend/girlfriend | Ya tengo novio/a |
| | yah tehngoh nohbyoh/ah |
| I'm not ready for that_____ | Yo no estoy preparado(a) |
| | yoh noh ehstoy prehpahrahdoh/ah |
| This is going too fast _____ for me | Vamos demasiado rápido |
| | bahmohs dehmahsyahdoh rahpeedoh |
| Take your hands off me____ | No me toque(s) |
| | noh meh tohkeh(s) |
| Okay, no problem _____ | No importa |
| | noh eempohrtah |
| Will you stay with me _____ tonight? | ¿Te quedas a dormir? |
| | teh kehdahs ah dohrmeer? |
| I'd like to go to bed_____ with you | Me gustaría acostarme contigo |
| | meh goostahreeah ahkohstahrmeh |
| | kohnteegoh |

| Only if we use a condom __ | Sólo si usamos condón |
| | *sohloh see oosahmohs kohndohn* |
| We have to be careful _____ about AIDS | Hay que tener cuidado por lo del Sida |
| | *ay keh tehnehr kweedahdoh pohr loh dehl seedah* |
| That's what they all say ____ | Eso es lo que dicen todos |
| | *ehsoh ehs loh keh deesehn tohdohs* |
| We shouldn't take any _____ risks | Más vale no arriesgarse |
| | *mahs bahleh noh ahrryehsgahrseh* |
| Do you have a condom? ___ | ¿Tienes condones? |
| | *tyehnehs kohndohnehs?* |
| No? In that case we _____ won't do it | ¿No? Pues entonces no |
| | *noh? pwehs ehntohnsehs noh* |

## .11 Arrangements

| When will I see_____ you again? | ¿Cuándo nos volvemos a ver? |
| | *kwahndoh nohs bohlbehmohs ah behr?* |
| Are you free over the _____ weekend? | ¿Tiene tiempo este fin de semana? |
| | *tyehneh tyehmpoh ehsteh feen deh sehmahnah?* |
| What shall we do?_____ | ¿Cómo quedamos? |
| | *kohmoh kehdahmohs?* |
| Where shall we meet? ____ | ¿Dónde nos encontramos? |
| | *dohndeh nohs ehnkohntrahmohs?* |
| Will you pick me/us up? ___ | ¿Me/nos pasa a buscar? |
| | *meh/nohs pahsah ah booskahr?* |
| Shall I pick you up?_____ | ¿Lo/la paso a buscar? |
| | *loh/lah pahsoh ah booskahr?* |
| I have to be home by... ____ | Tengo que estar en casa a las... |
| | *tehngoh keh ehstahr ehn kahsah ah lahs...* |
| I don't want to see _____ you anymore | No quiero volver a verlo/verla |
| | *noh kyehroh bohlbehr ah behrloh/behrlah* |

## .12 Saying good-bye

| Can I take you home? _____ | ¿Lo/la acompaño a su casa? |
| | *loh/lah ahkohmpahnyoh ah soo kahsah?* |
| Can I write/call you? _____ | ¿Puedo escribirle/llamarlo/llamarla por teléfono? |
| | *pwehdoh ehskreebeerleh /lyahmahrloh/ lyahmahrlah pohr tehlehfohnoh?* |
| Will you write/call me? ____ | ¿Me escribirá/llamará por teléfono? |
| | *meh ehskreebeerah/lyahmahrah pohr tehlehfohnoh?* |
| Can I have your _____ address/phone number? | ¿Me da su dirección/número de teléfono? |
| | *meh dah soo deerehksyohn/noomehroh deh tehlehfohnoh?* |
| Thanks for everything _____ | Gracias por todo |
| | *grahsyahs pohr tohdoh* |
| It was very nice _____ | Lo hemos pasado muy bien |
| | *loh ehmohs pahsahdoh mwee byehn* |
| Say hello to... _____ | Saludos a... |
| | *sahloodohs ah...* |
| All the best _____ | Te deseo lo mejor |
| | *teh dehsehoh loh meh<u>h</u>ohr* |

**3 Conversation**

| | |
|---|---|
| Good luck_____ | Buena suerte |
| | *bwehnah swehrteh* |
| When will you be back?____ | ¿Cuándo regresas? |
| | *kwahndoh rehgrehsahs?* |
| I'll be waiting for you _____ | Te esperaré |
| | *teh ehspehrahreh* |
| I'd like to see you again ____ | Me gustaría volver a verte |
| | *meh goostahreeah bohlbehr ah behrteh* |
| I hope we meet _____ | Espero que nos volvamos a ver pronto |
| again soon | *ehspehroh keh nohs bohlbahmohs ah behr* |
| | *prohntoh* |
| This is our address. _____ | Esta es nuestra dirección. Si alguna vez |
| If you're ever in the U.S. | pasa por los Estados Unidos... |
| | *ehstah ehs nwehstrah deerehksyohn. see* |
| | *ahlgoonah behs pahsah pohr lohs* |
| | *Ehstahthos Ooneethohs* |
| You'd be more than _____ | Está cordialmente invitado |
| welcome | *ehstah kohrdyahlmehnteh eenbeetahdoh* |

# **E**ating out

# 4 **E**ating out

● **In Latin American countries** people usually have three meals:
1 *El desayuno* (breakfast) approximately between 7 and 9am. Breakfast is light and consists of *café con leche* (white coffee), croissants or *pan tostado* (toast).
2 *El almuerzo* (lunch) approx. between 12 and 2pm. Lunch always includes a hot dish and is the most important meal of the day. Office workers and schoolchildren still lunch at home. It usually consists of four courses:
– starter (which can be a plate of greens)
– main course
– dessert
– fruit
3 *La cena* (dinner) between 8 and 10pm. Dinner is usually a light, hot meal, taken with the family.
At around 5pm, a snack (*la merienda,* called 'once' in Chile) is often served.

## 4 .1 **O**n arrival

| | |
|---|---|
| I'd like to reserve a table for seven o'clock, please | ¿Podría reservar una mesa para las siete? *pohdreeah rehsehrbahr oonah mehsah pahrah lahs syehteh?* |
| I'd like a table for two, _____ please | Quisiera una mesa para dos personas *keesyehrah oonah mehsah pahrah dohs pehrsohnahs* |
| We've/we haven't reserved_ | (No) hemos reservado *(noh) ehmohs rehsehrbahdoh* |
| Is the restaurant open _____ yet? | ¿Ya está abierto el restaurante? *yah ehstah ahbyehrtoh ehl rehstahoorahnteh?* |
| What time does the _____ restaurant open/close? | ¿A qué hora abre/cierra el restaurante? *ah keh ohrah ahbreh/syehrah ehl rehstahoorahnteh?* |
| Can we wait for a table? ___ | ¿Podemos esperar hasta que se desocupe una mesa? *pohdehmohs ehspehrahr ahstah keh seh dehsohkoopeh oonah mehsah?* |
| Do we have to wait long? __ | ¿Tenemos que esperar mucho? *tehnehmohs keh ehspehrahr moochoh?* |
| Is this seat taken? _____ | ¿Está ocupada esta silla? *ehstah ohkoopahdah ehstah seelyah?* |
| Could we sit here/there? ___ | ¿Podemos sentarnos aquí/allí? *pohdemohs sehntahrnohs ahkee/ahlyee?* |

| | |
|---|---|
| ¿Ha reservado mesa? _____ | Do you have a reservation? |
| ¿A nombre de quién? _____ | What name, please? |
| Por aquí, por favor. _____ | This way, please |
| Esta mesa está reservada _____ | This table is reserved |
| En quince minutos quedará libre una mesa | We'll have a table free in fifteen minutes. |
| ¿Le importaría esperar (en la barra) ____ | Would you like to wait (at the bar)? |

| Can we sit by the window? | ¿Podemos sentarnos junto a la ventana? |
|---|---|
| | *pohdehmohs sehntahrnohs hoontoh ah lah behntahnah?* |
| Can we eat outside? | ¿Podemos comer afuera? |
| | *pohdehmohs kohmehr ahfwehrah?* |
| Do you have another chair for us? | ¿Podría traernos otra silla? |
| | *pohdreeah trahehrnohs ohtrah seelyah?* |
| Do you have a highchair? | ¿Podría traernos una silla para niños? |
| | *pohdreeah trahehrnohs oonah seelyah pahrah neenyohs?* |
| Is there an outlet for this bottle-warmer? | ¿Hay un enchufe para este calentador de biberones? |
| | *ay oon ehnchoofeh pahrah ehsteh kahlehntahdohr deh beebehrohnehs?* |
| Could you warm up this bottle/jar for me? | ¿Podría calentarme este biberón/este bote? |
| | *pohdreeah kahlehntahrmeh ehsteh beebehrohn/ehsteh bohteh?* |
| Not too hot, please | Que no esté muy caliente, por favor |
| | *keh noh ehsteh mwee kahlyehnteh pohr fahbohr* |
| Is there somewhere I can change the baby's diaper? | ¿Hay algún lugar para cambiar al bebé? |
| | *ay ahlgoon loogahr pahrah kahmbyahr ahl behbeh?* |
| Where are the bathrooms? | ¿Dónde están los baños/aseos? |
| | *dohnde ehstahn lohs bahnyos/ahsehohs?* |

## 4 .2 Ordering

| Waiter! | ¡Mozo (mesero)! |
|---|---|
| | *mohsoh (mehsehroh)!* |
| Madam!/Sir! | ¡Oiga, (por favor)! |
| | *oygah (pohr fahbohr)!* |
| We'd like something to eat/a drink | Quisiéramos comer/beber algo |
| | *keesyehrahmohs kohmehr/behber ahlgoh* |
| Could I have a quick meal? | ¿Podría comer algo rápido? |
| | *pohdreeah kohmehr ahlgoh rahpeedoh?* |
| We don't have much time | Tenemos poco tiempo |
| | *tehnehmohs pohkoh tyehmpoh* |
| We'd like to have a drink first | Antes quisiéramos beber algo |
| | *ahntehs keesyehrahmohs behbehr ahlgoh* |
| Could we see the menu/wine list, please? | ¿Nos podría traer la carta/la carta de vinos? |
| | *nohs pohdreeah trahehr lah kahrtah/lah kahrtah deh beenohs?* |
| Do you have a menu in English? | ¿Tienen menú en inglés? |
| | *tyehnehn mehnoo ehn eenglehs?* |
| Do you have a dish of the day? | ¿Tienen menú del día/menú turístico? |
| | *tyehnehn mehnoo dehl deeah/mehnoo tooreesteekoh?* |
| We haven't made a choice yet | Todavía no hemos elegido |
| | *tohdahbeeah noh ehmohs ehlehheedoh* |
| What do you recommend? | ¿Qué nos recomienda? |
| | *keh nohs rehkohmyehndah?* |

**Eating out**

| | |
|---|---|
| What are the specialities of the region/the house? | ¿Cuáles son las especialidades de la región/de la casa? |
| | *kwahlehs sohn lahs ehspehsyahleedahdehs deh lah rehhyohn/deh lah kahsah?* |
| I like strawberries/olives | Me gustan las fresas/las aceitunas |
| | *meh goostahn lahs frehsahs/lahs ahseeheetoonahs* |
| I don't like meat/fish/... | No me gusta el pescado/la carne/... |
| | *noh meh goostah ehl pehskahdoh/lah kahrneh/...* |
| What's this? | ¿Qué es esto? |
| | *keh ehs ehstoh?* |
| Does it have...in it? | ¿Tiene...? |
| | *tyehneh...?* |
| What does it taste like? | ¿A qué sabe? |
| | *ah keh sahbeh?* |
| Is this a hot or a cold dish? | ¿Es un plato caliente o frío? |
| | *ehs oon plahtoh kahlyehnyteh oh freeoh?* |
| Is this sweet? | ¿Es un plato dulce? |
| | *ehs oon plahtoh doolse?* |
| Is this spicy? | ¿Es un plato picante? |
| | *ehs oon plahtoh peekahnteh?* |
| Do you have anything else, please? | ¿Tendría otra cosa? |
| | *tehndreeah ohtrah kohsah?* |
| I'm on a salt-free diet | No puedo comer sal |
| | *noh pwehdoh kohmehr sahl* |
| I can't eat pork | No puedo comer carne de cerdo |
| | *noh pwehdoh kohmehr kahrneh deh sehrdoh* |
| – sugar | No puedo comer azúcar |
| | *noh pwehdo kohmehr ahsookahr* |
| – fatty foods | No puedo comer grasa |
| | *noh pwehdoh kohmehr grahsah* |
| – (hot) spices | No puedo comer cosas picantes |
| | *noh pwehdoh kohmehr kohsahs peekahntehs* |
| I'll/we'll have what those people are having | Lo mismo que esos señores, por favor |
| | *loh meesmoh keh ehsohs sehnyohrehs pohr fahbohr* |
| I'd like... | Para mí... |
| | *pahrah mee...* |

| | |
|---|---|
| ¿Van a tomar un aperitivo? | Would you like a drink first? |
| ¿Ya han elegido? | Have you decided? |
| ¿Qué van a tomar? | What would you like to eat? |
| Que aproveche | Enjoy your meal. |
| ¿Quiere su bistec rojo, mediano o bien? | Would you like your steak rare, medium or well done? |
| ¿Van a comer postre/tomar café? | Would you like a dessert/coffee? |

| | |
|---|---|
| We're not having a _____ starter | No vamos a comer entrada |
| | *noh bahmohs ah kohmehr ehntrahdah* |
| The child will share_____ what we're having | El niño/la niña comerá de nuestro menú |
| | *ehl neenyoh/lah neenyah kohmehrah deh nwehstroh mehnoo* |
| Could I have some _____ more bread, please? | Más pan, por favor |
| | *mahs pahn pohr fahbohr* |
| – a bottle of water/wine ____ | Otra botella de agua/de vino, por favor |
| | *ohtrah bohtehlyah deh ahgwah/deh beenoh, pohr fahbohr* |
| – another helping of... ____ | Otra ración de..., por favor |
| | *ohtrah rahsyohn deh..., pohr fahbohr* |
| – some salt and pepper ____ | ¿Podría traerme sal y pimienta? |
| | *pohdreeah trahehrmeh sahl ee peemyehntah?* |
| – a napkin _____ | ¿Podría traerme una servilleta? |
| | *pohdreeah trahehrmeh oonah sehrbeelyehtah?* |
| – a spoon _____ | ¿Podría traerme una cuchara? |
| | *pohdreeah trahehrmeh oonah koochahrah?* |
| – an ashtray _____ | ¿Podría traerme un cenicero? |
| | *pohdreeah trahehrmeh oon sehneesehroh?* |
| – some matches_____ | ¿Podría traerme cerillas fósforos? |
| | *pohdreeah trahehrmeh sehreelyahs fohsfohrohs?* |
| – some toothpicks _____ | ¿Podría traerme unos palillos? |
| | *pohdreeah trahehrmeh oonohs pahleelyohs?* |
| – a glass of water _____ | ¿Podría traerme un vaso de agua? |
| | *pohdreeah trahehrmeh oon bahsoh deh ahgwah?* |
| – a straw (for the child) ____ | ¿Podría traerme una pajita (para el niño/la niña)? |
| | *pohdreeah trahehrmeh oonah pahheetah (pahrah ehl neenyoh/lah neenyah)?* |
| Enjoy your meal!_____ | ¡Que aproveche! |
| | *keh ahprohbehcheh!* |
| You too! _____ | Igualmente |
| | *eegwahlmehnteh* |
| Cheers!_____ | ¡Salud! |
| | *sahloodh!* |
| The next round's on me ___ | La próxima ronda me toca a mí |
| | *lah prohxeemah rohndah meh tohkah ah mee* |
| Could we have a doggy____ bag, please? | ¿Podemos llevarnos las sobras? |
| | *pohdehmohs lyehbarnohs lahs sohbrahs?* |

## 4 .3 The bill

*See also 8.2 Settling the bill*

| | |
|---|---|
| How much is this dish? ____ | ¿Cuánto vale este plato? |
| | *kwahntoh bahleh ehsteh plahtoh?* |
| Could I have the bill, _____ please? | La cuenta, por favor |
| | *lah kwehntah, pohr fahbohr* |
| All together _____ | Todo junto |
| | *tohdoh hoontoh* |
| Everyone pays separately__ | Cada uno paga lo suyo |
| | *kahdah oonoh pahgah loh sooyoh* |

| Could we have the menu again, please? | ¿Podría traernos otra vez la carta? |
| | *pohdreeah trahehrnohs ohtrah behs lah kahrtah?* |
| The...is not on the bill | Olvidó apuntar el/la... |
| | *olbeedoh ahpoontahr ehl/lah...* |

## .4 Complaints

| It's taking a very long time | Están tardando mucho |
| | *ehstahn tahrdahndoh moochoh* |
| We've been here an hour already | Ya llevamos una hora aquí |
| | *yah lyebahmohs oonah ohrah ahkee* |
| This must be a mistake | Esto tiene que ser una equivocación |
| | *ehstoh tyehneh keh sehr oonah ehkeebohkahsyohn* |
| This is not what I ordered | Esto no es lo que pedí |
| | *ehstoh noh ehs loh keh pehdee* |
| I ordered... | Pedí... |
| | *pehdee* |
| There's a dish missing | Falta un plato |
| | *fahltah oon plahtoh* |
| This is broken/not clean | Esto está roto/no está limpio |
| | *ehstoh ehstah rohtoh/noh ehstah leempyoh* |
| The food's cold | La comida está fría |
| | *lah kohmeedah ehstah freeah* |
| – not fresh | La comida no es fresca |
| | *lah kohmeedah noh ehs frehskah* |
| – too salty/sweet/spicy | La comida está muy salada/dulce/picante |
| | *lah kohmeedah ehstah mwee sahlahdah/doolseh/peekahnteh* |
| The meat's not done | La carne está cruda |
| | *lah kahrneh ehstah kroodah* |
| – overdone | La carne está muy cocida |
| | *lah kahrneh ehstah mwee kohseedah* |
| – tough | La carne está dura |
| | *lah kahrneh ehstah doorah* |
| – off | La carne está podrida |
| | *lah kahrneh ehstah pohdreedah* |
| Could I have something else instead of this? | ¿Me podría traer otra cosa en lugar de esto? |
| | *meh pohdreeah trahehr ohtrah kohsah ehn loogahr deh ehstoh?* |
| The bill/this amount is not right | La cuenta/este precio está mal |
| | *lah kwehntah/ehsteh prehsyoh ehstah mahl* |
| We didn't have this | Esto no lo hemos comido/bebido |
| | *ehstoh noh loh ehmohs kohmeedoh/behbeedoh* |
| There's no toiletpaper in the restroom | No hay papel en el baño |
| | *noh ay pahpehl ehn ehl bahnyoh* |
| Do you have a complaints book? | ¿Tienen libro de quejas? |
| | *tyehnen leebroh deh kehhas?* |
| Will you call the manager, please? | Haga el favor de llamar al jefe |
| | *ahgah ehl fahbohr deh lyamahr ahl hehfeh* |

## .5 Paying a compliment

| | |
|---|---|
| That was a wonderful _____ meal | Comimos muy bien |
| | _kohmeemohs mwee byehn_ |
| The food was excellent _____ | La comida ha estado exquisita |
| | _lah kohmeedah ah ehstahdoh ehxkeeseetah_ |
| The...in particular was _____ delicious | Sobre todo nos gustó el/la... |
| | _sohbreh tohdoh nohs goostoh ehl/lah..._ |

## .6 The menu

aperitivo
**apéritif**

aves
**poultry**

azúcar
**sugar**

bebidas alcohólicas
**alcoholic beverages**

bebidas calientes
**hot beverages**

carta de vinos
**wine list**

cócteles
**cocktails**

cubierto
**cover charge**

entremeses variados
**hors d'oeuvres**

mariscos
**seafood**

pastelería
**pastry**

pescados
**fish**

platos calientes
**hot dishes**

platos combinados
**combined dishes**

plato del día
**dish of the day**

platos fríos
**cold dishes**

platos principales
**main courses**

platos típicos
**regional specialities**

postres
**sweets/dessert**

primeros platos
**starters**

raciones
**portions**

servicio incluido
**tip included**

sopas
**soups**

tapas
**tapas**

venado
**game**

verduras
**vegetables**

## .7 Alphabetical list of drinks and dishes

aceituna
**olive**

aguacate/palta
**avocado**

ajo
**garlic**

albóndigas
**meat balls**

alcachofa/alcaucil
**artichoke**

almejas
**clams**

almendras
**almonds**

ancas de rana
**frog's legs**

anchoa/boquerón
**anchovy**

anguila
**eel**

anís
**aniseed**

apio
**celery**

arenque
**herring**

arroz
**rice**

asado
**roast, roasted**

atún/bonito
**tuna**

avellana
**hazelnut**

bacalao
**cod**

barbacoa asado
**barbecued meat**

licuado/batido de...
**...milk shake**

berenjena
**eggplant**

biftec/bife/bistec
**steak**

bizcocho
**sponge cake**

blanquillo/huevo
**egg**

buey/vaca
**beef**

cabrito
**kid**

café (solo/con leche)
**coffee (black/white)**

calamares (en su tinta)
**squid (cooked in their ink)**

caldo
**broth**

39

**Eating out**

callos
tripe
cangrejo
crab
caracoles
snails
carne
meat
carpa
carp
castaña
chestnut
cebolla
onion
cerdo/puerco
pork
cerezas
cherries
cerveza
beer
ceviche
marinated raw
  seafood
chile
chili pepper
chorizo
chorizo (paprika
  flavoured salami
  sausage)
chucrut
sauerkraut
chuleta/costilla
chop (meat)
churros
fritters
ciervo
venison
cigalas
Dublin Bay prawns
ciruela
plum
cochinillo asado
roast suckling pig
cocido
boiled
codorniz
quail
col/berza/repollo
cabbage
coles repollitos de
Bruselas
Brussels sprouts
coliflor
cauliflower

coñac
brandy
conejo
rabbit
copa helada/helado
ice cream
cordero
lamb
crema/nata
cream
criadillas/mollejas
sweetbreads
crudo
raw
cuba libre
rum and coke
dátil
date
dulce
sweet
enchiladas
stuffed tortillas
en escabeche
pickled
endibia
chicory/endive
ensalada (mixta)
mixed salad
ensaladilla rusa
Russian salad
escalope
escalope
espárragos
asparagus
especias
spices
espinaca
spinach
fideos
noodles
filete
fillet
flan
cream caramel
frambuesa
raspberry
fresa/frutilla
strawberry
frito
fried
fruta (del tiempo)
seasonal fruit
galleta
cracker (saltine)

gambas/camarones
prawns
garbanzos
chick peas
gazpacho andaluz
gazpacho (cold
  soup)
granizado de
  limón/café
iced drink
  (lemon/coffee)
grosellas
red/black currants
guacamole
avocado dip
guisado
stew
guisantes/arvejas
peas
habas
broad beans
harina
flour
hígado de ganso
goose liver
higo
fig
huevos al plato/
  duros/revueltos
fried/hard
  boiled/scrambled
  eggs
jamón de
  York/serrano
ham (cooked/Parma
  style)
jerez (seco, dulce)
sherry (dry, sweet)
jugo
fruit juice
langosta
lobster
langostino
crayfish
leche
milk
lechuga
lettuce
legumbres
vegetables
  (legumes)
lengua
tongue

lenguado
sole
lentejas
lentils
licor
liqueur
liebre
hare
limón
lemon
lomo de
cerdo/puerco
pork tenderloin
maíz (mazorca)/
elote/choclo
corn (on the cob)
mantequilla
butter
manzana
apple
mazapán
marzipan
mejillones
mussels
melocotón durazno
(en almíbar)
peach (in syrup)
melón
melon
membrillo
quince
merluza
hake
mermelada
jam
mero
sea bass
mole
chili and chocolate
sauce
morcilla
black pudding
(sausage)
mostaza
mustard
muslo de pollo
drumstick
nuez
walnut
ostras
oysters
paella
paella
pan
bread

pastel/queque
cake
papas/patatas fritas
French fries
pato (silvestre)
(wild) duck
pechuga (de pollo)
(chicken) breast
pepino
cucumber
pepinillos
gherkins
pera
pear
perdiz
partridge
perejil
parsley
pescado
fish
picadillo de ternera
chopped veal
pierna (de cordero)
leg (of lamb)
pimentón/chile
paprika
pimienta
pepper
pimientos
green/red peppers
piña
pineapple
plancha (a la)
grilled
plátano/banana
banana
plato principal
main course
platos típicos
regional specialities
pollo
chicken
puerro/poro
leek
pulpo
octopus
queso
cheese
rábanos
radishes
rabo de buey
oxtail
rape
monkfish

remolacha
beetroot
riñones
kidneys
rodaballo
turbot
romana (a la)
deep fried
vino rosado
rosé wine
salchicha
sausage
salchichón/salame
salami
salmón
salmon
salmón ahumado
smoked salmon
salmonete
red mullet
sandía
water melon
sandwich
sandwich
sangría
sangría
sardinas
sardines
setas/champiñones
mushrooms
solomillo/lomo de
buey/vaca
fillet of beef
sopa
soup
taco
stuffed maize/corn
pancake
tarta helada
ice cream cake
tequila
tequila
ternera
veal
tinto
red wine
tocino
bacon
tortilla
maize/corn pancake
tortilla española
Spanish omelette
(potato)

| | | |
|---|---|---|
| tortilla francesa | turrón | vinagre |
| **plain omelette** | **nougat** | **vinegar** |
| tortitas | uvas | zanahorias |
| **waffles** | **grapes** | **carrots** |
| trucha | vainitas/chauchas | jugo de naranja |
| **trout** | **French beans** | **orange juice** |
| trufas | verduras | |
| **truffles** | **green vegetables** | |

**Eating out**

# On the road

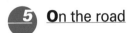

## 5 On the road

### 5.1 Asking for directions

| | |
|---|---|
| Excuse me, could I ask you something? | Perdone, ¿podría preguntarle algo? *pehrdohneh, pohdreeah prehgoontahrleh ahlgoh?* |
| I've lost my way | Me he perdido *meh eh pehrdeedoh* |
| Is there a(n)... around here? | ¿Sabe dónde hay un(a)...por aquí? *sahbeh dohndeh ay oon(ah)...pohr ahkee?* |
| Is this the way to...? | ¿Se va por aquí a...? *seh bah pohr ahkee ah...?* |
| Could you tell me how to get to the... (name of place) by car/on foot? | ¿Podría decirme cómo llegar a... (en coche/a pie)? *pohdreeah dehseermeh kohmoh lyehgahr ah... (ehn kohcheh/ah pyeh)?* |
| What's the quickest way to...? | ¿Cómo hago para llegar lo antes posible a...? *kohmoh ahgoh pahrah lyehgahr loh ahntehs pohseebleh ah...?* |
| How many kilometers is it to...? | ¿Cuántos kilómetros faltan para llegar a...? *kwahntohs keelohmehtrohs fahltahn pahrah lyehgahr ah...?* |
| Could you point it out on the map? | ¿Podría señalarlo en el mapa? *pohdreeah sehnyahlahrloh ehn ehl mahpah?* |

| | |
|---|---|
| No sé; no soy de aquí | I don't know, I don't know my way around here |
| Por aquí no es | You're going the wrong way |
| Tiene que volver a... | You have to go back to... |
| Allí los carteles le indicarán | From there on just follow the signs |
| Vuelva a preguntar allí | When you get there, ask again |

| | | |
|---|---|---|
| derecho **straight ahead** | la calle **the street** | a desnivel **the overpass** |
| a la izquierda **left** | el semáforo **the traffic light** | el puente **the bridge** |
| a la derecha **right** | el túnel **the tunnel** | el paso a nivel/ las barreras **the grade crossing/ the crossing gates** |
| doblar **turn** | el stop **the "yield" sign** | el cartel en dirección de... **the sign pointing to...** |
| seguir **follow** | el edificio **the building** | la flecha **the arrow** |
| cruzar **cross** | en la esquina **at the corner** | |
| el cruce **the intersection** | el río **the river** | |

| | |
|---|---|
| Su pasaporte, por favor _____ | Your passport, please |
| La tarjeta verde, por favor _____ | Your green card, please |
| El permiso de circulación/la carta _____ gris, por favor | Your vehicle documents, please |
| ¿Adónde va? _____ | Where are you heading? |
| ¿Cuánto tiempo piensa quedarse? _____ | How long are you planning to stay? |
| ¿Tiene algo que declarar? _____ | Do you have anything to declare? |
| ¿Puede abrir esto? _____ | Open this, please |

My children are entered ___ on this passport

Mis hijos están registrados en este pasaporte
*mees eehohs ehstahn rehheestrahdohs ehn ehsteh pahsahpohrteh*

I'm travelling through _____

Estoy de paso
*ehstoy deh pahsoh*

I'm going on vacation to... _

Voy de vacaciones a...
*boy deh bahkahsyohnehs ah...*

I'm on a business trip _____

He venido en viaje de negocios
*eh behneedoh ehn byahheh deh nehgohsyohs*

I don't know how long_____ I'll be staying yet

Todavía no sé cuánto tiempo me quedaré
*tohdahbeeah noh seh kwahntoh tyehmpoh meh kehdahreh*

I'll be staying here for _____ a weekend

Pienso quedarme un fin de semana
*pyehnsoh kehdahrmeh oon feen deh sehmahnah*

– for a few days _____

Pienso quedarme unos días
*pyehnsoh kehdahrmeh oonohs deeahs*

– for a week_____

Pienso quedarme una semana
*pyehnsoh kehdahrmeh oonah sehmahnah*

– for two weeks _____

Pienso quedarme dos semanas
*pyehnsoh kehdahrmeh dohs sehmahnahs*

I've got nothing to_____ declare

No tengo nada que declarar
*noh tehngoh nahdah keh dehklahrahr*

I've got...with me_____

Traigo...
*trahygoh...*

– ...cartons of cigarettes_____

Traigo...cartones de cigarros
*trahygoh...kahrtohnehs deh seegahrrohs*

– ...bottles of... _____

Traigo...botellas de...
*trahygoh...bohtehlyahs deh...*

– some souvenirs _____

Traigo algunos recuerdos de viaje
*trahygoh ahlgoonohs rehkwehrdohs deh byahheh*

These are personal_____ effects

Estos son artículos personales
*ehstohs sohn ahrteekoolohs pehrsohnahlehs*

These are not new _____

Estas cosas no son nuevas
*ehstahs kohsahs noh sohn nwehbahs*

| | |
|---|---|
| Here's the receipt _____ | Aquí está el recibo |
| | *ahkee ehstah ehl rehseeboh* |
| This is for private use _____ | Esto es para uso personal |
| | *ehstoh ehs pahrah oosoh pehrsohnahl* |
| How much import duty _____ do I have to pay? | ¿Cuánto tengo que pagar por derechos de aduana? |
| | *kwahntoh tehngoh keh pahgahr pohr dehrehchohs deh ahdwahnah?* |
| Can I go now? _____ | ¿Puedo seguir? |
| | *pwehdoh sehgheer?* |

| | |
|---|---|
| Porter! _____ | ¡Mozo! |
| | *mohsoh!* |
| Could you take this _____ luggage to...? | ¿Podría llevar este equipaje a...? |
| | *pohdreeah lyehbahr ehsteh ehkeepahheh ah...?* |
| How much do I _____ owe you? | ¿Cuánto le debo? |
| | *kwahntoh leh dehboh?* |
| Where can I find a _____ luggage cart? | ¿Dónde hay carritos para el equipaje? |
| | *dohndeh ay kahrreetohs pahrah ehl ehkeepahheh?* |
| Could you store this _____ luggage for me? | ¿Podría dejar este equipaje en la consigna? |
| | *pohdreeah dehhahr ehsteh ehkeepahheh ehn lah kohnseegnah?* |
| Where are the luggage _____ lockers? | ¿Dónde está la consigna automática? |
| | *dohndeh ehstah lah kohnseegnah ahootohmahteekah?* |
| I can't get the locker _____ open | No logro abrir la puerta de la consigna |
| | *noh lohgroh ahbreer lah pwehrtah deh lah kohnseegnah* |
| How much is it per item ____ per day? | ¿Cuánto sale por bulto y por día? |
| | *kwahntoh sahleh pohr booltoh ee pohr deeah?* |
| This is not my bag/ _____ suitcase | Este/ésta no es mi bolso/mi maleta |
| | *ehsteh/ehstah noh ehs mee bohlsoh/mee mahlehtah* |
| There's one item/bag/ _____ suitcase missing still | Todavía falta un bulto/un bolso/una maleta |
| | *tohdahbeeah fahltah oon booltoh/oon bohlsoh/oonah mahlehtah* |
| My suitcase is damaged ____ | Me han dañado la maleta/valija |
| | *meh ahn dahnyahdoh lah mahlehtah/bahleehah* |

## 5.4 Traffic signs

a la derecha
**right**
a la izquierda
**left**
abierto
**open**
altura máxima
**maximum height**
arcenes sin afirmar
**soft shoulders**
¡atención, peligro!
**danger**
autopista de peaje
**toll road**
autovía
**highway**
bajada peligrosa
**steep hill**
calzada resbaladiza
**slippery road**
cambio de sentido
**change of direction**
cañada
**animals crossing**
carretera comarcal
**secondary road**
carretera cortada
**road closed**
carretera en mal
 estado
**irregular road**
 **surface**
carretera nacional
**main road**

ceda el paso
**yield**
cerrado
**closed**
cruce peligroso
**dangerous crossing**
curvas en ... km
**curves for...km**
despacio
**drive slowly**
desprendimientos
**loose rocks**
desvío
**detour**
dirección prohibida
**no entry**
dirección única
**one-way traffic**
encender las luces
**turn on lights**
espere
**wait**
estacionamiento
 reglamentado
**limited parking zone**
excepto...
**except for...**
fin de...
**end of...**
hielo
**ice on road**
niebla
**beware fog**

obras
**roadworks ahead**
paso a nivel
 (sin barreras)
**grade crossing**
 **(no gates)**
paso de ganado
**cattle crossing**
peaje
**toll**
peatones
**pedestrian crossing**
precaución
**caution**
prohibido estacionar
**no parking**
prohibido adelantar/
 rebasar
**no passing**
puesto de socorro
**first aid**
salida
**exit**
salida de camiones
**trucks exit**
substancias
 peligrosas
**dangerous**
 **substances**
travesía peligrosa
**dangerous crossing**
zona peatonal
**pedestrian zone**

**On the road**

## 5.5 The car

*See the diagram on page 51.*

## 5.6 The gas station

| | |
|---|---|
| How many kilometers to ___ the next gas station, please? | ¿Cuántos kilómetros faltan para la próxima gasolinera? *kwahntohs keelohmehtrohs fahltahn pahrah lah prohxeemah gahsohleenehrah?* |
| I would like...liters of..., ___ please | Póngame...litros de..., por favor *pohngahmeh...leetrohs deh..., pohr fahbohr* |
| – super _____ | Póngame...litros de gasolina súper *pohngahmeh...leetrohs de gahsohleenah soopehr* |
| – leaded _____ | Póngame...litros de gasolina normal *pohngahmeh...leetrohs deh gahsohleenah nohrmahl* |

47

| – unleaded_____ | Póngame...litros de gasolina sin plomo |
| | *pohngahmeh...leetrohs deh gahsohleenah* |
| | *seen plohmoh* |
| – diesel _____ | Póngame...litros de gasóleo |
| | *pohngahmeh...leetrohs deh gahsohlehoh* |

| I would like... _____ | Póngame gasolina por... |
| worth of gas, please | *pohngahmeh gahsohleenah pohr...* |
| Fill her up, please _____ | Lléneme el depósito/tanque, por favor |
| | *lyehnehmeh ehl dehpohseetoh/tahnkeh,* |
| | *pohr fahbohr* |
| Could you check...? _____ | ¿Podría controlar/revisar...? |
| | *pohdreeah kohntrohlahr/rehbeesar?* |
| – the oil level _____ | ¿Podría controlar/revisar el nivel del |
| | aceite? |
| | *pohdreeah kohntrohlahr/rehbeesar ehl* |
| | *neebehl dehl ahseheeteh?* |
| – the tire pressure _____ | ¿Podría controlar/revisar la presión de los |
| | neumáticos? |
| | *pohdreeah kohntrohlahr/rehbeesar lah* |
| | *prehsyohn deh lohs nehoomahteekohs?* |
| Could you change the ____ | ¿Podría cambiar el aceite? |
| oil, please? | *pohdreeah kahmbyahr ehl ahseheeteh?* |
| Could you clean the ____ | ¿Podría limpiar los cristales/el parabrisas? |
| windows/the windshield, | *pohdreeah leempyahr lohs kreestahlehs/ehl* |
| please? | *pahrahbreesahs?* |
| Could you please wash ____ | ¿Podría lavar el carro/auto/coche? |
| the car? | *pohdreeah lahbahr ehl kahrroh/ahootoh/* |
| | *kohcheh?* |

## 5 .7 Breakdown and repairs

| I'm having car trouble.____ | Tengo una avería. ¿Podría ayudarme? |
| Could you give me a | *tehngoh oonah ahbehreeah. pohdreeah* |
| hand? | *ahyoodahrmeh?* |
| I've run out of gas _____ | Me quedé sin gasolina/bencina/nafta |
| | *meh kehdeh seen gahsohleenah/* |
| | *behnseenah/nahftah* |
| I've locked the keys_____ | Me he dejado las llaves en el carro/auto/ |
| in the car | coche |
| | *meh eh dehhahdoh lahs lyabehs ehn ehl* |
| | *kahrroh/ahootoh/kohcheh* |
| The car/motorbike/ _____ | El carro/coche/la moto/el ciclomotor no |
| moped won't start | arranca |
| | *ehl kahrroh/kohcheh/lah mohtoh/ehl* |
| | *seeklohmohtohr noh ahrrahnkah* |
| Could you contact the ____ | ¿Podría avisar al auxilio en carretera? |
| road assistance service | *pohdreeah ahbeesar ahl ahooxeelyoh ehn* |
| for me, please? | *kahrrehtehrah?* |
| Could you call a garage____ | ¿Podría llamar por teléfono a un taller |
| for me, please? | mecánico? |
| | *pohdreeah lyahmahr pohr tehlehfohnoh ah* |
| | *oon tahlyehr mehkahneekoh?* |
| Could you give me _____ | ¿Me podría llevar a...? |
| a lift to...? | *meh pohdreeah lyehbahr ah...?* |

|  |  |
|---|---|
| – a garage/into town? | ¿Me podría llevar a un taller mecánico/a la ciudad? _meh pohdreeah lyehbahr ah oon tahlyehr mehkahneekoh/ah lah syoodahdh?_ |
| – a phone booth? | ¿Me podría llevar a una caseta/cabina de teléfonos? _meh pohdreeah lyehbahr ah oonah kahsehtah/ kahbeenah deh tehlehfohnohs?_ |
| – an emergency phone? | ¿Me podría llevar a un teléfono de emergencia? _meh pohdreeah lyehbahr ah oon tehlehfohnoh deh ehmehrḥehnsyah?_ |
| Can we take my bicycle/moped? | ¿Podríamos llevar la bicicleta/el ciclomotor? _pohdreeahmohs lyehbahr lah beeseeklehtah/ehl seeklohmohtohr?_ |
| Could you tow me to a garage? | ¿Podría remolcarme hasta un taller mecánico? _pohdreeah rehmohlkahrmeh ahstah oon tahlyehr mehkahneekoh?_ |
| There's probably something wrong with...(See 5.8). | Me parece que está fallando el/la... _meh pahrehseh keh ehstah fahlyahndoh ehl/lah..._ |
| Can you fix it? | ¿Podría arreglarlo? _pohdreeah ahrrehglahrloh?_ |
| Could you fix my tire? | ¿Podría arreglar el neumático? _pohdreeah ahrrehglahr ehl nehoomahteekoh?_ |
| Could you change this wheel? | ¿Podría cambiar esta rueda? _pohdreeah kahmbyahr ehstah rwehdah?_ |
| Can you fix it so it'll get me to...? | ¿Podría arreglarlo de tal manera que pueda seguir hasta...? _pohdreeah ahrrehglahrloh deh tahl mahnehrah keh pwehdah sehgheer ahstah...?_ |
| Which garage can help me? | ¿En qué taller me podrán ayudar entonces? _ehn keh tahlyehr meh pohdrahn ahyoodahr ehntohnsehs?_ |
| When will my car/bicycle be ready? | ¿Para cuándo estará mi coche/bicicleta? _pahrah kwahndoh ehstahrah mee kohcheh/beeseeklehtah?_ |
| Can I wait for it here? | ¿Puedo esperar aquí? _pwehdoh ehspehrahr ahkee?_ |
| How much will it cost? | ¿Cuánto me va a salir? _kwahntoh meh bah ah sahleer?_ |
| Could you itemize the bill? | ¿Podría especificar la cuenta? _pohdreeah ehspehseefeekahr lah kwehntah?_ |
| Can I have a receipt for the insurance? | ¿Me podría dar un recibo para el seguro? _meh pohdreeah dahr oon rehseeboh pahrah ehl sehgooroh?_ |

5

**On the road**

## The parts of a car
(the diagram shows the numbered parts)

| | | |
|---|---|---|
| 1 battery | la batería | *lah bahtehreeah* |
| 2 rear light | el faro piloto | *ehl fahroh peelohtoh* |
| 3 rear-view mirror | el retrovisor | *ehl rehtrohbeesohr* |
| backup light | la luz de marcha atrás | *lah loos deh mahrchah ahtrahs* |
| 4 aerial | la antena | *lah ahntehnah* |
| car radio | la autorradio | *lah ahootohrrahdyoh* |
| 5 gas tank | el depósito/tanque de gasolina | *ehl dehpohseetoh/tahnkeh deh gahsohleenah* |
| inside mirror | el espejo interior | *ehl ehspehhoh eentehreeohr* |
| 6 spark plugs | las bujías | *lahs booheeahs* |
| fuel filter/pump | el separador de gasolina | *ehl sehpahrahdohr deh gahsohleenah* |
| 7 side mirror | el espejo exterior | *ehl ehspehoh ehxtehryohr* |
| 8 bumper | el parachoques | *ehl pahrahchohkehs* |
| carburetor | el carburador | *ehl kahrboorahdohr* |
| crankcase | el cárter | *ehl kahrtehr* |
| cylinder | el cilindro | *ehl seeleendroh* |
| ignition | los contactos del ruptor | *lohs kohntahktohs dehl rooptohr* |
| warning light | la luz piloto | *lah loos peelohtoh* |
| generator | la dinamo | *lah deenahmoh* |
| accelerator | el pedal del acelerador | *ehl pehdahl dehl ahsehlehrahdohr* |
| handbrake | el freno de mano | *ehl frehnoh deh mahnoh* |
| valve | la válvula | *lah bahlboolah* |
| 9 muffler | el silenciador | *ehl seelehnsyahdohr* |
| 10 trunk | el maletero/la cajuela | *ehl mahlehtehroh lah kahhwehlah* |
| 11 headlight | el faro | *ehl fahroh* |
| crank shaft | el cigüeñal | *ehl seegwehnyahl* |
| 12 air filter | el filtro de aire | *ehl feeltroh deh ayreh* |
| fog lamp | la luz antiniebla trasera | *lah loos ahnteenyehblah trahsehrah* |
| 13 engine block | el bloque motor | *ehl blohkeh mohtohr* |
| camshaft | el árbol de levas | *ehl ahrbohl deh lehbahs* |
| oil filter/pump | el filtro de aceite | *ehl feeltroh deh ahseeteh* |
| dipstick | la varilla indicadora de nivel de aceite | *lah bahreelyah eendeekahdohrah deh neebehl deh ahseyteh* |
| pedal | el pedal | *ehl pehdahl* |
| 14 door | la puerta | *lah pwertah* |
| 15 radiator | el radiador | *ehl rahdyahdohr* |
| 16 brake disc | el disco del freno | *ehl deeskoh dehl frehnoh* |
| spare wheel | la rueda de auxilio | *lah rwehdah deh ahookseeleeoh* |
| 17 indicator | el intermitente | *ehl eentehrmeetehnteh* |
| steering wheel | el volante | *ehl bohlahnteh* |
| 18 windshield wiper | el limpiaparabrisas | *ehl leempyahpahrahbreesahs* |
| 19 shock absorbers | los amortiguadores | *lohs ahmohrteegwahdohrehs* |
| sunroof | el techo corredizo | *ehl tehchoh kohrrehdeesoh* |
| spoiler | el spoiler | *ehl spoheelehr* |

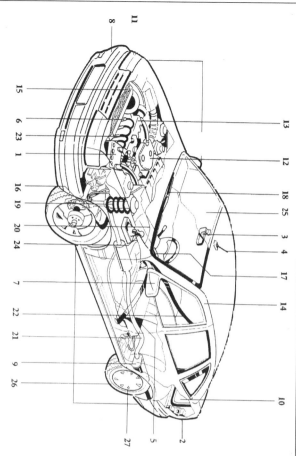

| | starter motor | el motor de arranque | *ehl mohtohr deh ahrrahnkeh* |
| 20 | steering column | el cárter de la dirección | *ehl kahrtehr deh lah deerehksyohn* |
| 21 | exhaust pipe | el tubo de escape | *ehl tooboh deh ehskahpeh* |
| 22 | seat belt | el cinturón de seguridad | *ehl seentoorohn deh sehgooreedahdh* |
| | fan | el ventilador | *ehl behnteelahdohr* |
| 23 | distributor cables | los cables del distribuidor | *lohs kahblehs dehl deestreebooeedohr* |
| 24 | gear shift | la palanca de cambios/velocidades | *lah pahlahnkah deh kahmbyohs/behlohseedahdes* |
| 25 | windshield | el parabrisas | *ehl pahrahbreesahs* |
| | water pump | la bomba de agua | *lah bohmbah deh ahgwah* |
| 26 | wheel | la rueda | *lah rwehdah* |
| 27 | hubcap | el tapacubos | *ehl tahpahkoobohs* |
| | piston | el émbolo/pistón | *ehl ehmbohloh/peestohn* |

51

### **5**.8 The bicycle/moped

*See the diagram on page 55.*
● **Bicycle paths** are rare in Latin American countries.

| | |
|---|---|
| No tengo piezas de repuesto para su ___ coche/su bicicleta | I don't have parts for your car/bicycle |
| Las piezas de repuesto me las tienen ___ que traer de otro sitio | I have to get the parts from somewhere else |
| Tengo que encargar las piezas de _____ repuesto | I have to order the parts |
| Eso llevará medio día _____ | That'll take half a day |
| Eso llevará un día _____ | That'll take a day |
| Eso llevará unos días _____ | That'll take a few days |
| Eso llevará una semana _____ | That'll take a week |
| Su coche ha quedado totalmente _____ destruido | Your car is a write-off |
| Ya no se puede hacer nada para_____ arreglarlo | It can't be repaired |
| El coche/la moto/el ciclomotor/la _____ bicicleta estará para las... | The car/motorbike/moped/ bicycle will be ready at... o'clock |

### **5**.9 Renting a vehicle

| | |
|---|---|
| I'd like to rent a... _____ | Quisiera alquilar un/una... *keesyehrah ahlkeelahr oon/oonah...* |
| Do I need a (special) _____ license for that? | ¿Hace falta un permiso de conducir (especial)? *ahse fahltah oon pehrmeesoh deh kohndooseer (ehspehsyahl)?* |
| I'd like to rent the...for... ____ | Quisiera alquilar el/la...por... *keesyehrah ahlkeelahr ehl/lah...pohr...* |
| – one day _____ | Quisiera alquilar el/la...por un día *keesyehrah ahlkeelahr ehl/lah...pohr oon deeah* |
| – two days _____ | Quisiera alquilar el/la...por dos días *keesyehrah ahlkeelahr ehl/lah...pohr dohs deeahs* |
| How much is that per_____ day/week? | ¿Cuánto sale por día/semana? *kwahntoh sahleh pohr deeah/pohr sehmahnah?* |
| How much is the _____ deposit? | ¿Cuánto es la fianza? *kwahntoh ehs lah fyahnsah?* |
| Could I have a receipt _____ for the deposit? | ¿Me podría dar un recibo por el pago de la fianza? *meh pohdreeah dahr oon rehseeboh pohr ehl pahgoh deh lah fyahnsah?* |
| How much is the _____ surcharge per kilometer? | ¿Cuánto hay que pagar extra por kilómetro? *kwahntoh ay keh pahgahr ehxtrah pohr keelohmehtroh?* |
| Does that include _____ gas ? | ¿Está incluida la gasolina? *ehstah eenklooeedah lah gahsohleenah?* |

| Does that include insurance? | ¿Está incluido el seguro? |
|---|---|
| | ehstah eenklooeedoh ehl sehgooroh? |
| What time can I pick the...up tomorrow? | ¿A qué hora puedo pasar mañana a buscar el/la...? |
| | ah keh ohrah pwehdoh pahsahr mahnyahnah ah booskahr ehl/lah...? |
| When does the...have to be back? | ¿A qué hora tengo que devolver el/la...? |
| | ah keh ohrah tehngoh keh dehbohlbehr ehl/lah...? |
| Where's the gas tank? | ¿Dónde está el depósito/tanque de gasolina? |
| | dohndeh ehstah ehl dehpohseetoh/tahnkeh deh gahsohleenah? |
| What sort of fuel does it take? | ¿Qué tipo de combustible hay que echarle? |
| | keh teepoh deh kohmboosteebleh ay keh ehchahrleh? |

## 5.10 Hitchhiking

| Where are you heading? | ¿Adónde va? |
|---|---|
| | ahdohndeh bah? |
| Can I come along? | ¿Me podría llevar? |
| | meh pohdreeah lyehbahr? |
| Can my boyfriend/ girlfriend come too? | ¿Podría llevar también a mi amigo/amiga? |
| | pohdreeah lyehbahr tahmbyehn ah mee ahmeegoh/ahmeegah? |
| I'm trying to get to... | Voy a... |
| | boy ah... |
| Is that on the way to...? | ¿Eso está camino de...? |
| | ehsoh ehstah kahmeenoh deh...? |
| Could you drop me off...? | ¿Me podría dejar...? |
| | meh pohdreeah dehhahr...? |
| – here? | ¿Me podría dejar aquí mismo? |
| | meh pohdreeah dehhahr ahkee meesmoh? |
| – at the...exit? | ¿Me podría dejar en la salida de...? |
| | meh pohdreeah dehhahr ehn lah sahleedah deh...? |
| – in the center? | ¿Me podría dejar en el centro? |
| | meh pohdreeah dehhahr ehn ehl sehntroh? |
| – at the next rotary? | ¿Me podría dejar en la próxima rotonda/glorieta? |
| | meh pohdreeah dehhahr ehn lah prohxeemah rohtohndah/glohryehtah? |
| Could you stop here, please? | ¿Podría pararse aquí? |
| | pohdreeah pahrahrseh ahkee? |
| I'd like to get out here | Quisiera bajarme aquí |
| | keesyehrah bahhahrmeh ahkee |
| Thanks for the lift | Gracias por llevarme |
| | grahsyahs pohr lyehbahrmeh |

5

On the road

# The parts of a bicycle
(the diagram shows the numbered parts)

|  |  |  |
|---|---|---|
| 1 rear light | el piloto | *ehl peelohtoh* |
| 2 rear wheel | la rueda trasera | *lah rwehdah trahsehrah* |
| 3 (luggage) carrier | el portaequipajes | *ehl pohrtahehkeepahhehs* |
| 4 bicycle fork | la cabeza | *lah kahbehsah* |
| 5 bell | el timbre | *ehl teembreh* |
| inner tube | la cámara | *lah kahmahrah* |
| tire | el neumático/la cubierta | *ehl nehoomahteekoh/lah koobyehrtah* |
| 6 crank | la biela | *lah byehlah* |
| 7 gear change | el cambio de velocidades | *ehl kahmbyoh deh behloseedahdehs* |
| wire | el hilo | *ehl eeloh* |
| generator | la dinamo | *lah deenahmoh* |
| bicycle trailer | el remolque de bicicleta | *ehl rehmohlkeh deh beeseeklehtah* |
| frame | el cuadro | *ehl kwahdroh* |
| 8 dress guard | el guardafaldas | *ehl gwardahfahldahs* |
| 9 chain | la cadena de rodillos | *lah kahdehnah deh rohdeelyohs* |
| chain guard | el cubrecadena/el cárter | *ehl koobrehkahdehnah/ehl kahrtehr* |
| chain lock | la cadena antirrobo | *lah kahdehnah ahnteerrohboh* |
| odometer | el contador kilométrico | *ehl kohntahdohr keelohmehtreekoh* |
| child's seat | la silla para niños | *lah seelyah pahrah neenyohs* |
| 10 headlight | el faro | *ehl fahroh* |
| bulb | la bombilla | *lah bohmbeelyah* |
| 11 pedal | el pedal | *ehl pehdahl* |
| 12 pump | la bombilla | *lah bohmbeelyah* |
| 13 reflector | el cristal reflectante | |
| 14 brake pad | | *rehflehktahnteh* |
| 15 brake cable | la zapatilla del freno | *lah thahpahteelyah dehl frehnoh* |
| 16 ring lock | el cable del freno | *ehl kahbleh dehl frehnoh* |
| 17 carrier straps | la cerradura | *lah sehrrahdoorah* |
| tachometer | las bandas elásticas | *lahs bahndahs ehlahsteekahs* |
| 18 spoke | el velocímetro | *ehl behlohseemehtroh* |
| 19 mudguard | el radio/el rayo | *ehl rahdyoh/ehl rahyoh* |
| 20 handlebar | el guardabarros | *ehl gwahrdahbahrrohs* |
| 21 chain wheel | el manillar | *ehl mahneelyahr* |
| toe clip | el piñón | *ehl peenyohn* |
| 22 crank axle | el calapiés | *ehl kahlahpyehs* |
| drum brake | el eje del cigueñal | *ehl ehheh dehl seegwehnyal* |
| rim | el freno de tambor | *ehl frehnoh deh tahmbohr* |
| 23 tube | la llanta | *lah lyahntah* |
| 24 valve | la válvula | *lah bahlboolah* |
| valve tube | el tubo de la válvula | *ehl tooboh deh lah bahlboolah* |

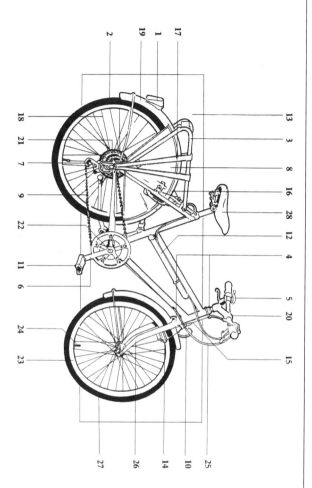

| 25 gear cable | | |
| --- | --- | --- |
| | el cable de | *ehl kahbleh deh* |
| 26 fork | velocidades | *behlohseedahdehs* |
| 27 front wheel | la horquilla | *lah ohrkeelyah* |
| 28 seat | la rueda delantera | *lah rwehdah dehlahntehrah* |
| | la silla | *la seelyah* |

# Public transportation

# **P**ublic transportation

## .1 In general

● **In general,** trains in Latin American countries are cheaper than buses, but slower and less comfortable. In countries where the railway network to remote areas has not been updated, the visitor has to rely on buses for land transportation, or on air services.

### *Announcements*

| | |
|---|---|
| El tren [de las 10:40] con destino a..., ___ ..., saldrá con (unos)...minutos de retraso | The [10:40] train to...has been delayed by 15 minutes |
| Por la vía 5 entrará el tren _____ [de las 10:40] con destino a.../ procedente de... | The train now arriving at platform 5 is the [10:40] train to .../from... |
| En la vía 5 está por partir el tren _____ [de las 10:40]... | The [10:40] train to...is about to leave from platform 5 |
| Su atención, por favor _____ Manténganse lejos de la vía; un tren rápido pasará por la plataforma... | Attention please! Keep your distance from the rail track, an express train will pass on platform... |
| Nos estamos aproximando a la _____ estación de... | We're now approaching... |

| | |
|---|---|
| Where does this train___ go to? | ¿Adónde va este tren? *ahdohndeh bah ehsteh trehn?* |
| Does this boat go to...? ___ | ¿Este barco va a...? *ehsteh bahrkoh bah ah...?* |
| Can I take this bus to...? ___ | ¿Puedo tomar este omnibús/autobús/ camión para ir a...? *pwehdoh tohmahr ehsteh ohmneeboos/ ahootohboos/kahmeeohn pahrah eer ah...?* |
| Does this train stop at...? ___ | ¿Este tren para en...? *ehsteh trehn pahrah ehn...?* |
| Is this seat taken/free _____ /reserved? | ¿Está ocupado/libre/reservado este asiento? *ehstah ohkoopahdoh/leebreh/rehsehrbahdoh ehsteh ahsyehntoh?* |
| I've reserved... _____ | He reservado... *eh rehsehrbahdoh...* |
| Could you tell me _____ where I have to get off for... ? | ¿Me podría decir dónde me tengo que bajar para ir a...? *meh pohdreeah dehseer dohndeh meh tehngoh keh bahhar pahrah eer ah...?* |
| Could you let me_____ know when we get to...? | ¿Me podría avisar cuando lleguemos a...? *meh pohdreeah ahbeesahr kwahndoh lyehghehmohs ah...?* |
| Could you stop at the_____ next stop, please? | La próxima parada, por favor *lah prohxeemah pahrahdah pohr fahbohr* |

| | | |
|---|---|---|
| Where are we now? _____ | ¿Dónde estamos? | |
| | *dohndeh ehstahmohs?* | |
| Do I have to get off here? __ | ¿Tengo que bajarme aquí? | |
| | *tehngoh keh bahhahrmeh ahkee?* | |
| Have we already _____ passed...? | ¿Ya hemos pasado...? | |
| | *yah ehmohs pahsahdoh...?* | |
| How long have I been _____ asleep? | ¿Cuánto tiempo he dormido? | |
| | *kwahntoh tyehmpoh eh dohrmeedoh?* | |
| How long does... _____ stop here? | ¿Cuánto tiempo se queda aquí...? | |
| | *kwahntoh tyehmpoh seh kehdah ahkee?* | |
| Can I come back on the _____ same ticket? | ¿Este boleto me sirve para volver? | |
| | *ehsteh bohlehtoh meh seerbeh pahrah bohlbehr?* | |
| Can I change on this_____ ticket? | ¿Se puede hacer trasbordo con este boleto? | |
| | *seh pwehdeh ahtehehr trahsbohrdoh kohn ehsteh bohlehtoh?* | |
| How long is this ticket _____ valid for? | ¿Hasta cuándo es válido este boleto? | |
| | *ahstah kwahndoh ehs bahleedoh ehsteh bohlehtoh* | |

## 6 .2 Questions to passengers

### Ticket types

| ¿Primera o segunda clase? _____ | First or second class? |
|---|---|
| ¿Boleto de ida o de ida y vuelta?_____ | Single or return? |
| ¿Fumadores o no fumadores? _____ | Smoking or nonsmoking? |
| ¿Ventanilla o pasillo?_____ | Window or aisle? |
| ¿Adelante o atrás? _____ | Front or back? |
| ¿Asiento o litera? _____ | Seat or berth? |
| ¿Arriba, en el medio o abajo?_____ | Top, middle or bottom? |
| ¿Clase turista o preferente?_____ | Tourist class or business class? |
| ¿Camarin o butaca? _____ | Cabin or seat? |
| ¿Individual o doble? _____ | Single or double? |
| ¿Cuántas personas viajan? _____ | How many are travelling? |

### Destination

| ¿Adónde quiere ir? _____ | Where are you travelling? |
|---|---|
| ¿Qué día sale? _____ | When are you leaving? |
| Su...sale a las... _____ | Your...leaves at... |
| Tiene que hacer trasbordo _____ | You have to change trains |
| Tiene que bajarse en... _____ | You have to get off at... |
| Tiene que pasar por... _____ | You have to travel via... |
| El viaje de ida es el día... _____ | The outward journey is on... |
| El viaje de vuelta es el día... _____ | The return journey is on... |
| Tiene que embarcar a las...a _____ más tardar | You have to be on board by... |

*Inside the vehicle*

| | |
|---|---|
| Boletos, por favor _____ | Your ticket, please |
| Su reserva/reservación, por favor _____ | Your reservation, please |
| Su pasaporte, por favor _____ | Your passport, please |
| Se ha equivocado de asiento _____ | You're in the wrong seat |
| Se ha equivocado de... _____ | You're on/in the wrong... |
| Este asiento está reservado _____ | This seat is reserved |
| Tiene que pagar un suplemento _____ | You'll have to pay an extra charge |
| El...tiene un retraso de...minutos _____ | The...has been delayed by...minutes |

## 6.3 Tickets

| | |
|---|---|
| Where can I...? _____ | ¿Dónde...?<br>*dohndeh...?* |
| – buy a ticket? _____ | ¿Dónde se compran los boletos?<br>*dohndeh seh kohmprahn lohs bohlehtohs?* |
| – make a reservation? _____ | ¿Dónde se hacen las reservas/reservaciones?<br>*dohndeh seh ahsehn lahs rehsehrbahs/rehsehrbahsyohnes?* |
| – reserve a flight? _____ | ¿Dónde puedo hacer una reserva para un vuelo?<br>*dohndeh pwehdoh ahsehr oonah rehsehrbah pahrah oon bwehloh?* |
| Could I have a...to...., please? | Quiero un/una...a...<br>*kyehroh oon/oonah...ah...* |
| – a single _____ | Quiero un boleto de ida a...<br>*kyehroh oon bohlehtoh deh eedah ah...* |
| – a return _____ | Quiero un boleto de ida y vuelta a...<br>*kyehroh oon bohlehtoh deh eedah ee bwehltah ah...* |
| first class _____ | en primera clase<br>*ehn preemehrah klahseh* |
| second class _____ | en segunda clase<br>*ehn sehgoondah klahseh* |
| tourist class _____ | en clase turista<br>*ehn klahseh tooreestah* |
| business class _____ | en clase preferente<br>*ehn klahseh prehfehrehnteh* |
| I'd like to reserve a seat/berth/cabin | Quisiera reservar un asiento/una litera/un camarín<br>*keesyehrah rehsehrbahr oon ahsyehntoh/oonah leetehrah/oon kahmahreen* |
| I'd like to book a berth in the sleeping car | Quisiera reservar un camarín/una alcoba en un coche cama<br>*keesyehrah rehsehrbahr oon kahmahreen/oonah ahlkohbah ehn oon kohcheh kahmah* |
| top/middle/bottom _____ | arriba/en el medio/abajo<br>*ahrreebah/ehn ehl mehdyoh/ahbahhoh* |
| smoking/no smoking _____ | fumadores/no fumadores<br>*foomahdohrehs/noh foomahdohrehs* |

| by the window _____ | ventanilla |
| | *behntahneelyah* |
| single/double _____ | individual/doble |
| | *eendeebeedwahl/dohbleh* |
| at the front/back_____ | adelante/atrás |
| | *ahdehlahnteh/ahtrahs* |
| There are...of us_____ | Somos...personas |
| | *sohmohs...pehrsohnahs* |
| a car _____ | un carro/auto |
| | *oon kahrroh/ahootoh* |
| a camper/RV _____ | una caravana/casa rodante |
| | *oonah kahrahbahnah/kahsah rohdahnteh* |
| ...bicycles_____ | ...bicicletas |
| | *...beeseeklehtahs* |
| Do you also have...? _____ | ¿Tienen...? |
| | *tyehnehn...?* |
| – season tickets? _____ | ¿Tienen abonos? |
| | *tyehnen ahbohnohs?* |
| – weekly tickets? _____ | ¿Tienen abonos semanales? |
| | *tyehnehn ahbohnohs sehmahnahlehs?* |
| – monthly season _____ | ¿Tienen abonos mensuales? |
| tickets? | *tyehnehn ahbohnohs mehnswahlehs?* |

## 6 .4 Information

| Where's...? _____ | ¿Dónde hay...? |
| | *dohndeh ay...?* |
| Where's the information ___ | ¿Dónde está la oficina de información? |
| desk? | *dohndeh ehstah lah ohfeeseenah deh* |
| | *eenfohrmahsyohn?* |
| Where can I find a_____ | ¿Dónde hay un horario? |
| timetable? | *dohndeh ay oon ohrahryoh?* |
| Where's the...desk? _____ | ¿Dónde está el mostrador de...? |
| | *dohndeh ehstah ehl mohstrahdohr deh...?* |
| Do you have a city map___ | ¿Tendría un plano de la ciudad con la red |
| with the bus/the subway | de autobuses/metro? |
| routes on it? | *tehndreeah oon plahnoh deh lah syoodahdh* |
| | *kohn lah rehd deh ahootohboosehs/* |
| Do you have a _____ | *mehtroh?* |
| timetable? | ¿Tendría un horario? |
| I'd like to confirm/ _____ | *tehndreeah oon ohrahryoh?* |
| cancel/change my | Quisiera confirmar/cancelar/cambiar mi |
| reservation for/trip to... | reserva/mi viaje a... |
| | *keesyehrah kohnfeermahr/kahnsehlahr/* |
| | *kahmbyahr mee rehsehrbah/mee byahheh* |
| | *ah...* |
| Will I get my money_____ | ¿Me devuelven el dinero? |
| back? | *meh dehbwehlbehn ehl deenehroh?* |
| I want to go to..._____ | Tengo que ir a...¿Cómo hago para llegar |
| How do I get there? | (lo más rápido posible)? |
| (What's the quickest way | *tehngoh keh eer ah...kohmoh ahgoh pahrah* |
| there?) | *lyehgahr(loh mahs rahpeedoh pohseebleh)?* |
| How much is a _____ | ¿Cuánto vale un boleto de ida/de ida y |
| single/return to...? | vuelta a...? |
| | *kwahntoh bahleh oon bohlehtoh deh eedah* |
| | *ee bwehltah ah...?* |

60

| | |
|---|---|
| Do I have to pay an _____ extra charge? | ¿Tengo que pagar algún suplemento? *tehngoh keh pahgahr ahlgoon sooplehmehntoh?* |
| Can I interrupt my _____ journey with this ticket? | ¿Con este boleto puedo hacer una parada intermedia? *kohn ehsteh bohlehtoh pwehdoh ahthehr oonah pahrahdah eentehrmehdyah?* |
| How much luggage _____ am I allowed? | ¿Cuánto equipaje puedo llevar? *kwahntoh ehkeepahheh pwehdoh lyebahr?* |
| Can I send my luggage _____ in advance? | ¿Puedo enviar mi equipaje por anticipado? *pwehdoh ehnbeeahr mee ehkeepahheh pohr ahnteeseepahdoh?* |
| Does this...travel direct? ___ | ¿Este...va directo? *ehsteh...bah deerehktoh?* |
| Do I have to change? _____ Where? | ¿Tengo que hacer trasbordo? ¿Dónde? *tehngoh keh ahthehr trahsbohrdoh? dohndeh?* |
| Will there be any _____ stopovers? | ¿Habrá escalas? *ahbrah ehskahlahs?* |
| Does the boat stop at_____ any ports on the way? | ¿El barco hace alguna escala? *ehl bahrkoh ahseh ahlgoonah ehskahlah?* |
| Does the train/ _____ bus stop at...? | ¿Este tren/este autobús para en...? *ehsteh trehn/ehsteh ahootohboos pahrah ehn...?* |
| Where should I get off? ____ | ¿Dónde me tengo que bajar? *dohndeh meh tehngoh keh bahhahr?* |
| Is there a connection _____ to...? | ¿Hay enlace para...? *ay ehnlahseh pahrah...?* |
| How long do I have to ____ wait? | ¿Cuánto tengo que esperar? *kwahntoh tehngoh keh ehspehrahr?* |
| When does...leave? _____ | ¿Cuándo sale...? *kwahndoh sahleh...?* |
| What time does the _____ first/next/last...leave? | ¿A qué hora sale el primer/próximo/último...? *ah keh ohrah sahleh ehl preemehr/prohxeemoh/oolteemoh...?* |
| How long does...take? ____ | ¿Cuánto tarda...en llegar? *kwahntoh tahrdah...ehn lyehgahr?* |
| What time does...arrive ____ in...? | ¿A qué hora llega...a...? *ah keh ohrah lyegah...ah...?* |
| Where does the...to... _____ leave from? | ¿De dónde sale el...a...? *deh dohndeh sahleh ehl...ah...?* |
| Is this...to...? _____ | ¿Este es...a...? *ehsteh ehs...ah...?* |

## 6 .5 Airplanes

● **On arrival** at an airport in Spanish speaking countries, you will find the following signs:

| | |
|---|---|
| llegadas | salidas |
| arrivals | departures |

### 6 .6 Trains

● **In some countries** first and second class are available, and even sleeping berths for long distance train services. In others, local trains servicing urban areas are the fastest and most reliable public transportation, along with modern subway.

### 6 .7 Taxis

● **There are plenty of taxis** in most cities. Extra charges are payable for luggage and travel to stations or airports. It is advisable to inquire about the price in advance and make sure that you are hiring a city taxi.

| libre<br>for hire | ocupado<br>occupied | parada de taxis<br>taxi stand |
|---|---|---|

| | |
|---|---|
| Taxi! _____ | ¡Taxi!<br>_tahxee!_ |
| Could you get me a taxi, ___<br>please? | ¿Me podría llamar un taxi?<br>_meh pohdreeah lyahmahr oon tahksee?_ |
| Where can I find a taxi_____<br>around here? | ¿Dónde se puede tomar un taxi por aquí?<br>_dohndeh seh pwehdeh tohmahr oon tahxee<br>pohr ahkee?_ |
| Could you take me to..., ___<br>please? | A..., por favor<br>_ah..., pohr fahbohr_ |
| – this address _____ | A esta dirección, por favor<br>_ah ehstah deerehksyohn, pohr fahbohr_ |
| – the...hotel _____ | Al hotel..., por favor<br>_ahl ohtehl..., pohr fahbohr_ |
| – the town/center of _____<br>the city | Al centro, por favor<br>_ahl sehntroh, pohr fahbohr_ |
| – the station _____ | A la estación, por favor<br>_ah lah ehstahsyohn, pohr fahbohr_ |
| – the airport_____ | Al aeropuerto, por favor<br>_ahl ahehrohpwehrtoh, pohr fahbohr_ |
| How much is the _____<br>trip to...? | ¿Cuánto sale el recorrido hasta...?<br>_kwahntoh sahleh ehl rehkohrreedoh<br>ahstah...?_ |
| How far is it to...? _____ | ¿Cuánto es hasta...?<br>_kwahntoh ehs ahstah...?_ |
| Could you turn on the _____<br>meter, please? | ¿Podría poner en marcha el taxímetro?<br>_pohdreeah pohnehr ehn mahrchah ehl<br>tahxeemehtroh?_ |
| I'm in a hurry _____ | Estoy apurado<br>_ehstoy ahpoorahdoh_ |
| Could you speed up/slow ___<br>down a little? | ¿Podría ir más rápido/más despacio?<br>_pohdreeah eer mahs rahpeedoh/mahs<br>dehspasyoh?_ |
| Could you take a _____<br>different route? | ¿Podría ir por otro camino?<br>_pohdreeah eer pohr ohtroh kahmeenoh?_ |
| I'd like to get out here, _____<br>please | Déjeme aquí<br>_dehhehmeh ahkee_ |

Public transportation

| You have to go...here _____ | Siga...aquí |
| | *seegah...ahkee* |
| You have to go straight _____ here | Siga derecho aquí |
| | *seegah dehrehchoh akee* |
| You have to turn left _____ here | Doble a la izquierda aquí |
| | *dohbleh ah lah eeskyehrdah ahkee* |
| You have to turn right _____ here | Doble a la derecha aquí |
| | *dohbleh ah lah dehrehchah ahkee* |
| This is it _____ | Es aquí |
| | *ehs ahkee* |
| Could you wait a minute _____ for me, please? | Espéreme un momentito/tantito, por favor |
| | *ehspehrehmeh oon mohmehnteetoh/ tahnteetoh, pohr fahbohr* |

# 7

## Overnight accommodation

# Overnight accommodation

## 7 .1 General

● **In most of the** Latin American countries, cheap hotels are located around train and bus stations, while expensive international hotels can be found in the center of large cities, near airports or in residential districts. Tourist resorts normally offer a good variety of overnight accommodation.

| | |
|---|---|
| ¿Cuánto tiempo piensa quedarse? _____ | How long will you be staying? |
| Rellene este formulario, por favor _____ | Fill in this form, please |
| ¿Me permite su pasaporte? _____ | Could I see your passport? |
| Tiene que pagar una fianza _____ | I'll need a deposit |
| Tiene que pagar por adelantado _____ | You'll have to pay in advance |

| | |
|---|---|
| My name's...I've made a reservation over the phone/by mail | Me llamo...Reservé una habitación por teléfono/por carta _meh lyahmoh...eh rehsehrbeh oonah ahbeetahsyohn pohr tehlehfohnoh/pohr kahrtah_ |
| How much is it per night/week/month? | ¿Cuánto sale por noche/semana/mes? _kwahntoh sahleh pohr nohcheh/sehmahnah/ mehs?_ |
| We'll be staying at least...nights/weeks | Pensamos quedarnos al menos...noches/semanas _pehnsahmohs kehdahrnohs ahl mehnohs...nohchehs/sehmahnahs_ |
| We don't know yet | Todavía no lo sabemos exactamente _tohdahbeeah noh loh sahbehmohs ehxahktahmehnteh_ |
| Do you allow pets (cats/dogs)? | ¿Están permitidos los animales domésticos (perros/gatos)? _ehstahn pehrmeeteedohs lohs ahneemahlehs dohmehsteekohs (pehrrohs/gahtohs)?_ |
| What time does the gate/door open/close? | ¿A qué hora cierran/abren la verja/la puerta de entrada? _ah keh ohrah syehrrahn/ahbrehn lah behr<u>h</u>ah/lah pwehrtah deh ehntrahdah?_ |
| Could you get me a taxi, please? | ¿Podría llamar un taxi? _pohdreeah lyahmahr oon tahxee?_ |
| Is there any mail for me? | ¿Hay carta para mí? _ay kahrtah pahrah mee?_ |

**7 Overnight accommodation**

## .2 Camping

*See the diagram on page 69.*

| | |
|---|---|
| Puede elegir el sitio usted mismo _____ | You can pick your own site |
| El sitio se lo asignamos nosotros _____ | You'll be allocated a site |
| Este es el número de su _____ emplazamiento | This is your site number |
| Por favor pegue esto en el parabrisas ___ del carro/auto | Stick this on your car, please |
| No pierda esta tarjeta _____ | Please don't lose this card |

| | |
|---|---|
| Where's the manager? _____ | ¿Dónde está el encargado? *dohndeh ehstah ehl ehnkahrgahdoh?* |
| Are we allowed to camp here? | ¿Podemos acampar aquí? *pohdehmohs ahkahmpahr ahkee?* |
| There are...of us and ...tents | Somos...personas y...tiendas/carpas *sohmohs...pehrsohnahs ee...tyehndahs/ kahrpahs* |
| Can we pick our own site? | ¿Podemos elegir el sitio nosotros mismos? *pohdehmohs ehlehheer ehl seetyoh nohsohtrohs meesmohs?* |
| Do you have a quiet spot for us? | ¿Nos podría dar un sitio tranquilo? *nohs pohdreeah dahr oon seetyoh trahnkeeloh?* |
| Do you have any other sites available? | ¿No tiene otro sitio libre? *noh tyehneh ohtroh seetyoh leebreh?* |
| It's too windy/sunny/ shady here. | Hay mucho viento/mucho sol/mucha sombra *ay moochoh byehntoh/moochoh sohl/moochah sohmbrah* |
| It's too crowded here | Hay mucha gente *ay moochah hehnteh* |
| The ground's too hard/uneven | El suelo es muy duro/muy desigual *ehl swehloh ehs mwee dooroh/mwee dehseegwahl* |
| Do you have a level spot for the camper/trailer/folding trailer? | ¿Tiene un sitio plano para el autocaravana/la caravana/el remolque tienda? *tyehneh oon seetyoh plahnoh pahrah ehl ahootohkahrahbahnah/lah kahrahbahnah/ehl rehmohlkeh-tyehndah?* |
| Could we have adjoining sites? | ¿Tiene dos plazas juntas? *tyehneh dohs plahsahs hoontahs?* |
| Can we park the car next to the tent? | ¿Podemos estacionar el carro/auto/coche junto a la tienda/carpa? *pohdehmohs ehstahsyohnahr ehl karroh/ahootoh/kohcheh hoontoh ah lah tyehndah/kahrpah?* |
| How much is it per person/tent/trailer/car? | ¿Cuánto sale por persona/tienda/caravana/coche? *kwahntoh sahleh pohr pehrsohnah/tyehndah/ kahrahbahnah/kohcheh?* |

**Overnight accommodation**

**7**

66

| Are there any...? | ¿Hay...? |
| | *ay...?* |
| – any hot showers? | ¿Hay duchas con agua caliente? |
| | *ay doochahs kohn ahgwah kahlyehnteh?* |
| – washing machines? | ¿Hay lavadoras? |
| | *ay lahbahdohrahs?* |
| Is there a...on the site? | ¿En este camping hay...? |
| | *ehn ehsteh kahmpeen ay...?* |
| Is there a children's play area on the site? | ¿En este camping hay un sitio para que jueguen los niños? |
| | *ehn ehsteh kahmpeen ay oon seetyoh pahrah keh hwehghehn lohs neenyohs?* |
| Are there covered cooking facilities on the site? | ¿En este camping hay un sitio cubierto para cocinar? |
| | *ehn ehsteh kahmpeen ay oon seetyoh koobyehrtoh pahrah kohseenahr?* |
| Can I rent a safe here? | ¿Tienen caja fuerte para alquilar? |
| | *tyehnehn kahhah fwehrteh pahrah ahlkeelahr?* |
| Are we allowed to barbecue here? | ¿Se pueden hacer barbacoas? |
| | *seh pwehdehn ahsehr bahrbahkohahs?* |
| Are there any power outlets? | ¿Hay tomas de corriente eléctrica? |
| | *ay tohmahs deh kohrryehnteh ehlehktreekah?* |
| Is there drinking water? | ¿Hay agua potable? |
| | *ay ahgwah pohtahbleh?* |
| When's the trash/garbage collected? | ¿Cuándo pasan a recoger la basura? |
| | *kwahndoh pahsahn ah rehkohhehr lah bahsoorah?* |
| Do you sell gas bottles (butane gas/propane gas)? | ¿Venden bombas de gas (butano/propano)? |
| | *behndehn bohmbahs deh gahs(bootahnoh/prohpahnoh)?* |

## 7 Overnight accommodation

## 7.3 Hotel/B&B/apartment/holiday rental

| Do you have a single/double room available? | ¿Le queda alguna habitación individual/doble? |
| | *leh kehdah ahlgoonah ahbeetahsyohn eendeebeedwahl/dohbleh?* |
| per person/per room | por persona/por habitación |
| | *pohr pehrsohnah/pohr ahbeetahsyohn* |
| Does that include breakfast/lunch/dinner? | ¿Incluye desayuno/comida/cena? |
| | *eenklooyeh dehsahyoonoh/kohmeedah/sehnah?* |
| Could we have two adjoining rooms? | ¿Nos puede dar dos habitaciones una al lado de la otra? |
| | *nohs pwehdeh dahr dohs ahbeetahsyohnehs oonah ahl lahdoh deh lah ohtrah?* |
| with/without toilet/bath/shower | con/sin wáter/baño propio/ducha propia |
| | *kohn/seen bahtehr prohpyoh/bahnyoh prohpyoh/doochah prohpyah?* |
| (not) facing the street | que (no) dé a la calle |
| | *keh (noh) deh ah lah kahlyeh* |
| with/without a view of the sea | con/sin vista al mar |
| | *kohn/seen beestah ahl mahr* |
| Is there...in the hotel? | ¿El hotel tiene...? |
| | *ehl ohtehl tyehneh...?* |

67

## Camping equipment
(the diagram shows the numbered parts)

| | luggage space | el compartimiento de equipaje | *ehl kohmpahrteemyehntoh de ehkeepah<u>h</u>eh* |
|---|---|---|---|
| | can opener | el abrelatas | *ehl ahbrehlahtahs* |
| | butane gas bottle | la bomba garrafa (de gas butano) | *lah bohmbah gahrrahfah (deh gahs bootahnoh)* |
| 1 | pannier | la ciclobolsa | *lah theeklohbohlsah* |
| 2 | gas cooker | el hornillo de gas | *ehl ohrneelyoh deh gahs* |
| 3 | groundsheet | la lona del suelo | *lah lohnah dehl swehloh* |
| | hammer | el martillo | *ehl mahrteelyoh* |
| | hammock | la hamaca | *lah ahmahkah* |
| 4 | jerry can | el bidón | *ehl beedohn* |
| | campfire | la fogata | *lah fohgahtah* |
| 5 | folding chair | la silla plegable | *lah seelyah plehgahbleh* |
| 6 | insulated picnic box | la bolsa refrigeradora | *lah bohlsah rehfree<u>h</u>ehrahdohrah* |
| | compass | la brújula | *lah broo<u>h</u>oolah* |
| | wick | la mecha | *lah mehchah* |
| | corkscrew | el sacacorchos | *ehl sahkahkohrchohs* |
| 7 | airbed | el colchón neumático | *ehl kohlchohn nehoomahteekoh* |
| 8 | airbed plug | el taponcito de la válvula del colchón | *ehl tahpohnseetoh deh lah bahlboolah dehl kohlchohn* |
| | pump | la bomba neumática | *lah bohmbah nehoomahteekah* |
| 9 | awning | el tejadillo | *ehl teh<u>h</u>ahdeelyoh* |
| 10 | mat | la esterilla | *lah ehstehreelyah* |
| 11 | pan | la olla | *lah ohlyah* |
| 12 | pan handle | el mango de la olla | *ehl mahngoh deh lah ohlyah* |
| | primus stove | el hornillo de querosén | *ehl ohrneelyoh deh kehrohsehn* |
| | zip | la cremallera | *lah krehmalyehrah* |
| 13 | backpack | la mochila | *lah mohcheelah* |
| 14 | guy rope | el viento | *ehl byehntoh* |
| | sleeping bag | el saco de dormir | *ehl sahkoh deh dohrmeer* |
| 15 | storm lantern | el farol de tormentas | *ehl fahrohl deh tohrmehntahs* |
| | camp bed | el catre (de tijera) | *ehl kahtreh (deh teehehrah)* |
| | table | la mesa | *lah mehsah* |
| 16 | tent | la tienda | *lah tyehndah* |
| 17 | tent peg | la estaca | *lah ehstakah* |
| 18 | tent pole | el palo de tienda | *ehl pahloh deh tyehndah* |
| | vacuum | el termo | *ehl tehrmoh* |
| 19 | water bottle | la cantimplora | *lah kahnteemplohrah* |
| | clothes pin | la pinza | *lah peensah* |
| | clothes line | la cuerda de tender ropa | *lah kwehrdah deh tehndehr rohpah* |
| | windbreak | el paravientos/el paraván | *ehl pahrahbyehntohs/ehl pahrahbahn* |
| 20 | flashlight | la linterna de bolsillo | *lah leentehrnah deh bohlseelyoh* |
| | pocket knife | la navaja | *lah nahbah<u>h</u>ah* |

**Overnight accommodation** 7

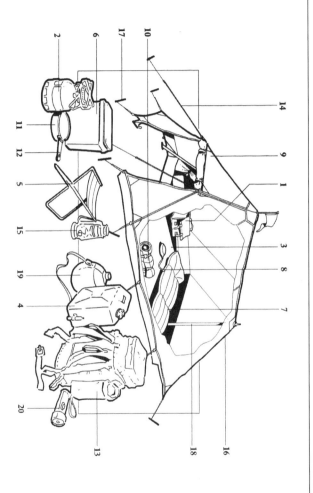

| Is there an elevator in the hotel? | ¿El hotel tiene ascensor/elevador? *ehl ohtehl tyehneh ahssehnsohr/ ehlehbahdohr?* |
| Do you have room service? | ¿El hotel tiene servicio de habitación? *ehl ohtehl tyehneh sehrbeethyoh deh ahbeetahthyohn?* |

---

🖐

| Tiene WC y ducha en el mismo piso/en su habitación | You can find the toilet and shower on the same floor/in the room |
| Por aquí, por favor | This way, please |
| Su habitación está en el...piso; es la número... | Your room is on the...floor, number... |

---

| Could I see the room? | ¿Puedo ver la habitación? *pwehdoh behr lah ahbeetahsyohn?* |
| I'll take this room | Me quedo con esta habitación *meh kehdoh kohn ehstah abeetahsyohn* |
| We don't like this one | Esta no nos gusta *ehstah noh nohs goostah* |
| Do you have a larger/ less expensive room? | ¿Tiene una habitación más grande/más barata? *tyehneh oonah ahbeetahsyohn mahs grahnde/mahs bahrahtah?* |
| Could you put in a cot? | ¿Puede agregar una cuna? *pwehde ahgrehgahr oonah koonah?* |
| What time's breakfast? | ¿A qué hora es el desayuno? *ah keh ohrah ehs ehl dehsahyoonoh?* |
| Where's the dining room? | ¿Dónde está el comedor? *dohndeh ehstah ehl kohmehdohr?* |
| Can I have breakfast in my room? | ¿Me pueden traer el desayuno a la habitación? *meh pwehdehn trahehr ehl dehsahyoonoh ah lah ahbeetahsyohn?* |
| Where's the emergency exit/fire escape? | ¿Dónde está la salida de emergencia/la escalera de incendios? *dohndeh ehstah lah sahleedah deh ehmehrhehnsyah/lah ehskahlehrah de eensehndyohs?* |
| Where can I park my car (safely)? | ¿Dónde hay un sitio (seguro) para estacionar el carro/auto? *dohndeh ay oon seetyoh sehgooroh pahrah ehstahsyohnahr ehl kahrroh/ahootoh?* |
| The key to room..., please | La llave de la habitación..., por favor *lah lyahbeh deh lah ahbeetahsyohn..., pohr fahbohr* |
| Could you put this in the safe, please? | ¿Podría dejar esto en la caja fuerte? *pohdreeah dehhahr ehstoh ehn lah cahhah fwehrteh?* |
| Could you wake me at...tomorrow? | ¿Me podría despertar mañana a las...? *meh pohdreeah dehspehrtahr mahnyahnah ah lahs...?* |

Overnight accommodation

| Could you find a _____ babysitter for me? | ¿Me podría conseguir una niñera para el bebé? |
| | *meh pohdreeah kohnsehguer oonah neenyehrah pahrah ehl behbeh?* |
| Could I have an extra _____ blanket? | ¿Tendría una manta extra? |
| | *tehndreeah oonah mahntah ehxtrah?* |
| What days do the _____ cleaners come in? | ¿Qué días limpian la habitación? |
| | *keh deeahs leempyahn lah ahbeetahsyohn?* |
| When are the sheets/ _____ towels/dish towels changed? | ¿Cuándo cambian las sábanas/las toallas/los paños de cocina? |
| | *kwahndoh kahmbyahn lahs sahbahnahs/lahs tohahllahs/lohs pahnyohs deh kohseenah?* |

 **.4 C**omplaints

| We can't sleep for _____ the noise | No podemos dormir por el ruido |
| | *noh pohdehmohs dohrmeer pohr ehl rweedoh* |
| Could you turn the _____ radio down, please? | ¿Podría bajar el volumen de la radio? |
| | *pohdreeah bahhar ehl vohloomehn deh lah rahdyoh?* |
| We're out of toilet paper ___ | Se acabó el papel higiénico. |
| | *seh ahkahboh ehl pahpehl eehyehneekoh* |
| There aren't any.../ _____ there's not enough... | No hay.../no hay suficientes... |
| | *noh ay.../noh ay soofeesyehntehs...* |
| The bed linen's dirty _____ | La ropa de cama está sucia |
| | *lah rohpah deh kahmah ehstah soosyah* |
| The room hasn't been _____ cleaned | No han limpiado la habitación |
| | *noh ahn leempyahdoh lah ahbeetahsyohn* |
| The kitchen is not clean _____ | La cocina no está limpia |
| | *lah kohseenah noh ehstah leempyah* |
| The kitchen utensils are _____ dirty | Los utensilios de cocina están sucios |
| | *lohs ootehnseelyohs deh kohseenah ehstahn soosyohs* |
| The heater's not _____ working | La calefacción no funciona |
| | *lah kahlehfahksyohn noh foonsyohnah* |
| There's no (hot) _____ water/electricity | No hay agua (caliente)/electricidad |
| | *noh ay ahgwah(kahlyehnteh)/ehlehktreeseedahdh* |
| ...is broken _____ | ...está estropeado |
| | *...ehstah ehstrohpehahdoh* |
| Could you have that _____ seen to? | ¿Podrían verlo? |
| | *pohdreeahn behrloh?* |
| Could I have another _____ room/camp site? | ¿Tendría otra habitación/sitio para la tienda? |
| | *tehndreeah ohtrah ahbeetahsyohn/seetyoh pahrah lah tyehndah?* |
| The bed creaks terribly _____ | La cama hace mucho ruido |
| | *lah kahmah ahseh moochoh rweedoh* |
| The bed sags _____ | La cama es demasiado blanda |
| | *lah kahmah ehs dehmahsyahdoh blahndah* |
| There are bugs/insects _____ in our room | Hay muchos bichos/insectos en nuestra habitación |
| | *ay moochohs beechohs/eensehktohs ehn nooehstrah ahbeetahsyohn* |

| | |
|---|---|
| This place is full of mosquitos | Está lleno de mosquitos |
| | *ehstah lyehnoh deh mohskeetohs* |
| – cockroaches | Está lleno de cucarachas |
| | *ehstah lyehnoh deh kookahrahchahs* |

## .5 Departure

*See also 8.2 Settling the bill*

| | |
|---|---|
| I'm leaving tomorrow. Could I pay my bill, please? | Mañana me voy. ¿Podría pagar la cuenta ahora? |
| | *mahnyahnah meh boy. pohdreeah pahgahr lah kwehntah ahohrah?* |
| What time should we check out? | ¿A qué hora tenemos que dejar...? |
| | *ah keh ohrah tehnehmohs keh dehhahr...?* |
| Could I have my deposit/passport back, please? | ¿Me devuelve la fianza/el pasaporte? |
| | *meh dehbwehlbeh lah fyahnsah/ehl pahsahpohrteh?* |
| We're in a terrible hurry | Estamos muy apurados |
| | *ehstahmohs mwee ahpoorahdohs* |
| Could you forward my mail to this address? | ¿Podría enviarme la correspondencia a esta dirección? |
| | *pohdreeah ehnbyahrmeh lah kohrrehspohndehnsyah ah ehstah deerehksyohn?* |
| Could we leave our luggage here until we leave? | ¿Podríamos dejar el equipaje aquí hasta que nos marchemos? |
| | *pohdreeahmohs dehhahr ehl ehkeepahheh ahkee ahstah keh nohs mahrchehmohs?* |
| Thanks for your hospitality | Muchas gracias por la hospitalidad |
| | *moochahs grahsyahs pohr lah ohspeetahleedahdh* |

Overnight accommodation

# Money matters

# 8 Money matters

● Bank opening hours vary in Latin American countries. In large cities exchange bureaus and ATMs for the major credit and debit cards can also be found. To exchange currency a passport is required. It is most advisable to take American dollars when travelling to Latin America, instead of any other foreign currency, since they may even be accepted as a local currency in some countries.

| Country | Currency |
| --- | --- |
| Argentina | peso |
| Bolivia | boliviano |
| Chile | peso |
| Colombia | peso |
| Costa Rica | colón |
| Cuba | peso |
| Dominican Republic | peso |
| Ecuador | sucre |
| El Salvador | colón |
| Guatemala | quetzal |
| Honduras | lempira |
| Mexico | peso |
| Nicaragua | oro |
| Panama | balboa |
| Paraguay | guaraní |
| Peru | sol |
| Uruguay | peso |

## 8.1 Banks

Where can I find a bank/an exchange office around here?
¿Dónde hay un banco/una oficina de cambios por aquí?
*dohndeh ay oon bahnkoh/oonah ohfeeseenah deh kahmbyohs pohr ahkee?*

Where can I cash this traveler's check/giro check?
¿Dónde puedo cambiar este cheque de viajero/este cheque postal?
*dohndeh pwehdoh kahmbyahr ehsteh chehkeh deh byahhehroh/ehsteh chehkeh pohstahl?*

Can I cash this...here?
¿Puedo cambiar aquí este...?
*pwehdoh kahmbyahr ahkee ehsteh...?*

Can I withdraw money on my credit card here?
¿Se puede sacar dinero con una tarjeta de crédito?
*seh pwehdeh sahkahr deenehroh kohn oonah tahrhehtah deh krehdeetoh?*

What's the minimum/ maximum amount?
¿Cuál es el mínimo/el máximo?
*kwahl ehs ehl meeneemoh/ehl mahxeemoh?*

Can I take out less than that?
¿También puedo sacar menos?
*tahmbyehn pwehdoh sahkahr mehnohs?*

I've had some money transferred here. Has it arrived yet?
He pedido un giro telegráfico. ¿Me ha llegado ya?
*eh pehdeedoh oon heeroh tehlehgrahfeekoh. meh ah lyehgahdoh yah?*

| | |
|---|---|
| These are the details _____ of my bank in the U.S. | Estos son los datos de mi banco en los Estados Unidos *ehstohs sohn lohs dahtohs deh mee bahnkoh ehn lohs Ehstahdohs Ooneedohs* |
| This is my bank/giro _____ number | Este es mi número de cuenta bancaria/de la caja postal *ehsteh ehs mee noomehroh deh kwehntah bahnkahryah/deh lah kah<u>h</u>ah pohstahl* |
| I'd like to change _____ some money | Quisiera cambiar dinero *keesyehrah kahmbyahr deenehroh* |
| – pounds into... _____ | Libras esterlinas por... *leebrahs ehstehrleenahs pohr...* |
| – dollars into... _____ | Dólares estadounidenses por... *dohlahrehs ehstahdohooneedehnsehs pohr...* |
| What's the exchange _____ rate? | ¿A cuánto está el cambio? *ah kwahntoh ehstah ehl kahmbyoh?* |
| Could you give me _____ some small change with it? | ¿Me podría dar sencillo/cambio? *meh pohdreeah dahr sehnseelyoh/kahmbyoh?* |
| This is not right _____ | Esto está mal *ehstoh ehstah mahl* |

| | |
|---|---|
| Firme aquí _____ | Sign here, please |
| Tiene que rellenar esto _____ | Fill this out, please |
| ¿Me permite su pasaporte? _____ | Could I see your passport, please? |
| ¿Me permite su carnet de identidad? _____ | Could I see some identification, please? |
| ¿Me permite su tarjeta de la _____ caja postal? | Could I see your girobank card, please? |
| ¿Me permite su tarjeta del banco? _____ | Could I see your bank card, please? |

## 8 .2 Settling the bill

| | |
|---|---|
| Could you put it on _____ my bill? | ¿Podría cargarlo a mi cuenta? *pohdreeah kahrgahrloh ah mee kwehntah?* |
| Does this amount _____ include tip? | ¿Está incluido el servicio en esta cifra? *ehstah eenklooeedoh ehl sehrbeesyoh ehn ehstah seefrah?* |
| Can I pay by...? _____ | ¿Puedo pagar con...? *pwehdoh pahgahr kohn...?* |
| Can I pay by credit card? _____ | ¿Puedo pagar con tarjeta de crédito? *pwehdoh pahgahr kohn tahr<u>h</u>ehtah deh krehdeetoh?* |
| Can I pay by traveler's _____ check? | ¿Puedo pagar con un cheque de viajero? *pwehdoh pahgahr kohn oon chehkeh de byah<u>h</u>ehroh?* |
| Can I pay with foreign _____ currency? | ¿Puedo pagar con moneda extranjera? *pwehdoh pahgahr kohn mohnehdah ehxtrahnhehrah?* |

| | |
|---|---|
| You've given me too_____ much/you haven't given me enough change | Me ha devuelto de más/de menos *meh ah dehbwehltoh deh mahs/deh mehnohs* |
| Could you check the _____ bill again, please? | ¿Puede volver a hacer la cuenta? *pwehdeh bohlbehr ah ahsehr lah kwehntah?* |
| Could I have a receipt,____ please? | ¿Podría darme un recibo? *pohdreeah dahrmeh oon rehseeboh?* |
| I don't have enough _____ money on me | No me alcanza el dinero *noh meh ahlkahnsah ehl deenehroh* |
| This is for you _____ | Tenga, esto es para usted *tehngah, ehstoh ehs pahrah oostehdh* |
| Keep the change _____ | Quédese con el vuelto *kehdehseh kohn ehl bwehltoh* |

| | |
|---|---|
| No aceptamos tarjetas de _____ crédito/cheques de viajero/moneda extranjera | **We don't accept credit cards/traveler's checks/ foreign currency** |

# Mail and telephone

9

# 9 **M**ail and telephone

## 9 .1 **M**ail

*For giros, see 8 Money matters*

● **Post offices** are open from Monday to Saturday although opening hours vary from country to country. However, some hotels also provide stamps (*estampillas, timbres*). It is advisable to post letters at a post office, rather than in the mailboxes (*buzón*).

| | | |
|---|---|---|
| giros postales<br>money orders | telegramas<br>telegrams | sellos<br>stamps |
| paquetes<br>parcels | | |

| | |
|---|---|
| Where's...? | ¿Dónde está...?<br>*dohndeh ehstah...?* |
| Where's the post office? | ¿Dónde hay una oficina de correos por aquí?<br>*dohndeh ay oonah ohfeeseenah deh kohrrehohs pohr ahkee?* |
| Where's the main post office? | ¿Dónde está la oficina central de correos?<br>*dohndeh ehstah lah ohfeeseenah sehntrahl deh kohrrehohs?* |
| Where's the mailbox? | ¿Dónde hay un buzón por aquí?<br>*dohndeh ay oon boosohn pohr ahkee?* |
| Which counter should I go to...? | ¿Cuál es la ventanilla para...?<br>*kwahl ehs lah behntahneelyah pahrah...?* |
| – to send a fax | ¿Cuál es la ventanilla para enviar un fax?<br>*kwahl ehs lah behntahneelyah pahrah ehnbyahr oon fahx?* |
| – to change money | ¿Cuál es la ventanilla para cambiar dinero?<br>*kwahl ehs lah behntahneelyah pahrah kahmbyahr deenehroh?* |
| – to change giro checks | ¿Cuál es la ventanilla para los cheques postales?<br>*kwahl ehs lah behntahneelyah pahrah lohs chehkehs pohstahlehs?* |
| – for a Telegraph Money Order? | ¿Cuál es la ventanilla para los giros telegráficos?<br>*kwahl ehs lah behntahneelyah pahrah lohs heerohs tehlehgrahfeekohs?* |
| General delivery | Lista de correos<br>*leestah deh kohrrehohs* |
| Is there any mail for me? My name's... | ¿Hay carta para mí? Me llamo...<br>*ay kahrtah pahrah mee? meh lyahmoh...* |

### Stamps

| | |
|---|---|
| What's the postage _____ for a...to...? | ¿Cuánto se le pone a un(a)...para...? *kwahntoh seh leh pohneh ah oon(ah)...pahrah...?* |
| Are there enough _____ stamps on it? | ¿Lleva suficiente franqueo? *lyehbah soofeesyehnteh frahnkehoh?* |
| I'd like... ... stamps_____ | Déme... estampillas/timbres de... *dehmeh... ehstahmpeelyahs/teembrehs deh...* |
| I'd like to send this..._____ | Quisiera enviar esto... *keesyehrah ehnbyahr ehstoh...* |
| – express _____ | Quisiera enviar esto por correo urgente *keesyehrah ehnbyahr ehstoh pohr kohrrehoh oorhehnteh* |
| – by air mail _____ | Quisiera enviar esto por avión *keesyehrah ehnbyahr ehstoh pohr ahbyohn* |
| – by registered mail _____ | Quisiera enviar esto certificado *keesyehrah ehnbyahr ehstoh sehrteefeekahdoh* |

### Telegram / fax

| | |
|---|---|
| I'd like to send a_____ telegram to... | Quisiera mandar un telegrama a... *keesyehrah mahndahr oon tehlehgrahmah ah...* |
| How much is that _____ per word? | ¿Cuánto cuesta por palabra? *kwahntoh kwehstah pohr pahlahbrah?* |
| This is the text I want_____ to send | Este es el texto que quiero enviar *ehsteh ehs ehl tehxtoh keh kyehroh ehnbyahr* |
| Shall I fill in the form _____ myself? | ¿Relleno yo mismo el formulario? *rehlyehnoh yoh meesmoh ehl fohrmoolahryoh?* |
| Can I make photocopies/___ send a fax here? | ¿Se pueden hacer fotocopias/se puede enviar un fax aquí? *seh pwehdehn ahsehr fohtohkohpyahs/seh pwehdeh ehnbyahr oon fahx ahkee?* |
| How much is it _____ per page? | ¿Cuánto cuesta por página? *kwahntoh kwehstah pohr pahheenah?* |

## .2 Telephone

*See also 1.8 Telephone alphabet*

● **For international calls** you may have to go to a telephone office in some Latin American countries, since telephone booths normally offer access to the local or the interurban network only. The country code for the UK is 44 and 1 for the USA and Canada.

| | |
|---|---|
| Is there a phone booth _____ around here? | ¿Hay alguna caseta/cabina telefónica por aquí? *ay ahlgoonah kahsehtah/kahbeenah tehlehfohneekah pohr ahkee?* |
| Could I use your _____ phone, please? | ¿Podría usar su teléfono? *pohdreeah oosahr soo tehlehfohnoh?* |

| | |
|---|---|
| Do you have a _____ (city/region)...phone directory? | ¿Tiene una guía de teléfonos de la ciudad/la provincia de...? |
| | *tyehneh oonah gheeah deh tehlehfohnohs deh lah syoodahdh/lah prohbeensyah deh...?* |
| Where can I get a _____ phone card? | ¿Dónde puedo conseguir una tarjeta de teléfonos? |
| | *dohndeh pwehdoh kohnsehgheer oonah tahrhehtah deh tehlehfohnohs?* |
| Could you give me...? _____ | ¿Me podría dar...? |
| | *meh pohdreeah dahr...?* |
| – the number for _____ international directory assistance | ¿Me podría dar el número de información internacional? |
| | *meh pohdreeah dahr ehl noomehroh deh eenfohrmahsyohn eentehrnahsyohnahl?* |
| – the number of room... \_\_\_ | ¿Me podría dar el número de la habitación...? |
| | *meh pohdreeah dahr ehl noomehroh deh lah ahbeetahsyohn...?* |
| – the international _____ access code | ¿Me podría dar el código internacional? |
| | *meh pohdreeah dahr ehl kohdeegoh eentehrnahsyonahl...?* |
| – the country code for...\_\_\_\_ | ¿Me podría dar el código de...? |
| | *meh pohdreeah dahr ehl kohdeegoh deh...?* |
| – the area code for..._____ | ¿Me podría dar el prefijo de...? |
| | *meh pohdreeah dahr ehl prehfeehoh deh...?* |
| – the number of... _____ | ¿Me podría dar el número de...? |
| | *meh pohdreeah dahr ehl noomehroh deh...?* |
| Could you check if this\_\_\_\_\_ number's correct? | ¿Podría controlar/revisar si está bien este número? |
| | *pohdreeah kohntrohlahr/rehbeesar see ehstah byehn ehsteh noomehroh?* |
| Can I dial international\_\_\_\_\_ direct? | ¿Se puede llamar directamente al extranjero? |
| | *seh pwehdeh lyahmahr deerehktahmehnteh ahl ehxtrahnhehroh?* |
| Do I have to go through \_\_\_ the switchboard? | ¿Hay que llamar por operadora? |
| | *ay keh lyahmahr pohr ohpehrahdohrah?* |
| Do I have to dial '0'_____ first? | ¿Hay que marcar primero el cero? |
| | *ay keh mahrkahr preemehroh ehl sehroh?* |
| Do I have to reserve _____ my calls? | ¿Hay que pedir línea? |
| | *ay keh pehdeer leenehah?* |
| Could you dial this _____ number for me, please? | ¿Podría usted llamar a este número? |
| | *pohdreeah oostehdh lyahmahr ah ehsteh noomehroh?* |
| Could you put me _____ through to.../extension..., please? | ¿Me podría poner con.../con la extensión...? |
| | *meh pohdreeah pohnehr kohn.../kohn lah ehxtehnsyohn...?* |
| I'd like to place a _____ collect call to... | Quisiera una llamada de cobro revertido/por cobrar a... |
| | *keesyehrah oonah lyahmahdah deh kohbroh rehbehrteedoh/pohr kohbrahr ah...* |
| What's the charge per \_\_\_\_ minute? | ¿Cuánto cuesta por minuto? |
| | *kwahntoh kwehstah pohr meenootoh?* |
| Have there been any \_\_\_\_\_ calls for me? | ¿Ha habido alguna llamada para mí? |
| | *ah ahbeedoh ahlgoonah lyahmahdah pahrah mee?* |

### The conversation

Hello, this is... _____ Buenos días, soy...
*bwehnohs deeahs, soy...*

Who is this, please? _____ ¿Con quién hablo?
*kohn kyehn ahbloh?*

Is this...? _____ ¿Hablo con...?
*ahbloh kohn...?*

I'm sorry, I've dialed _____ Perdone, me he equivocado de número
the wrong number *pehrdohneh, meh eh ehkeebohkahdoh deh noomehroh*

I can't hear you _____ No le oigo bien
*noh leh oygoh byehn*

I'd like to speak to... _____ Quisiera hablar con...
*keesyehrah ahblahr kohn...*

Is there anybody _____ ¿Hay alguien que hable inglés?
who speaks English? *ay ahlghyehn keh ahbleh eenglehs?*

Extension..., please _____ ¿Me pone con la extensión...?
*meh pohneh kohn lah ehxtehnsyohn...?*

Could you ask him/her _____ ¿Podría decirle que me llame?
to call me back? *pohdreeah dehseerleh keh meh lyahmeh?*

My name's... _____ Me llamo...Mi número es...
My number's... *meh lyahmoh...mee noomehroh ehs...*

Could you tell him/her _____ ¿Puede decirle que llamé?
I called? *pwehdeh dehseerleh keh lyahmeh?*

I'll call back tomorrow _____ Lo/la volveré a llamar mañana
*loh/lah bohlbehreh ah lyahmahr mahnyahnah*

---

Lo llaman por teléfono _____ There's a phone call for you

Primero tiene que marcar el cero _____ You have to dial '0' first

Un momento, por favor _____ One moment, please

No contestan _____ There's no answer

Está ocupado _____ The line's busy

¿Quiere esperar? _____ Do you want to hold?

Ahora le paso _____ Connecting you

Se ha equivocado de número _____ You've got a wrong number

El señor/la señora...no está en estos _____ He's/she's not here
momentos. right now

El señor/la señora...no estará hasta... _____ He'll/she'll be back...

Este es el contestador _____ This is the answering
automático de... machine of...

# **S**hopping

● **Opening times** for shopping vary in Latin American countries. In large cities, shops and offices remain open at lunch time, but in provinces they may close for long breaks, until late in the afternoon (*siesta*).

Drugstores may display the list of *farmacias de guardia* (those open on Sundays and after hours).

---

almacén
department store

antigüedades
antiques

artículos de deporte
sports shop

artículos del hogar
household goods

artículos dietéticos
health food shop

artículos fotográficos
camera shop

artículos de limpieza
household products
  and cosmetics

artículos usados
second-hand shop

autoservicio
self service

bicicletas
bicycle shop

bodega
liquor store

bricolaje
Do-it-yourself-store

carnicería
butcher's shop

casa de música
music shop

centro comercial
shopping centre

comestibles
grocery store

decoración
  (de interiores)
interior design shop

droguería
drugstore

electrodomésticos
electrical appliances

farmacia
pharmacy

ferretería
hardware shop

floristería/florería
florist

frutas y verduras
greengrocer

galería comercial
shopping center

heladería
ice cream parlour

joyería
jeweler

juguetería
toy shop

lavandería
laundry

lechería
dairy

librería
book shop

mercado
market

mercería
notions

óptica
optician

panadería
bakery

pastelería/confitería
cake shop

peluquería (señoras,
  caballeros)
hairdresser

perfumería
cosmetics

pescadería
fishmonger

quiosco
news stand

recuerdos de viaje
souvenir shop

reparación de
  bicicletas
bicycle repair shop

revistas y prensa
newsagent

salón de belleza
beauty parlor

supermercado
supermarket

tienda/negocio
shop

tienda de modas
clothes shop

tintorería
drycleaner

zapatería
shoe shop

zapatero
cobbler

## 10 .1 Shopping conversations

| | |
|---|---|
| Where can I get...? _____ | ¿Dónde puedo conseguir...? |
| | *dohndeh pwehdoh kohnsehgheer...?* |
| When does this shop _____ open? | ¿De qué hora a qué hora abren? |
| | *deh keh ohrah ah keh ohrah ahbrehn?* |
| Could you tell me _____ where the...department is? | ¿Me podría indicar la sección de...? |
| | *meh pohdreeah eendeekahr lah sehksyohn deh...?* |
| Could you help me, _____ please? I'm looking for... | ¿Podría ayudarme? Busco... |
| | *pohdreeah ahyoodahrmeh? booskoh...* |
| Do you sell British/ _____ American newspapers? | ¿Venden periódicos/diarios británicos/americanos? |
| | *behndehn pehryohdeekohs/dyahryohs breetahneekohs/ahmehreekahnohs?* |

---

¿Lo/la atienden? _____ **Are you being served?**

| | |
|---|---|
| No. I'd like... _____ | No. Quisiera... |
| | *noh. keesyehrah...* |
| I'm just looking, _____ if that's all right | Sólo estoy mirando, gracias |
| | *sohloh ehstoy meerahndoh, grahsyahs* |

---

¿Algo más? _____ **Anything else?**

| | |
|---|---|
| Yes, I'd also like... _____ | Sí, también déme... |
| | *see, tahmbyehn dehmeh...* |
| No, thank you. That's all ___ | No, gracias. Es todo |
| | *noh, grahsyahs, ehs tohdoh* |
| Could you show me...? ____ | ¿Me podría mostrar...? |
| | *meh pohdreeah mohstrahr...?* |
| I'd prefer... _____ | Prefiero... |
| | *prehfyehroh...* |
| This is not what I'm _____ looking for | No es lo que busco |
| | *noh ehs loh keh booskoh* |
| Thank you. I'll keep_____ looking | Gracias. Voy a seguir mirando |
| | *grahsyahs. boy ah sehgheer meerahndoh* |
| Do you have _____ something...? | ¿No tendría algo ...? |
| | *noh tehndreeah ahlgoh ...?* |
| – less expensive?_____ | ¿No tendría algo más barato? |
| | *noh tehndreeah ahlgoh mahs bahrahtoh?* |
| – smaller? _____ | ¿No tendría algo más pequeño? |
| | *noh tehndreeah ahlgoh mahs pehkehnyoh?* |
| – larger? _____ | ¿No tendría algo más grande? |
| | *noh tehndreeah ahlgoh mahs grahndeh?* |
| I'll take this one _____ | Me llevo éste/ésta |
| | *meh lyehboh ehsteh/ehstah* |
| Does it come with _____ instructions? | ¿Viene con instrucciones? |
| | *byehneh kohn eenstrooksyohnehs?* |
| It's too expensive_____ | Me parece muy caro |
| | *meh pahrehseh mwee kahroh* |

| I'll give you... _____ | Le doy... |
|---|---|
| | *leh doy...* |
| Could you keep this for ___ me? I'll come back for it later | ¿Me lo/la podría guardar? Volveré más tarde a buscarlo |
| | *meh loh/lah pohdreeah gwahrdahr? bohlbehreh mahs tahrdeh ah booskahrloh* |
| Have you got a bag _____ for me, please? | ¿Tendría una bolsita? |
| | *tehndreeah oonah bohlseetah?* |
| Could you gift wrap _____ it, please? | ¿Me lo podría envolver para regalo? |
| | *meh loh pohdreeah ehnbohlbehr pahrah rehgahloh?* |

| Lo siento; no lo tenemos _____ | I'm sorry, we don't have that |
|---|---|
| Lo siento; ya no queda _____ | I'm sorry, we're sold out |
| Lo siento, hasta el...no lo _____ tendremos | I'm sorry, that won't be in until... |
| Pague en la caja, por favor _____ | You can pay at the cash desk |
| No aceptamos tarjetas de crédito _____ | We don't accept credit cards |
| No aceptamos cheques de viajero_____ | We don't accept traveler's checks |
| No aceptamos moneda extranjera _____ | We don't accept foreign currency |

## 10 .2 Food

| I'd like a hundred_____ grams of..., please | Quisiera cien gramos de... |
|---|---|
| | *keesyehrah syehn grahmohs deh...* |
| – half a kilo of... _____ | Quisiera medio kilo de... |
| | *keesyehrah mehdyoh keeloh deh...* |
| – a kilo of... _____ | Quisiera un kilo de... |
| | *keesyehrah oon keeloh deh...* |
| Could you...it for me, _____ please? | ¿Me lo podría...? |
| | *meh loh pohdreeah...?* |
| Could you slice it/_____ chop (grind) it for me, please? | ¿Me lo podría cortar en tajadas/lonchas/ rebanadas/trozos? |
| | *meh loh pohdreeah kohrtahr ehn tahhahdahs/lohnchahs/rehbahnahdahs/ trohsohs?* |
| Could you grate it _____ for me, please? | ¿Me lo podría rallar? |
| | *meh loh pohdreeah rahlyahr?* |
| Can I order it?_____ | ¿Se lo podría encargar? |
| | *seh loh pohdreeah ehnkahrgahr?* |
| I'll pick it up tomorrow/ ____ at... | Pasaré a buscarlo mañana/a las... |
| | *pahsahreh ah booskahrloh mahnyahnah/ah lahs...* |
| Can you eat/drink this? ____ | ¿Es para comer/beber? |
| | *ehs pahrah kohmehr/behbehr?* |
| What's in it? _____ | ¿Qué lleva dentro? |
| | *keh lyehbah dehntroh?* |

| | |
|---|---|
| I saw something in the _____ window. Shall I point it out? | Vi algo en el escaparate/la vidriera. ¿Se lo enseño? *bee ahlgoh ehn ehl ehskahpahrahteh/ lah beedryehrah, seh loh ehnsehnyoh?* |
| I'd like something to _____ go with this | Busco algo que haga juego con esto *booskoh ahlgoh keh ahgah hwehgoh kohn ehstoh* |
| Do you have shoes _____ in this colour? | ¿Tiene zapatos de este color? *tyehneh sahpahtohs deh ehsteh kohlohr?* |
| I'm a size...in the U.S._____ | En los Estados Unidos tengo el número... *ehn lohs ehstahdohs ooneedohs tehngoh ehl noomehroh...* |
| Can I try this on? _____ | ¿Me lo podría probar? *meh loh pohdreeah prohbahr?* |
| Where's the fitting _____ room? | ¿Dónde está el probador? *dohndeh ehstah ehl prohbahdohr?* |
| It doesn't fit _____ | No me queda bien *noh meh kehdah byehn* |
| This is the right size _____ | Este es mi número *ehsteh ehs mee noomehroh* |
| It doesn't suit me _____ | No me está bien *noh meh ehstah byehn* |
| Do you have this/ _____ these in...? | ¿Tiene éste/ésta, pero en...? *tyehneh ehsteh/ehstah pehroh ehn...?* |
| The heel's too high/low _____ | El tacó/tacón me parece muy alto/bajo *ehl tahkoh/tahkohn meh pahrehtheh mwee ahltoh/bahhoh* |
| Is this/are these _____ genuine leather? | ¿Es/son de piel/cuero auténtico/a? *ehs/sohn deh pyehl/kwehroh ahootehnteekoh/ah?* |
| I'm looking for a... _____ for a...-year-old baby/child | Busco un/una...para un bebé/niño de...años *booskoh oon/oonah...pahrah oon behbeh/neenyoh deh...ahnyohs* |
| I'd like a... ... _____ | Quisiera un/una...de... *keesyehrah oon/oonah...deh...* |
| – silk _____ | Quisiera un/una...de seda *keesyehrah oon/oonah...deh sehdah* |
| – cotton _____ | Quisiera un/una...de algodón *keesyehrah oon/oonah...deh ahlgohdohn* |
| – woolen _____ | Quisiera un/una...de lana *keesyehrah oon/oonah...deh lahnah* |
| – linen _____ | Quisiera un/una...de hilo/lino *keesyehrah oon/oonah...deh eeloh/leenoh* |
| What temperature _____ can I wash it at? | ¿A qué temperatura lo puedo lavar? *ah keh tehmpehrahtoorah loh pwehdoh lahbahr?* |
| Will it shrink in the _____ wash? | ¿Encoge al lavarlo? *enkohheh ahl lahbahrloh?* |

| | | |
|---|---|---|
| No planchar | Colgar mojado | Lavado a mano |
| Do not iron | Drip dry | Hand wash |
| No centrifugar | Lavado en seco | Lavado a máquina |
| Do not spin dry | Dry clean | Machine wash |

**Shopping**

**10**

**At the cobbler**

| | |
|---|---|
| Could you mend these shoes? | ¿Podría arreglar estos zapatos? |
| | *pohdreeah ahrrehglahr ehstohs sahpahtohs?* |
| Could you put new soles/heels on these? | ¿Podría ponerle suelas nuevas/tacones nuevos? |
| | *pohdreeah pohnehrle swehlahs nwehbahs/ tahkohnehs nwehbohs?* |
| When will they be ready? | ¿Para cuándo van a estar? |
| | *pahrah kwahndoh bahn ah ehstahr?* |
| I'd like..., please | Quisiera..., por favor |
| | *keesyehrah..., pohr fahbohr* |
| – a can of shoe polish | Quisiera una crema para zapatos |
| | *keesyehrah oonah krehmah pahrah sahpahtohs* |
| – a pair of shoelaces | Quisiera un par de cordones |
| | *keesyehrah oon pahr deh kohrdohnehs* |

## 🔟 .4 Photographs and video

| | |
|---|---|
| I'd like a film for this camera, please | Quisiera un rollo/carrete para esta cámara |
| | *keesyehrah oon rohlyoh/kahrrehteh pahrah ehstah kahmahrah* |
| – a 126 cartridge | Quisiera una película en cassette de 126 |
| | *keesyehrah oonah pehleekoolah ehn kahseht deh syehntoh beheenteesehsees* |
| – a 35mm color slide | Quisiera un rollo/carrete de 35mm para diapositivas en color |
| | *keesyehrah oon rohlyoh/kahrrehteh deh treyntah ee seenkoh meeleemehtrohs pahrah deeapohseeteebahs ehn kohlohr* |
| – a 35mm color print | Quisiera un rollo/carrete de 35mm en color |
| | *keesyehrah oon rohlyoh/kahrrehteh deh treyntah ee seenkoh meeleemehtrohs ehn kohlohr* |
| – a 35mm black and white | Quisiera un rollo/carrete de 35mm en blanco y negro |
| | *keesyehrah oon rohlyoh/kahrrehteh deh treyntah ee seenkoh meeleemehtrohs ehn blahnkoh ee nehgroh* |
| – a videotape | Quisiera una cinta de vídeo |
| | *keesyehrah oonah seentah deh veedehoh* |
| color/black and white | color/blanco y negro |
| | *kohlohr/blahnkoh ee nehgroh* |
| super eight | superocho |
| | *soopehrohchoh* |
| 12/24/36 exposures | doce/veinticuatro/treinta y seis fotos |
| | *dohseh/beheenteekwahtroh/treheentah ee sehees fohtohs* |
| ASA/DIN number | valor ISO |
| | *bahlohr eesoh* |
| daylight film | película para luz natural |
| | *pehleekoolah pahrah loos nahtoorahl* |
| film for artificial light | película para luz artificial |
| | *pehleekoolah pahrah loos ahrteefeesyahl* |

### Problems

Could you load the _____ film for me, please?
¿Me podría poner el rollo/carrete en la cámara?
*meh pohdreeah pohnehr ehl rohlyoh/kahrrehteh ehn lah kahmahrah?*

Could you take the film ____ out for me, please?
¿Me podría sacar el rollo/carrete de la cámara?
*meh pohdreeah sahkahr ehl rohlyoh/kahrrehteh deh lah kahmahrah?*

Should I replace_____ the batteries?
¿Tengo que cambiar las pilas?
*tehngoh keh kahmbyahr lahs peelahs?*

Could you have a look_____ at my camera, please? It's not working
¿Me podría revisar la cámara? Ya no funciona
*meh pohdreeah rehbeesahr lah kahmahrah? yah noh foonsyohnah*

The...is broken _____
Está estropeado el...
*ehstah ehstrohpehahdoh ehl...*

The film's jammed _____
Se ha atascado el rollo/carrete
*seh ah ahtahskahdoh ehl rohlyoh /kahrrehteh*

The film's broken_____
Se ha roto el rollo/carrete
*seh ah rohtoh ehl rohlyoh/kahrrehteh*

The flash isn't working ____
No funciona el flash
*noh foonsyohnah ehl flahsh*

### Processing and prints

I'd like to have this film ____ developed/printed, please
Quisiera mandar a revelar/copiar este rollo/carrete
*keesyehrah mahndahr ah rehbehlahr/kohpyahr ehsteh rohlyoh/kahrrehteh*

I'd like...prints from _____ each negative
Quisiera...copias de cada negativo
*keesyehrah...kohpyahs deh kahdah nehgahteeboh*

glossy/matte _____
brillante/mate
*breelyahnte/mahteh*

I'd like to reorder _____ these photos
Quisiera encargar más copias de estas fotos
*keesyehrah ehnkahrgahr mahs kohpyahs deh ehstahs fohtohs*

I'd like to have this _____ photo enlarged
Quisiera una ampliación de esta foto
*keesyehrah oonah ahmplyahsyohn deh ehstah fohtoh*

How much is_____ processing?
¿Cuánto sale el revelado?
*kwahntoh sahleh ehl rehbehlahdoh?*

– printing? _____
¿Cuánto sale el copiado?
*kwahntoh sahleh ehl kohpyahdoh?*

– extra copies? _____
¿Cuánto salen las copias adicionales?
*kwahntoh sahlehn lahs kohpyahs ahdeesyohnahlehs?*

– the enlargement? _____
¿Cuánto sale la ampliación?
*kwahntoh sahleh lah ahmplyahsyohn?*

When will they_____ be ready?
¿Para cuándo van a estar?
*pahrah kwahndoh bahn ah ehstahr?*

| | |
|---|---|
| Do I have to make an appointment? | ¿Tengo que pedir hora/cita? *tehngoh keh pehdeer ohrah/seetah?* |
| Can I come in now? | ¿Podría atenderme enseguida? *pohdreeah ahtehndehrmeh ehnsehgheedah?* |
| How long will I have to wait? | ¿Cuánto tengo que esperar? *kwahntoh tehngoh keh ehspehrahr?* |
| I'd like a shampoo/ haircut | Quisiera lavarme/cortarme el pelo *keesyehrah lahbahrmeh/kohrtahrmeh ehl pehloh* |
| I'd like a shampoo for oily/dry hair, please | Quisiera un champú para cabello graso/seco *keesyehrah oon chahmpoo pahrah kahbehlyoh grahsoh/sehkoh* |
| – an anti-dandruff shampoo | Quisiera un champú anticaspa *keesyehrah oon chahmpoo ahnteekahspah* |
| – a shampoo for permed/colored hair | Quisiera un champú para cabello con permanente/teñido. *keesyehrah oon chahmpoo pahrah kahbehlyoh kohn pehrmahnehnteh/tehnyeedoh* |
| – a color rinse shampoo | Quisiera un champú color *keesyehrah oon chahmpoo kohlohr* |
| – a shampoo with conditioner | Quisiera un champú con acondicionador *keesyehrah oon chahmpoo kohn ahkohndeesyohnahdohr* |
| – highlights | Quisiera que me hagan claritos/luces *keesyehrah keh meh ahgahn klahreetohs/loosehs* |
| Do you have a colour chart, please? | ¿Tendría una carta de colores? *tehndreeah oonah kahrtah deh kohlohrehs?* |
| I want to keep it the same color | Quiero conservar el mismo color *kyehroh kohnsehrbahr ehl meesmoh kohlohr* |
| I'd like it darker/lighter | Quisiera un color más oscuro/más claro *keesyehrah oon kohlohr mahs ohskooroh/mahs klahroh* |
| I'd like/I don't want hairspray | (No) quiero fijador *(noh) kyehroh feehahdohr* |
| – gel | (No) quiero gel *(noh) kyehroh hehl* |
| – lotion | (No) quiero loción *(noh) kyehroh lohsyohn* |
| I'd like short bangs | Quisiera el flequillo corto *keesyehrah ehl flehkeelyoh kohrtoh* |
| Not too short at the back | No lo quisiera demasiado corto por detrás *noh loh keesyehrah dehmahsyahdoh kohrtoh pohr dehtrahs* |
| Not too long here | No lo quisiera demasiado largo aquí *noh loh keesyehrah dehmahsyahdoh lahrgoh ahkee* |
| I'd like/I don't want (many) curls | (No) quisiera (demasiados) rizos *(noh) keesyehrah (dehmahsyadohs) reesohs* |

| It needs a little/_____ a lot taken off | Hay que cortar sólo un trocito/un buen trozo |
| | *ay keh kohrtahr sohloh oon trohseetoh/oon bwehn trohsoh* |
| I want a completely _____ different style | Quisiera un modelo totalmente diferente |
| | *keesyehrah oon mohdehloh tohtahlmehnteh deefehrehnteh* |
| I'd like it the same as... ____ | Quisiera el pelo como... |
| | *keesyehrah ehl pehloh kohmoh...* |
| – as that lady's _____ | Quisiera el pelo como esa señora |
| | *keesyehrah ehl pehloh kohmoh ehsah sehnyohrah* |
| – as in this photo_____ | Quisiera el pelo como en esta foto |
| | *keesyehrah ehl pehloh kohmoh ehn ehstah fohtoh* |
| Could you put the _____ drier up/down a bit? | ¿Podría poner el casco más alto/bajo? |
| | *pohdreeah pohnehr ehl kahskoh mahs ahltoh/mahs bah<u>h</u>oh?* |
| I'd like a facial_____ | Quisiera una máscara facial |
| | *keesyehrah oonah mahskahrah fahsyahl* |
| – a manicure_____ | Quisiera que me hagan manicura |
| | *keesyehrah keh meh ahgahn mahneekoorah* |
| – a massage _____ | Quisiera que me hagan masaje |
| | *keesyehrah keh meh ahgahn mahsahheh* |
| Could you trim _____ my bangs? | ¿Me podría recortar el flequillo? |
| | *meh pohdreeah rehkohrtahr ehl flehkeelyoh?* |
| – my beard? _____ | ¿Me podría recortar la barba? |
| | *meh pohdreeah rehkohrtahr lah bahrbah?* |
| – my moustache? _____ | ¿Me podría recortar el bigote? |
| | *meh pohdreeah rehkohrtahr ehl beegohteh?* |
| I'd like a shave, please ____ | Aféiteme/rasúreme, por favor |
| | *ahfeheetehmeh/rahsoorehmeh, pohr fahbohr* |
| I'd like a wet shave,_____ please | Aféiteme/rasúreme a navaja, por favor |
| | *ahfeheetehmeh/rahsoorehmeh ah nahbah<u>h</u>ah, pohr fahbohr* |

| ¿Cómo quiere el corte de pelo? _____ | How do you want it cut? |
| ¿Qué modelo deseaba? _____ | What style did you have in mind? |
| ¿Qué color quiere?_____ | What color do you want it? |
| ¿Esta temperatura le va bien?_____ | Is the temperature all right for you? |
| ¿Quiere algo para leer?_____ | Would you like something to read? |
| ¿Quiere algo para beber? _____ | Would you like a drink? |
| ¿Así está bien? _____ | Is this what you had in mind? |

# **A**t the Tourist Information Center

## **11** **A**t the Tourist Information Center

### **11** .1 **P**laces of interest

| | |
|---|---|
| Where's the Tourist _____ Information, please? | ¿Dónde está la oficina de turismo? *dohndeh ehstah lah ohfeeseenah deh tooreesmoh?* |
| Do you have a city map?___ | ¿Tendría un plano de la ciudad? *tehndreeah oon plahnoh deh lah syoodahdh?* |
| Where is the museum? ____ | ¿Dónde está el museo? *dohndeh ehstah ehl moosehoh?* |
| Where can I find _____ a church? | ¿Dónde podría encontrar una iglesia? *dohndeh pohdreeah ehnkohntrahr oonah eeglehsyah?* |
| Could you give me _____ some information about...? | ¿Me podría dar información sobre...? *meh pohdreeah dahr eenfohrmahsyohn sohbreh...?* |
| How much is that? _____ | ¿Cuánto le debemos por esto? *kwahntoh leh dehbehmohs pohr ehstoh?* |
| What are the main _____ places of interest? | ¿Cuáles son los sitios más interesantes para visitar? *kwahlehs sohn lohs seetyohs mahs eentehrehsahntehs pahrah veeseetahr?* |
| Could you point them _____ out on the map? | ¿Me los podría señalar en el plano? *meh lohs pohdreeah sehnyahlahr ehn ehl plahnoh?* |
| What do you _____ recommend? | ¿Qué nos recomienda? *keh nohs rehkohmyehndah?* |
| We'll be here for a_____ few hours | Pensamos quedarnos unas horas *pehnsahmohs kehdahrnohs oonahs ohrahs* |
| – a day _____ | Pensamos quedarnos un día *pehnsahmohs kehdahrnohs oon deeah* |
| – a week_____ | Pensamos quedarnos una semana *pehnsahmohs kehdahrnohs oonah sehmahnah* |
| We're interested in..._____ | Nos interesa... *nohs eentehrehsah...* |
| Is there a scenic walk _____ around the city? | ¿Hay algún circuito turístico para visitar la ciudad a pie? *ay ahlgoon seerkweetoh tooreesteekoh pahrah veeseetar lah syoodahdh ah pyeh?* |
| How long does it take? ____ | ¿Cuánto dura? *kwahntoh doorah?* |
| Where does it start/end? ___ | ¿De dónde sale?/¿Dónde termina? *deh dohndeh sahleh?/dohndeh tehrmeenah?* |
| Are there any boat _____ cruises here? | ¿Hay excursiones en barco? *ay ehxkoorsyohnehs ehn bahrkoh?* |
| Where can we board? _____ | ¿Dónde se puede embarcar? *dohndeh seh pwehdeh ehmbahrkahr?* |
| Are there any bus tours?___ | ¿Hay excursiones en autocar? *ay ehxkoorsyohnehs ehn ahootohkahr?* |
| Where do we get on?_____ | ¿De dónde salen? *deh dohndeh sahlehn?* |
| Is there a guide who_____ speaks English? | ¿Hay algún guía que hable inglés? *ay ahlgoon gheeah keh ahbleh eenglehs?* |

| | |
|---|---|
| What trips can we take around the area? | ¿Qué excursiones se pueden hacer en los alrededores? |
| | *keh ehxkoorsyohnehs seh pwehdehn ahsehr ehn lohs ahlrehdehdohrehs?* |
| Are there any _____ excursions? | ¿Hay excursiones organizadas? |
| | *ay ehxkoorsyohnehs ohrgahneesahdahs?* |
| Where do they go to? ____ | ¿Hacia dónde van? |
| | *ahsyah dohndeh bahn?* |
| We'd like to go to... _____ | Quisiéramos ir a... |
| | *keesyehrahmohs eer ah...* |
| How long is the trip? _____ | ¿Cuánto se tarda en llegar? |
| | *kwahntoh seh tahrdah ehn lyehgahr?* |
| How long do we _____ stay in...? | ¿Cuánto dura la visita a...? |
| | *kwahntoh doorah lah beeseetah ah...* |
| Are there any guided _____ tours? | ¿Hay visitas guiadas? |
| | *ay beeseetahs gheeahdahs?* |
| How much free time_____ will we have there? | ¿Cuánto tiempo libre tenemos allí? |
| | *kwahntoh tyehmpoh leebreh tehnehmohs ahlyee?* |
| We want to go hiking _____ | Nos gustaría hacer una excursión a pie |
| | *nohs goostahreeah ahsehr oonah ehxkoorsyohn ah pyeh* |
| Can we hire a guide? _____ | ¿Es posible contratar un guía? |
| | *ehs pohseebleh kohntrahtahr oon gheeah?* |
| Can I reserve mountain ____ huts? | ¿Se puede hacer una reserva/reservación para un refugio (en la montaña)? |
| | *seh pwehdeh ahsehr oonah rehsehrbah/ rehsehrbahsyohn pahrah oon rehfoohyoh (ehn lah mohntahnyah)?* |
| What time does... _____ open/close? | ¿A qué hora abre/cierra...? |
| | *ah keh ohrah ahbreh/syehrrah...?* |
| What days is...open/_____ closed? | ¿Qué días tiene abierto/cerrado...? |
| | *keh deeahs tyehneh ahbyehrtoh/sehrrahdoh...?* |
| What's the admission_____ price? | ¿Cuánto sale la entrada? |
| | *kwahntoh sahleh lah ehntrahdah?* |
| Is there a group _____ discount? | ¿Hay descuento para grupos? |
| | *ay dehskwehntoh pahrah groopohs?* |
| Is there a child _____ discount? | ¿Hay descuento para niños? |
| | *ay dehskwehntoh pahrah neenyohs?* |
| Is there a discount_____ for seniors? | ¿Hay descuento para jubilados? |
| | *ay dehskwehntoh pahrah hoobeelahdohs?* |
| Can I take (flash) _____ photos/can I film here? | ¿Se pueden sacar fotos (con flash)/ filmar aquí? |
| | *seh pwehdehn sahkahr fohtohs(kohn flahsh)/feelmahr ahkee?* |
| Do you have any _____ postcards of...? | ¿Venden postales de...? |
| | *behndehn pohstahlehs deh...?* |
| Do you have an _____ English...? | ¿Tiene un...en inglés? |
| | *tyehneh oon...ehn eenglehs?* |
| – an English catalogue?____ | ¿Tiene un catálogo en inglés? |
| | *tyehneh oon kahtahlohgoh ehn eenglehs?* |
| – an English program?____ | ¿Tiene un programa en inglés? |
| | *tyehneh oon prohgrahmah ehn eenglehs?* |
| – an English brochure? ____ | ¿Tiene un folleto en inglés? |
| | *tyehneh oon fohlyehtoh ehn eenglehs?* |

| | |
|---|---|
| Do you have this _____ week's/month's entertainment guide? | ¿Tiene la guía de los espectáculos de esta semana/este mes? *tyehneh lah gheeah deh lohs ehspehktahkoolohs deh ehstah sehmahnah/ehsteh mehs?* |
| What's on tonight? _____ | ¿Adónde podríamos ir esta noche? *ahdohndeh pohdreeahmohs eer ehstah nohcheh?* |
| We want to go to... _____ | Nos gustaría ir a... *nohs goostahreeah eer ah...* |
| Which films are _____ showing? | ¿Qué películas dan? *keh pehleekoolahs dahn?* |
| What sort of film is that?___ | ¿Qué clase de película es? *keh klahseh deh pehleekoolah ehs?* |
| suitable for everyone _____ | para todos los públicos *pahrah tohdohs lohs poobleekohs* |
| not suitable for_____ children | prohibido para menores de 12/16 años *proheebeedoh pahrah mehnohrehs deh dohseh/dyehseesehees ahnyohs* |
| original version _____ | versión original *behrsyohn ohreeheenahl* |
| subtitled _____ | subtitulada *soobteetoolahdah* |
| dubbed _____ | doblada *dohblahdah* |
| Is it a continuous_____ showing? | ¿Es sesión continua? *ehs sehsyohn kohnteenooah?* |
| What's on at...?_____ | ¿Qué dan en...? *keh dahn ehn...?* |
| – the theater? _____ | ¿Qué dan en el teatro? *keh dahn ehn ehl tehahtroh?* |
| – the concert hall? _____ | ¿Qué tocan en la sala de conciertos? *keh tohkahn ehn lah sahlah deh kohnsyehrtohs?* |
| – the opera? _____ | ¿Qué dan en la ópera? *keh dahn ehn lah ohpehrah?* |
| Where can I find a good _____ disco around here? | ¿Dónde hay una buena discoteca por aquí? *dohndeh ay oonah bwehnah deeskohtehkah pohr ahkee?* |
| Is it for members only? _____ | ¿Hay que ser socio? *ay keh sehr sohsyoh?* |
| Where can I find a good _____ nightclub around here? | ¿Dónde hay un buen cabaret por aquí? *dohndeh ay oon bwehn kahbahreh pohr ahkee?* |
| Is it evening wear only? _____ | ¿Hay que ir en traje de etiqueta? *ay keh eer ehn trahheh deh ehteekehtah?* ¿Es recomendable ir en traje de etiqueta? |
| Should I/we dress up? _____ | *ehs rehkohmehndahbleh eer ehn trahheh deh ehteekehtah?* ¿A qué hora empieza el espectáculo? |
| What time does the _____ show start? | *ah keh ohrah ehmpyehsah ehl ehspehktahkooloh?* |
| When's the next soccer _____ match? | ¿Cuándo es el próximo partido de fútbol? *kwahlndoh ehs ehl prohxeemoh pahrteedoh deh footbohl?* |

94

Who's playing? _____ ¿Quiénes juegan?
*kyehnehs hwehgahn?*

I'd like an escort for _____ Quisiera contratar un/una acompañante
tonight. Could you para esta noche. ¿Podría hacerme una
arrange that for me? reserva/reservación?
*keesyehrah kohntrahtahr oon/oonah
ahkohmpahnyahnteh pahrah ehstah
nohcheh. podreeah ahsehrmeh oonah
rehsehrbah/rehsehrbahsyohn?*

## 11 .3 Reserving tickets

Could you reserve some ___ ¿Podría hacernos una reserva/reservación?
tickets for us? *pohdreeah ahsehrnohs oonah rehsehrbah/
rehsehrbahsyohn?*

We'd like to reserve... _____ Quisiéramos...entradas/una mesa...
tickets/a table... *keesyehrahmohs...ehntrahdahs/oonah
mehsah...*

– tickets/seats in the _____ Quisiéramos...entradas en la platea
orchestra *keesyehrahmohs...ehntrahdahs ehn lah
plahtehah*

– tickets/seats in the _____ Quisiéramos...entradas en el palco
balcony *keesyehrahmohs...ehntrahdahs ehn ehl
pahlkoh*

– box seats _____ Quisiéramos...entradas en el palco
privado
*keesyehrahmohs...ehntrahdahs ehn ehl
pahlkoh preebahdoh*

– a table at the front _____ Quisiéramos una mesa adelante
*keesyehrahmohs oonah mehsah
ahdehlahnteh*

– in the middle _____ Quisiéramos una mesa al centro
*keesyehrahmohs oonah mehsah ahl
sehntroh*

– at the back _____ Quisiéramos una mesa atrás
*keesyehrahmohs oonah mehsah ahtrahs*

Could I reserve...seats for __ ¿Podría reservar...entradas para la función
the...o'clock de las...?
performance? *pohdreeah rehsehrbahr...ehntrahdahs pahrah
lah foonsyohn deh lahs...?*

Are there any seats left ____ ¿Quedan entradas para esta noche?
for tonight? *kehdahn ehntrahdahs pahrah ehstah
nohcheh?*

How much is a ticket? _____ ¿Cuánto sale la entrada?
*kwahntoh sahleh lah ehntrahdah?*

When can I pick the _____ ¿Cuándo puedo pasar a retirar/recoger
tickets up? las entradas?
*kwahndoh pwehdoh pahsahr ah rehteerahr/
rehkohhehr lahs ehntrahdahs?*

I've got a reservation _____ Tengo una reserva/reservación
*tehngoh oonah rehsehrbah/rehsehrbahsyohn*

My name's... _____ Me llamo...
*meh lyahmoh...*

| | |
|---|---|
| ¿Para qué función desea reservar? _____ | Which performance do you want to reserve for? |
| ¿Qué sector prefiere? _____ | Where would you like to sit? |
| No hay entradas _____ | Everything's sold out |
| Sólo quedan entradas de pie _____ | It's standing room only |
| Sólo quedan entradas en el palco _____ | We've only got balcony seats left |
| Sólo quedan entradas en la galería _____ | We've only got seats left in the gallery |
| Sólo quedan entradas en la platea _____ | We've only got orchestra seats left |
| Sólo quedan entradas adelante _____ | We've only got seats left at the front |
| Sólo quedan entradas atrás _____ | We've only got seats left at the back |
| ¿Cuántas entradas quiere? _____ | How many seats would you like? |
| Tiene que retirar/recoger las entradas antes de las... _____ | You'll have to pick up the tickets before...o'clock |
| ¿Me permite las entradas? _____ | Tickets, please |
| Este es su asiento _____ | This is your seat |

At the Tourist Information Center

11

# Sports

### 12.1 Sporting questions

| | |
|---|---|
| Where can we... _____ around here? | ¿Dónde se puede... por aquí? _dohndeh seh pwehdeh... pohr ahkee?_ |
| Is there a... _____ around here? | ¿Hay algún...por aquí cerca? _ahee ahlgoon...pohr ahkee sehrkah?_ |
| Can I hire a...here? _____ | ¿Alquilan...? _ahlkeelahn...?_ |
| Can I take...lessons? _____ | ¿Dan clases de...? _dahn klahsehs deh...?_ |
| How much is that per\_\_\_\_\_ hour/per day/class? | ¿Cuánto sale por hora/día/clase? _kwahntoh sahleh pohr ohrah/deeah/klahseh?_ |
| Do I need a permit _____ for that? | ¿Se necesita un permiso? _seh nehsehseetah oon pehrmeesoh?_ |
| Where can I get _____ the permit? | ¿Dónde se consiguen los permisos? _dohndeh seh kohnseeghehn lohs pehrmeesohs?_ |

### 12.2 By the waterfront

| | |
|---|---|
| Is it a long way to _____ the sea still? | ¿Falta mucho para llegar al mar? _fahltah moochoh pahrah lyehgahr ahl mahr?_ |
| Is there a...around here? \_\_\_ | ¿Hay algún...por aquí? _ay ahlgoon...pohr ahkee?_ |
| – an outdoor/indoor/_____ public swimming pool | ¿Hay alguna piscina por aquí? _ay ahlgoonah peesseenah pohr ahkee?_ |
| – a sandy beach _____ | ¿Hay alguna playa con arena por aquí? _ay ahlgoonah plahyah kohn ahrehnah pohr ahkee?_ |
| – a nudist beach_____ | ¿Hay alguna playa nudista por aquí? _ay ahlgoonah plahyah noodeestah pohr ahkee?_ |
| – mooring _____ | ¿Hay algún atracadero por aquí? _ay ahlgoon ahtrahkahdehroh pohr ahkee?_ |
| Are there any rocks_____ here? | ¿Hay rocas? _ay rohkahs?_ |
| When's high/low tide? \_\_\_\_\_ | ¿Cuándo sube/baja la marea? _kwahndoh soobeh/bahhah lah mahrehah?_ |
| What's the water _____ temperature? | ¿Qué temperatura tiene el agua? _keh tehmpehrahtoorah tyehneh ehl ahgwah?_ |
| Is it (very) deep here? \_\_\_\_\_ | ¿Es (muy) profundo? _ehs mwee prohfoondoh?_ |
| Can you stand here?_____ | ¿Se puede estar de pie? _seh pwehdeh ehstahr de pyeh?_ |
| Is it safe to swim here? \_\_\_\_ | ¿Es seguro para nadar? _ehs sehgooroh pahrah nahdahr?_ |
| Are there any currents? \_\_\_\_ | ¿Hay corriente? _ay kohrryehnteh?_ |
| Are there any rapids/ \_\_\_\_\_ waterfalls in this river? | ¿Este río tiene rápidos/cascadas? _ehsteh reeoh tyehneh rahpeedohs/kahskahdahs?_ |
| What does that flag/ _____ buoy mean? | ¿Qué significa aquella bandera/boya? _keh seegneefeekah ahkehlyah bahndehrah/bohyah?_ |

| Is there a life guard on duty here? | ¿Hay algún socorrista/guardavidas/salvavidas? |
| | *ay ahlgoon sohkohrreestah/ gwahrdahbeedahs/ sahlbahbeedahs?* |
| Are dogs allowed here? | ¿Está permitido traer perros? |
| | *ehstah pehrmeeteedoh trahehr pehrrohs?* |
| Is camping on the beach allowed? | ¿Está permitido acampar en la playa? |
| | *ehstah pehrmeeteedoh ahkahmpahr ehn lah plahyah?* |
| Are we allowed to build a fire here? | ¿Está permitido hacer fuego? |
| | *ehstah pehrmeeteedoh ahsehr fwehgoh?* |

| Peligro | Prohibido pescar | Prohibido bañarse |
| **Danger** | **No fishing** | **No swimming** |
| Aguas de pesca | Prohibido hacer surfing | Permiso obligatorio |
| **Fishing water** | **No surfing** | **Permits only** |

# 12 .3 In the snow

| Can I take ski lessons here? | ¿Dan clases de esquí? |
| | *dahn klahsehs deh eskee?* |
| for beginners/advanced | para principiantes/avanzados |
| | *pahrah preenseepyahntehs/ahbahnsahdohs* |
| How large are the groups? | ¿De cuántas personas son los grupos? |
| | *deh kwahntahs pehrsohnahs sohn lohs groopohs?* |
| What language are the classes in? | ¿En qué idioma son las clases? |
| | *ehn keh eedyohmah sohn lahs klahsehs?* |
| I'd like a lift pass, please | Quisiera un pase para las telesillas |
| | *keesyehrah oon pahseh pahrah lahs tehlehseelyahs* |
| Must I give you a passport photo? | ¿Se necesita foto? |
| | *seh nehsehseetah fohtoh?* |
| Where can I have a passport photo taken? | ¿Dónde puedo sacarme fotos? |
| | *dohndeh pwehdoh sahkahrmeh fohtohs?* |
| Where are the beginners' slopes? | ¿Dónde están las pistas para principiantes? |
| | *dohndeh ehstahn lahs peestahs pahrah preenseepyahntehs?* |
| Are there any runs for cross-country skiing? | ¿Hay pistas de esquí de fondo por aquí? |
| | *ay peestahs deh ehskee deh fohndoh pohr ahkee?* |
| Have the cross-country runs been marked? | ¿Las pistas de esquí de fondo están señalizadas? |
| | *lahs peestahs deh ehskee deh fohndoh ehstahn sehnyahleesahdahs?* |
| Are the...in operation? | ¿Están abiertos los...? |
| | *ehstahn ahbyehrtohs lohs...?* |
| – the ski lifts | ¿Ya funcionan los telesquís? |
| | *yah foonsyohnahn lohs tehlehskees?* |
| – the chair lifts | ¿Ya funcionan las telesillas? |
| | *yah foonsyohnahn lahs tehlehseelyahs?* |
| Are the slopes usable? | ¿Están abiertas las pistas? |
| | *ehstahn ahbyehrtahs lahs peestahs?* |

Sports

12

99

# Sickness

# 13 Sickness

## 13 .1 Call (get) the doctor

| | |
|---|---|
| Could you call/get a _____ doctor quickly, please? | ¿Podría llamar/ir a buscar rápido a un médico, por favor?<br>*pohdreeah lyahmahr/eer ah booskahr rahpeedoh ah oon mehdeekoh, pohr fahbohr?* |
| When does the doctor _____ have office hours? | ¿Cuándo atiende/tiene consulta el médico?<br>*kwahndoh ahtyehndeh/tyehneh kohnsooltah ehl mehdeekoh?* |
| When can the doctor _____ come? | ¿Cuándo puede venir el médico?<br>*kwahndoh pwehdeh behneer ehl mehdeekoh?* |
| I'd like to make an _____ appointment to see the doctor | ¿Podría pedirme hora/cita con el médico?<br>*pohdreeah pehdeermeh ohrah/seetah kohn ehl mehdeekoh?* |
| I've got an appointment ___ to see the doctor at... | Tengo hora/cita con el médico para las...<br>*tehngoh ohrah/seetah kohn ehl mehdeekoh pahrah lahs...* |
| Which doctor/pharmacy _____ has night/weekend duty? | ¿Qué médico/farmacia está de guardia esta noche/este fin de semana?<br>*keh mehdeekoh/fahrmahsyah ehstah deh gwahrdyah ehstah nohcheh/ehsteh feen deh sehmahnah?* |

## 13 .2 Patient's ailments

| | |
|---|---|
| I don't feel well _____ | No me siento bien<br>*noh meh syehntoh byehn* |
| I'm dizzy _____ | Tengo mareos<br>*tehngoh mahrehohs* |
| – ill _____ | Estoy enfermo<br>*ehstoy ehnfehrmoh* |
| – sick _____ | Tengo náuseas<br>*tehngoh nahoosehahs* |
| I've got a cold _____ | Estoy acatarrado<br>*ehstoy ahkahtahrrahdoh* |
| It hurts here _____ | Me duele aquí<br>*meh dwehleh ahkee* |
| I've been throwing up _____ | He devuelto<br>*eh dehbwehltoh* |
| I've got... _____ | Tengo molestias de...<br>*tehngoh mohlehstyahs deh...* |
| I'm running a _____ temperature of...degrees | Tengo...grados de fiebre<br>*tehngoh...grahdohs deh fyehbreh* |
| I've been stung by _____ a wasp | Me picó una avispa<br>*meh peekoh oonah ahbeespah* |
| I've been stung by an _____ insect | Me picó un insecto<br>*meh peekoh oon eensehktoh* |
| I've been bitten by _____ a dog | Me mordó un perro<br>*meh mohrdoh oon pehrroh* |
| I've been stung by _____ a jellyfish | Me picó una medusa<br>*meh peekoh oonah mehdoosah* |

**Sickness**

**13**

101

| I've been bitten by a snake | Me mordó una serpiente |
| | *meh mohrdoh oonah sehrpyehnteh* |
| I've been bitten by an animal | Me picó un insecto |
| | *meh peekoh oon eensehktoh* |
| I've cut myself | Me corté |
| | *meh kohrteh* |
| I've burned myself | Me quemé |
| | *meh kehmeh* |
| I've grazed myself | Tengo una rozadura |
| | *tehngoh oonah rohsahdoorah* |
| I've had a fall | Me caí |
| | *meh kahee* |
| I've sprained my ankle | Me torcí el tobillo |
| | *meh tohrsee ehl tohbeelyoh* |
| I've come for the morning-after pill | Vengo a que me dé una píldora del día después |
| | *behngoh ah keh meh deh oonah peeldohrah dehl deeah dehspwehs* |

## 13 .3 The consultation

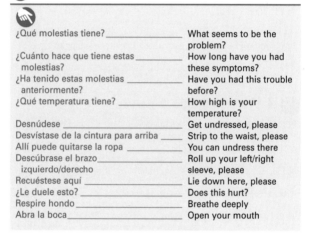

| ¿Qué molestias tiene? | What seems to be the problem? |
| ¿Cuánto hace que tiene estas molestias? | How long have you had these symptoms? |
| ¿Ha tenido estas molestias anteriormente? | Have you had this trouble before? |
| ¿Qué temperatura tiene? | How high is your temperature? |
| Desnúdese | Get undressed, please |
| Desvístase de la cintura para arriba | Strip to the waist, please |
| Allí puede quitarse la ropa | You can undress there |
| Descúbrase el brazo izquierdo/derecho | Roll up your left/right sleeve, please |
| Recuéstese aquí | Lie down here, please |
| ¿Le duele esto? | Does this hurt? |
| Respire hondo | Breathe deeply |
| Abra la boca | Open your mouth |

### Patient's medical history

| I'm a diabetic | Soy diabético |
| | *soy deeahbehteekoh* |
| I have a heart condition | Soy enfermo cardíaco |
| | *soy ehnfehrmoh kahrdeeahkoh* |
| I have asthma | Soy asmático |
| | *soy ahsmahteekoh* |
| I'm allergic to... | Soy alérgico a... |
| | *soy ahlehrheekoh ah...* |
| I'm...months pregnant | Estoy embarazada de...meses |
| | *ehstoy ehmbahrahsadah deh...mehsehs* |
| I'm on a diet | Sigo una dieta |
| | *seegoh oonah dyehtah* |

| I'm on medication/ _____ the pill | Tomo medicamentos/la píldora<br>*tohmoh mehdeekahmehntohs/lah peeldohrah* |
| I've had a heart attack _____ once before | Ya tuve un ataque cardíaco<br>*yah toobeh oon ahtahkeh kahrdeeeahkoh* |
| I've had a(n)...operation____ | Me operaron del/de la...<br>*meh ohpehrahrohn dehl/deh lah...* |
| I've been ill recently _____ | Estuve enfermo hace poco<br>*ehstoobeh ehnfehrmoh ahseh pohkoh* |
| I've got an ulcer _____ | Tengo una úlcera<br>*tehngoh oonah oolsehrah* |
| I've got my period_____ | Tengo la regla<br>*tehngoh lah rehglah* |

---

| ¿Padece alguna alergia? _____ | Do you have any allergies? |
| ¿Toma medicamentos? _____ | Are you on any medication? |
| ¿Sigue alguna dieta? _____ | Are you on a diet? |
| ¿Está embarazada? _____ | Are you pregnant? |
| ¿Está vacunado/a contra el tétanos?_____ | Have you had a tetanus injection? |

---

| No es nada grave _____ | It's nothing serious |
| Se fracturó el/la... _____ | Your...is broken |
| Se contusionó el/la _____ | You've got a/some bruised... |
| Se desgarró el/la... _____ | You've got (a) torn... |
| Tiene una inflamación _____ | You've got an infection |
| Tiene apendicitis_____ | You've got appendicitis |
| Tiene bronquitis _____ | You've got bronchitis |
| Tiene una enfermedad venérea _____ | You've got a venereal disease |
| Tiene gripe _____ | You've got the flu |
| Tuvo un ataque al corazón_____ | You've had a heart attack |
| Tiene una infección vírica/viral, _____ bacteriana | You've got an infection (viral..., bacterial...) |
| Tiene una pulmonía_____ | You've got pneumonia |
| Tiene una úlcera _____ | You've got an ulcer |
| Se distendió un músculo_____ | You've pulled a muscle |
| Tiene una infección vaginal_____ | You've got a vaginal infection |
| Tiene una intoxicación alimenticia _____ | You've got food poisoning |

**Sickness**

*13*

103

| Tiene una insolación _____ | You've got sunstroke |
| Es alérgico a... _____ | You're allergic to... |
| Está embarazada _____ | You're pregnant |
| Quisiera hacerle un análisis de sangre/de orina/de materia fecal | I'd like to have your blood/urine/stools tested |
| Hay que suturar la herida_____ | It needs stitching |
| Lo/la voy a derivar a un especialista/a ___ un hospital | I'm referring you to a specialist/sending you to the hospital |
| Tiene que hacerse radiografías _____ | You'll need to have some x-rays taken |
| Vuelva a tomar asiento en la sala de espera | Could you wait in the waiting room, please? |
| Hay que operarlo/operarla_____ | You'll need an operation |

### The diagnosis

| Is it contagious?_____ | ¿Es contagioso? |
| | *ehs kohntahhyohsoh?* |
| How long do I have to stay...? | ¿Hasta cuándo tengo que...? |
| | *ahstah kwahndoh tehngoh keh...?* |
| – in bed _____ | ¿Hasta cuándo tengo que guardar cama? |
| | *ahstah kwahndoh tehngoh keh gwahrdahr kahmah?* |
| – in the hospital _____ | ¿Hasta cuándo tengo que quedarme en el hospital? |
| | *ahstah kwahndoh tehngoh keh kehdahrmeh ehn ehl ohspeetahl?* |
| Do I have to go on a special diet? | ¿Tengo que seguir alguna dieta? |
| | *tehngoh keh sehgheer ahlgoonah dyehtah?* |
| Am I allowed to travel? ___ | ¿Puedo viajar? |
| | *pwehdoh byahhahr?* |
| Can I make a new appointment? | ¿Puedo volver a pedir hora/cita? |
| | *pwehdoh bohlbehr ah pehdeer ohrah/seetah?* |
| When do I have to come back? | ¿Cuándo tengo que volver? |
| | *kwahndoh tehngoh keh bohlbehr?* |
| I'll come back tomorrow | Vuelvo mañana |
| | *bwehlboh mahnyahnah* |

| Vuelva mañana/dentro de...días _____ | Come back tomorrow/in...days' time |

## 13 .4 Medication and prescriptions

| How do I take this medicine? | ¿Cómo se toman estos medicamentos? |
| | *kohmoh seh tohmahn ehstohs mehdeekahmehntohs?* |
| How many pills/ drops/injections/ spoonfuls/tablets each time? | ¿Cuántas cápsulas/gotas/inyecciones/ cucharadas/tabletas por vez? |
| | *kwahntahs kahpsoolahs/gohtahs/eenyehksyohnehs/koochahrahdahs pohr behs?* |

| How many times a day? ___ | ¿Cuántas veces al día? |
|---|---|
| | *kwahntahs behsehs ahl deeah?* |
| I've forgotten my _____ medication. At home I take... | Se me ha olvidado traer los medicamentos. En casa tomo... |
| | *seh meh ah olbeedahdoh trahehr lohs mehdeekahmehntohs. ehn kahsah tohmoh...* |
| Could you write a _____ prescription for me? | ¿Podría hacerme una receta? |
| | *pohdreeah ahsehrmeh oonah rehsehtah?* |

---

| Voy a recetarle unos antibióticos/un_____ jarabe/un calmante/ unos analgésicos | I'm prescribing antibiotics/a mixture/a tranquillizer/pain killers |
|---|---|
| Tiene que guardar reposo _____ | Have lots of rest |
| No tiene que salir a la calle _____ | Stay indoors |
| Tiene que guardar cama _____ | Stay in bed |

---

| | | |
|---|---|---|
| antes de cada comida **before meals** | inyecciones **injections** | tragar entero **swallow whole** |
| cápsulas **pills** | para uso externo exclusivamente **not for internal use** | tabletas **tablets** |
| diluir en agua **dissolve in water** | ungüento **ointment** | tomar/ingerir **take** |
| gotas **drops** | aplicar/embadurnar **rub on** | estos medicamentos afectan la capacidad de conducir |
| cada...horas **every...hours** | cucharadas (soperas/ cucharaditas) **spoonfuls** | **this medication impairs your driving** |
| seguir la cura hasta el final **finish the course** | (tablespoons/ teaspoons) | ...vez/veces cada 24 horas **...times a day** |
| durante...días **for...days** | | |

## 13.5 At the dentist's

| Do you know a good _____ dentist? | ¿Me podría recomendar un buen dentista? |
|---|---|
| | *meh pohdreeah rehkohmehndahr oon bwehn dehnteestah?* |
| Could you make a _____ dentist's appointment for me? It's urgent | ¿Me podría pedir hora/cita con el dentista? Es urgente |
| | *meh pohdreeah pehdeer ohrah/seetah kohn ehl dehnteestah? ehs oor<u>h</u>ehnteh* |
| Can I come in today, _____ please? | ¿Me podría atender hoy mismo? |
| | *meh pohdreeah ahtehndehr oy meesmoh?* |
| I have (terrible) _____ toothache | Tengo (un terrible) dolor de muelas |
| | *tehngoh (oon tehrreebleh) dohlohr deh mwehlahs* |
| Could you prescribe/ _____ give me a painkiller? | ¿Me podría recetar/dar un analgésico? |
| | *meh pohdreeah rehsehtahr/dahr oon ahnahl<u>h</u>ehseekoh?* |

| A piece of my tooth _____ has broken off | Se me cayó un pedazo de un diente *seh meh kahyoh oon pehdahsoh deh oon dyehnteh* |
|---|---|
| My filling's come out _____ | Se me salió un empaste *seh meh sahleeoh oon ehmpahsteh* |
| I've got a broken crown_____ | Se me rompió la corona *seh meh ah rohmpeeoh lah kohrohnah* |
| I'd like/I don't want a _____ local anaesthetic | Quisiera que/no quiero que me ponga anestesia local *keesyehrah keh/noh kyehroh keh meh pohngah ahnehstehsyah lohkahl* |
| Can you do a temporary ___ repair job? | ¿Me podría hacer un arreglo provisional? *meh pohdreeah ahsehr oon ahrrehgloh prohbeesyohnahl?* |
| I don't want this tooth _____ pulled | No quiero que me extraiga esta muela *noh kyehroh keh meh ehxtraheegah ehstah mwehlah* |
| My dentures are broken. ___ Can you fix them? | Se me ha roto la dentadura postiza ¿Podría arreglármela? *seh meh ah rohtoh lah dehntahdoorah pohsteesah. pohdreeah arrehglahrmehlah?* |

| ¿Qué diente/muela le duele?_____ | Which tooth hurts? |
|---|---|
| Tiene un absceso _____ | You've got an abscess |
| Tengo que tratarle el nervio _____ | I'll have to do a root canal |
| Voy a ponerle anestesia local _____ | I'm giving you a local anaesthetic |
| Tengo que empastarle/extraerle/ _____ pulirle este/esta... | I'll have to fill/pull this tooth/file this...down |
| Tengo que usar el torno _____ | I'll have to drill |
| Abra la boca_____ | Open wide, please |
| Cierre la boca_____ | Close your mouth, please |
| Enjuáguese_____ | Rinse, please |
| ¿Le sigue doliendo?_____ | Does it hurt still? |

**13 Sickness**

# In trouble

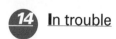

# 14 In trouble

## 14.1 Asking for help

| | |
|---|---|
| Help! _____ | ¡Socorro! ¡Ayuda! |
| | *sohkohrroh! iahyoodah!* |
| Fire! _____ | ¡Fuego! |
| | *fwehgoh!* |
| Police! _____ | ¡Policía! |
| | *pohleeseeah!* |
| Quick! _____ | ¡Rápido! |
| | *rahpeedoh!* |
| Danger! _____ | ¡Peligro! |
| | *pehleegroh!* |
| Watch out! _____ | ¡Cuidado! |
| | *kweedahdoh!* |
| Stop! _____ | ¡Alto! |
| | *ahltoh!* |
| Be careful! _____ | ¡Cuidado! |
| | *kweedahdoh!* |
| Don't! _____ | ¡No, no! |
| | *noh, noh!* |
| Let go! _____ | ¡Suelte! |
| | *swehlteh!* |
| Stop that thief! _____ | ¡Al ladrón! |
| | *ahl lahdrohn!* |
| Could you help me, _____ please? | ¿Podría ayudarme, por favor? |
| | *pohdreeah ahyoodahrmeh, pohr fahbohr?* |
| Where's the police _____ station/emergency exit/fire escape? | ¿Dónde está la comisaría/la salida de emergencia/la escalera de incendios? |
| | *dohndeh ehstah lah kohmeesahreeah/lah sahleedah deh ehmehrhehnsyah/lah ehskahlehrah deh eensehndyohs?* |
| Where's the nearest fire _____ extinguisher? | ¿Dónde hay un extintor? |
| | *dohndeh ay oon ehxteentohr?* |
| Call the fire department! _____ | ¡Llamen a los bomberos! |
| | *lyahmehn ah lohs bohmbehrohs!* |
| Call the police! _____ | ¡Llamen a la policía! |
| | *lyahmehn ah lah pohleeseeah!* |
| Call an ambulance! _____ | ¡Llamen a una ambulancia! |
| | *lyahmehn ah oonah ahmboolahnsyah!* |
| Where's the nearest _____ phone? | ¿Dónde hay un teléfono? |
| | *dohndeh ay oon tehlehfohnoh?* |
| Could I use your phone? _____ | ¿Podría llamar por teléfono? |
| | *pohdreeah lyahmahr pohr tehlehfohnoh?* |
| What's the emergency _____ number? | ¿Cuál es el número de urgencias? |
| | *kwahl ehs ehl noomehroh deh oorhehnsyahs?* |
| What's the number for _____ the police? | ¿Cuál es el número de la policía? |
| | *kwahl ehs ehl noomehroh deh lah pohleeseeah?* |

## 14 .2 Loss

| | |
|---|---|
| I've lost my purse/_____ wallet | Se me perdió el monedero/la cartera<br>*seh meh pehrdeeoh ehl mohnehdehroh/lah kahrtehrah* |
| I left my...behind _____ yesterday | Ayer dejé el/la...<br>*ahyehr dehheh ehl/lah...* |
| I left my...here_____ | Dejé el/la...aquí<br>*dehheh ehl/lah...ahkee* |
| Did you find my...? _____ | ¿Encontraron mi...?<br>*ehnkohntrahrohn mee...?* |
| It was right here_____ | Estaba aquí<br>*ehstahbah ahkee* |
| It's quite valuable _____ | Es muy valioso<br>*ehs mwee bahlyohsoh* |
| Where's the lost_____ and found office? | ¿Dónde está la oficina de objetos perdidos?<br>*dohndeh ehstah lah ohfeeseenah deh ohbhehtohs pehrdeedohs?* |

## 14 .3 Accidents

| | |
|---|---|
| There's been an _____ accident | Ha habido un accidente<br>*ah ahbeedoh oon ahkseedehnteh* |
| Someone's fallen into_____ the water | Se cayó alguien al agua<br>*seh kahyoh ahlghyehn ahl ahgwah* |
| There's a fire _____ | Hay un incendio<br>*ay oon eensehndyoh* |
| Is anyone hurt? _____ | ¿Hay algún herido?<br>*ay ahlgoon ehreedoh?* |
| Some people have _____ been/no one's been injured | (No) hay heridos<br>*(noh) ay ehreedohs* |
| There's someone in _____ the car/train still | Todavía queda alguien en el carro/tren<br>*tohdahbeeah kehdah ahlguyehn ehn ehl kahrroh/trehn* |
| It's not too bad. Don't_____ worry | No es grave. No se preocupe<br>*noh ehs grahbeh. noh seh prehohkoopeh* |
| Leave everything the _____ way it is, please | No toque nada<br>*noh tohkeh nahdah* |
| I want to talk to the_____ police first | Primero quisiera hablar con la policía<br>*preemehroh keesyehrah ahblahr kohn lah pohleeseeah* |
| I want to take a _____ photo first | Primero quisiera sacar una foto<br>*preemehroh keesyehrah sahkahr oonah fohtoh* |
| Here's my name_____ and address | Aquí tiene mi nombre y dirección<br>*ahkee tyehneh mee nohmbreh ee deerehksyohn* |
| Could I have your _____ name and address? | ¿Me da su nombre y dirección?<br>*meh dah soo nohmbreh ee deerehksyohn?* |
| Could I see some_____ identification/your insurance papers? | ¿Me permite su carnet de identidad/sus papeles del seguro?<br>*meh pehrmeeteh soo kahrneh deh eedehnteedah/soos pahpehlehs dehl sehgooroh?* |

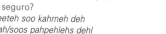

In trouble

14

| Will you act as a witness? | ¿Puede hacer de testigo? |
|---|---|
| | *pwehdeh ahsehr deh tehsteegoh?* |
| I need the details for the insurance | Necesito los datos para el seguro |
| | *nehsehseetoh lohs dahtohs pahrah ehl sehgooroh* |
| Are you insured? | ¿Está asegurado? |
| | *ehstah ahsehgoorahdoh?* |
| Third party or all inclusive? | ¿Responsabilidad civil o contra todo riesgo? |
| | *rehspohnsahbeeleedahd seebeel oh kohntrah tohdoh ryehsgoh?* |
| Could you sign here, please? | Firme aquí, por favor |
| | *feermeh ahkee, pohr fahbohr* |

## 14 .4 Theft

| I've been robbed | Me robaron |
|---|---|
| | *meh rohbahrohn* |
| My...has been stolen | Me robaron el/la... |
| | *meh rohbahrohn ehl/lah...* |
| My car's been broken into | Me abrieron el carro/auto/coche |
| | *meh ahbreeyehrohn ehl kahrroh/ahootoh/kohcheh* |

## 14 .5 Missing person

| I've lost my child/ grandmother | Se perdió mi hijo/mi hija/mi abuela |
|---|---|
| | *seh pehrdeeoh mee ee<u>h</u>oh/mee eehah/mee ahbwehlah* |
| Could you help me find him/her? | ¿Podría ayudarme a buscarlo/la? |
| | *pohdreeah ahyoodahrmeh ah booskahrloh/lah?* |
| Have you seen a small child? | ¿Ha visto a un niño pequeño/a una niña pequeña? |
| | *ah beestoh ah oon neenyoh pehkehnyoh/ah oonah neenyah pehkehnyah?* |
| He's/she's...years old | Tiene...años |
| | *tyehneh...ahnyohs* |
| He's/she's got short/long/blond/red/ brown/black/ gray/curly/ straight/frizzy hair | Tiene el pelo corto/largo/rubio/rojo/ castaño/negro/ canoso/rizado/liso/crespo |
| | *tyehneh ehl pehloh kohrtoh/lahrgoh/roobyoh/ kahstahnyoh/nehgroh/kahnohsoh/reesahdoh/ leesoh/krehspoh* |
| with a ponytail | con cola de caballo |
| | *kohn kohlah deh kahbahlyoh* |
| with braids | con trenzas |
| | *kohn trehnsahs* |
| in a bun | con moño rodete |
| | *kohn mohnyoh rohdehteh* |
| He's/she's got blue/brown/green eyes | Tiene ojos azules/marrones/verdes |
| | *tyehneh oh<u>h</u>ohs ahsoolehs/mahrrohnehs/behrdehs* |
| He's wearing swimming trunks/hiking boots | Lleva bañador/botas de montaña |
| | *lyehbah bahnyahdohr/bohtas deh mohntahnyah* |
| with/without glasses/ a bag | con/sin gafas/bolso |
| | *kohn/seen gahfahs/bohlsoh* |

| tall/short _____ | alto/bajito |
| | *ahltoh/bahheetoh* |
| This is a photo of _____ | Esta es su foto |
| him/her | *ehstah ehs soo fohtoh* |
| He/she must be lost _____ | Seguramente se habrá perdido |
| | *sehgoorahmehnteh seh ahbrah pehrdeedoh* |

## 14 .6 The police

### An arrest

| | |
|---|---|
| Los papeles del carro/auto/coche, por favor _____ | Your registration papers, please |
| Conducía demasiado rápido _____ | You were speeding |
| Tiene mal estacionado el coche _____ | You're not allowed to park here |
| No ha puesto monedas en el _____ parquímetro | You haven't put money in the meter |
| No le funcionan los faros _____ | Your lights aren't working |
| Le vamos a poner una multa de... _____ pesos | That's a...peso fine |
| ¿Va a pagar la multa en el acto? _____ | Do you want to pay now? |
| Tiene que pagar en el acto _____ | You'll have to pay now |

| I don't speak Spanish _____ | No hablo español |
| | *noh ahbloh ehspahnyohl* |
| I didn't see the sign _____ | No vi el cartel |
| | *noh bee ehl kahrtehl* |
| I don't understand _____ what it says | No entiendo lo que dice |
| | *noh ehntyehndoh loh keh deeseh* |
| I was only doing... _____ kilometers an hour | Sólo iba a...kilómetros por hora |
| | *sohloh eebah ah...keelohmehtrohs pohr ohrah* |
| I'll have my car checked ___ | Haré revisar el carro/auto/coche |
| | *ahreh rehbeesahr ehl kahrroh/ahootoh/ kohcheh* |
| I was blinded by _____ oncoming lights | Me cegó/encandiló un carro/auto/coche que venía de frente |
| | *meh sehgoh/ehnkahndeeloh oon kahrroh/ ahootoh/kohcheh keh behneeah deh frehnteh* |

### At the police station

| I want to report a _____ collision/missing person/rape | Vengo a hacer la denuncia de un choque/un extravío/una violación |
| | *behngoh ah ahsehr lah dehnoonsyah deh oon chohkeh/oon ehxtrahbeeoh/oonah beeohlahsyohn* |
| Could you make out _____ a report, please? | ¿Podría hacer un atestado/declaración? |
| | *pohdreeah ahsehr oon ahtehstahdoh/ dehklahrahsyohn?* |
| Could I have a copy _____ for the insurance? | ¿Me podría dar una copia para el seguro? |
| | *meh pohdreeah dahr oonah kohpyah pahrah ehl sehgooroh?* |

In trouble

14

111

| I've lost everything | He perdido todo |
| | *eh pehrdeedoh tohdoh* |
| I'd like an interpreter | Quisiera un intérprete |
| | *keesyehrah oon eentehrprehteh* |
| I'm innocent | Soy inocente |
| | *soy eenohsehnteh* |

---

| ¿Dónde fue? | Where did it happen? |
| ¿Qué se le perdió? | What's missing? |
| ¿Qué le robaron? | What's been taken? |
| ¿Me permite su documento de identidad? | Could I see some identification? |
| ¿A qué hora ocurrió? | What time did it happen? |
| ¿Quiénes estuvieron implicados? | Who was involved? |
| ¿Hay testigos? | Are there any witnesses? |
| Rellene este formulario | Fill this out, please |
| Firme aquí, por favor | Sign here, please |
| ¿Quiere un intérprete? | Do you want an interpreter? |

---

| I don't know anything about it | No sé nada |
| | *noh seh nahdah* |
| I want to speak to someone... | Quisiera hablar con alguien de... |
| | *keesyehrah ahblahr kohn ahlguyehn deh...* |
| from the American consulate | Quisiera hablar con alguien del Consulado Americàno |
| | *keesyehrah ahblahr kohn ahlguyehn dehl kohnsoolahdoh ahmehreekahno* |
| I need to see someone from the American embassy | Quisiera hablar con alguien de la Embajada Americàna |
| | *keesyehrah ahblahr kohn ahlguyehn deh lah ehmbah<u>h</u>ahdah ahmehreekahno* |
| I need a lawyer who speaks English | Necesito un abogado que habla inglés |
| | *nehsehseetoh oon ahbohgahdoh keh ahblah eenghlehs* |

# **W**ord list

# Word list English - Spanish

● **This word list** is meant to supplement the previous chapters.
Nouns are always accompanied by the Spanish definite article in order
to indicate whether it is a masculine (el) or feminine (la) word.
In a number of cases, words not contained in this list can be found
elsewhere in this booklet, namely alongside the diagrams of the car,
the bicycle and the tent. Many food terms can be found in the Spanish-
English list in 4.7.

## A

| | | |
|---|---|---|
| a little | un poco | *oon pohkoh* |
| above (up) | arriba | *ahrreebah* |
| abroad | el extranjero | *ehl ehxtrahnhehroh* |
| accident | el accidente | *ehl ahkseedehnteh* |
| adder | la víbora | *la veebohrah* |
| addition | la suma | *lah soomah* |
| address | la dirección | *lah deerehksyohn* |
| admission | la entrada | *lah ehntrahdah* |
| admission price | el precio de entrada | *ehl prehsyoh deh ehntrahdah* |
| admission ticket | la entrada | *lah ehntrahdah* |
| advice | el consejo | *ehl kohnsehhoh* |
| after | después de | *dehspwehs deh* |
| afternoon (in the) | (por) la tarde | *(pohr) lah tahrdeh* |
| aftershave | la loción para después de afeitarse | *lah lohthyohn pahrah dehspwehs deh ahfehytahrseh* |
| again | de nuevo | *deh nwehboh* |
| against | contra | *kohntrah* |
| age | la edad | *lah ehdahdh* |
| AIDS | el Sida | *ehl seedah* |
| air conditioning | el aire acondicionado | *ehl ayreh ahkohndeesyohnahdoh* |
| air mattress | el colchón neumático | *ehl kohlchohn nehoomahteekoh* |
| air sickness bag | bolsita para el mareo | *bohlseetah pahrah ehl mahrehoh* |
| aircraft | el avión | *ehl ahbyohn* |
| airport | el aeropuerto | *ehl ahehrohpwehrtoh* |
| alarm | la alarma | *lah ahlahrmah* |
| alarm clock | el despertador | *ehl dehspehrtahdohr* |
| alcohol | el alcohol | *ehl ahlkohohl* |
| all the time | cada vez | *kahdah behs* |
| allergic | alérgico | *ahlehrheekoh* |
| alone | solo | *sohloh* |
| always | siempre | *syehmpreh* |
| ambulance | la ambulancia | *lah ahmboolahnsyah* |
| American | Americano(a) | *ahmehreekahno(a)* |
| amount | el importe | *ehl eempohrteh* |
| amusement park | el parque de atracciones | *ehl pahrkeh deh ahtrahkthyohnehs* |
| anaesthetize | anestesiar | *ahnehstehsyahr* |
| anchovy | la anchoa | *lah ahnchohah* |

| | | |
|---|---|---|
| angry | enojado | *ehnohhdahdoh* |
| animal | el animal | *ehl ahneemahl* |
| ankle | el tobillo | *ehl tohbeelyoh* |
| answer | la respuesta | *lah rehspwehstah* |
| ant | la hormiga | *lah ohrmeegah* |
| antibiotics | los antibióticos | *lohs ahnteebyohteekohs* |
| antifreeze | el anticongelante | *ehl ahnteekohnhehlahnteh* |
| antique | antiguo | *ahnteegwoh* |
| antiques | las antigüedades | *lahs ahnteegwehdahdehs* |
| anus | el ano | *ehl ahnoh* |
| apartment | el departamento | *ehl dehpahrtahmehntoh* |
| aperitif | el aperitivo | *ehl ahpehreeteeboh* |
| apologies | las disculpas | *lahs deeskoolpahs* |
| apple | la manzana | *lah mahnsahnah* |
| apple juice | el jugo de manzana | *ehl hoogoh deh mahnsahnah* |
| apple pie | la tarta de manzana | *lah tahrtah deh mahnsahnah* |
| apple sauce | el puré de manzanas | *ehl pooreh deh mahnsahnahs* |
| appointment | la cita | *lah seetah* |
| approximately | más o menos | *mahs oh mehnohs* |
| April | abril | *ahbreel* |
| archbishop | el arzobispo | *ehl ahrsohbeespoh* |
| architecture | la arquitectura | *lah ahrkeetehktoorah* |
| area | los alrededores | *lohs ahlrehdehdohrehs* |
| area code | el prefijo | *ehl prehfeehoh* |
| arm | el brazo | *ehl brahsoh* |
| arrange to meet | quedar | *kehdahr* |
| arrive | llegar | *lyehgahr* |
| arrow | la flecha | *lah flehchah* |
| art | el arte | *ehl ahrteh* |
| artery | la arteria | *lah ahrtehryah* |
| artichokes | las alcachofas | *lahs ahlkahchohfahs* |
| article | el artículo | *ehl ahrteekooloh* |
| artificial respiration | la respiración artificial | *lah rehspeerahsyohn ahrteefeesyahl* |
| arts and crafts | la artesanía | *lah ahrtehsahneeah* |
| ashtray | el cenicero | *ehl sehneesehroh* |
| ask (a question) | preguntar | *prehgoontahr* |
| ask for | pedir | *pehdeer* |
| asparagus | los espárragos | *lohs ehspahrrahgohs* |
| aspirin | la aspirina | *lah ahspeereenah* |
| assault | la agresión | *lah ahgrehsyohn* |
| August | agosto | *ahgohstoh* |
| automatic | automático | *ahootohmahteekoh* |
| automatic car | el carro/auto/coche con cambio automático | *ehl kahrroh/ahootoh/kohcheh/ kohn kahmbyoh ahootohmahteekoh* |
| autumn | el otoño | *ehl ohtohnyoh* |
| avalanche | el alud | *ehl ahloodh* |
| awake (adj.) | despierto | *dehspyehrtoh* |
| awning | el toldo | *ehl tohldoh* |

# B

| baby | el bebé | *ehl behbeh* |
|---|---|---|
| baby food | la comida para bebés | *lah kohmeedah pahrah behbehs* |
| babysitter | la niñera | *lah neenyehrah* |
| back (at the) | atrás | *ahtrahs* |
| back | la espalda | *lah ehspahldah* |
| backpack | la mochila | *lah mohcheelah* |
| bacon | el tocino | *ehl tohseenoh* |
| bad | mal, malo | *mahl, mahloh* |
| bag | la bolsa | *lah bohlsah* |
| baker | la panadería | *lah pahnahdehreeah* |
| balcony (theater) | el palco (alto) | *ehl pahlkoh (ahltoh)* |
| balcony (to building) | el balcón | *ehl bahlkohn* |
| ball | la pelota | *lah pehlohtah* |
| ballet | el ballet | *ehl bahleh* |
| ballpoint pen | el bolígrafo | *ehl bohleegrahfoh* |
| banana | el plátano/la banana | *ehl plahtahnoh/ lah bahnahnah* |
| bandage | la gasa | *lah gahsah* |
| Bandaids | las tiritas, los esparadrapos | *lahs teereetahs, lohs ehspahrah-drahpohs* |
| bangs | el flequillo | *ehl flehkeelyoh* |
| bank (river) | la orilla | *lah ohreelyah* |
| bank | el banco | *ehl bahnkoh* |
| bank card | la tarjeta del banco | *lah tahrhehtah dehl bahnkoh* |
| bar (café) | el bar | *ehl bahr* |
| bar (in one's room) | el bar | *ehl bahr* |
| bar | la barra | *lah bahrrah* |
| barbecue | la barbacoa | *lah bahrbahkohah* |
| basketball | el baloncesto | *ehl bahlohnsehstoh* |
| bath | el baño | *ehl bahnyoh* |
| bath attendant | el bañista | *ehl bahnyeestah* |
| bath foam | el gel de baño | *ehl hehl deh bahnyoh* |
| bath towel | la toalla de baño | *lah tohahlyah deh bahnyoh* |
| bathing cap | el gorro de baño | *ehl gohrroh deh bahnyoh* |
| bathing suit | el bañador | *ehl bahnyahdohr* |
| bathroom | el cuarto de baño | *ehl kwahrtoh deh bahnyoh* |
| battery (car) | la batería | *lah bahtehreeah* |
| battery | la pila | *lah peelah* |
| beach | la playa | *lah plahyah* |
| beans | los frijoles/porotos blancos | *lohs freehohlehs/ pohrohtohs blahnkohs* |
| beautiful | bonito/lindo | *bohneetoh/leendoh* |
| beauty parlor | el salón de belleza | *ehl sahlohn deh behlyehsah* |
| bed | la cama | *lah kahmah* |
| bee | la abeja | *lah ahbehhah* |
| beef | la carne de vaca | *lah kahrneh deh bahkah* |
| beer | la cerveza | *lah sehrbehsah* |
| beet | la remolacha | *lah rehmohlahchah* |
| before | antes, delante de | *ahntehs, dehlahnteh deh* |

| | | |
|---|---|---|
| begin | empezar | ehmpehsahr |
| beginner | el principiante | ehl preenseepyahnteh |
| behind | atrás | ahtrahs |
| Belgian (f) | la belga | lah behlgah |
| Belgian (m) | el belga | ehl behlgah |
| Belgium | Bélgica | behl<u>h</u>eekah |
| bellboy | el mozo de cuerda/ | ehl mohsoh deh |
| | botones | kwehrdah/bohtohnehs |
| belt | el cinturón | ehl seentoorohn |
| berth | la litera | lah leetehrah |
| better | mejor | meh<u>h</u>ohr |
| bicarb | el bicarbonato | ehl beekahrbohnahtoh |
| bicycle | la bicicleta | lah beeseeklehtah |
| bicycle pump | el inflador | ehl eenflahdohr |
| bicycle repairman | el mecánico de | ehl mehkahneekoh |
| | bicicletas | deh beeseeklehtahs |
| bikini | el/la bikini | ehl/lah beekeenee |
| bill | la cuenta | lah kwehntah |
| billiards, to play | el juego de billar | ehl <u>h</u>wehgoh deh |
| | | beelyahr |
| birthday (to have a) | cumplir años | koompleer ahnyohs |
| birthday | el cumpleaños | ehl koomplehahnyohs |
| bite | morder | mohrdehr |
| bitter | amargo | ahmahrgoh |
| black | negro | nehgroh |
| bland | soso/desabrido | sohsoh/dehsahbreedoh |
| blanket | la manta/frazada | lah mahntah/frahsahdah |
| bleach | teñir de rubio | tehnyeer deh roobyoh |
| blister | la ampolla | lah ahmpohlyah |
| blond | rubio | roobyoh |
| blood | la sangre | lah sahngreh |
| blood pressure | la tensión/presión | lah tehnsyohn/prehsyohn |
| | sanguínea | sahngheenehah |
| blouse | la blusa | lah bloosah |
| blow dry | secar a mano | sehkahr ah mahnoh |
| blue | azul | ahsool |
| boat | el barco | ehl bahrkoh |
| body | el cuerpo | ehl kwehrpoh |
| body milk | la leche corporal | lah lehcheh kohrpohrahl |
| boiled | cocido | kohseedoh |
| boiled ham | el jamón de York/ | ehl <u>h</u>ahmohn deh |
| | cocido | yohrk/kohseedoh |
| bonbon | el bombón | ehl bohmbohn |
| bone | el hueso | ehl wehsoh |
| book | el libro | ehl leebroh |
| bookshop | la librería | lah leebrehreeah |
| border | la frontera | lah frohntehrah |
| bored (be) | aburrirse | ahboorreerseh |
| boring | aburrido | ahboorreedoh |
| born | nacido | nahseedoh |
| botanical gardens | el jardín botánico | ehl hahrdeen |
| | | bohtahneekoh |
| both | ambos/ambas | ahmbohs/ahmbahs |
| bottle (baby's) | el biberón | ehl beebehrohn |
| bottle | la botella | lah bohtehlyah |
| bottle-warmer | el calentador de | ehl kahlehntahdohr |
| | biberones | de beebehrohnehs |

117

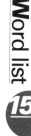

**Word list**

**15**

| | | |
|---|---|---|
| bowling | los bolos | *lohs bohlohs* |
| box (in theater) | el palco | *ehl pahlkoh* |
| box | la caja | *kahhah* |
| box office | la taquilla | *lah tahkeelyah* |
| boy | el chico | *ehl cheekoh* |
| bra | el sujetador | *ehl soohehtahdohr* |
| bracelet | la pulsera | *lah poolsehrah* |
| braised | estofado | *ehstohfahdoh* |
| brake | el freno | *ehl frehnoh* |
| brake fluid | el líquido de frenos | *ehl leekeedoh deh frehnohs* |
| bread | el pan | *ehl pahn* |
| breakdown service (auto) | el auxilio en carretera | *ehl ahooxeelyoh ehn kahrrehtehrah* |
| break (limb) | fracturarse | *frahktoorahrseh* |
| breakfast | el desayuno | *ehl dehsahyoonoh* |
| breast | el pecho | *ehl pehchoh* |
| bridge | el puente | *ehl pwehnteh* |
| bring | llevar | *lyehbahr* |
| brochure | el folleto | *ehl fohlyehtoh* |
| broken | roto, estropeado | *rohtoh, ehstrohpehahdoh* |
| broth | el caldo | *ehl kahldoh* |
| brother | el hermano | *ehl ehrmahnoh* |
| brown | marrón | *mahrrohn* |
| bruise (verb) | contusionarse | *kohntoosyohnahrseh* |
| brush | el cepillo | *ehl sehpeelyoh* |
| Brussels sprouts | las coles de Bruselas | *lahs kohlehs deh broosehlahs* |
| bucket | el cubo/el balde | *ehl koobooh/ehl bahldeh* |
| bug | el bicho | *ehl beechoh* |
| building | el edificio | *ehl ehdeefeesyoh* |
| bullfight | la corrida de toros | *lah kohrreedah deh tohrohs* |
| buoy | la boya | *lah boyah* |
| burglary | el robo en una casa | *ehl rohboh ehn oonah kahsah* |
| burn (verb) | quemar | *kehmahr* |
| burn | la quemadura | *lah kehmahdoorah* |
| burnt | quemado | *kehmahdoh* |
| bus | el autobús/ el camión/ el omnibús | *ehl ahootohboos/ ehl kahmyohn/ ehl ohmneeboos* |
| bus station | la estación de autobuses | *lah ehstahthyohn deh ahootohboosehs* |
| bus stop | la parada de autobús | *lah pahrahdah deh ahootohboosehs* |
| business class | la clase preferente | *lah klahseh prehfehrehnteh* |
| business trip | el viaje de negocios | *ehl byahheh deh nehgohsyohs* |
| busy (crowded) | hay mucha gente | *ay moochah hehnteh* |
| busy (telephone) | ocupado | *ohkoopahdoh* |
| butane camping gas | el gas butano | *ehl gahs bootahnoh* |
| butcher's | la carnicería | *lah kahrneesehreeah* |
| butter | la mantequilla | *lah mahntehkeelyah* |
| button | el botón | *ehl bohtohn* |

| | | |
|---|---|---|
| buy | comprar | kohmprahr |
| by airmail | el correo aéreo/<br>vía aérea | ehl kohrrehoh<br>ahehrehoh/beeah<br>ahehrehah |

## C

| | | |
|---|---|---|
| cabbage | la col, la berza | lah kohl, lah behrthah |
| cabin | la cabaña | lah kahbahnyah |
| cake | el pastel/queque | ehl pahstehl/kehkeh |
| cake shop | la pastelería, la<br>confitería | lah pahstehlehreeah,<br>lah kohnfeeteehreeah |
| call (by phone) | llamar por teléfono | lyahmahr pohr<br>tehlehfohnoh |
| called (name) | llamarse | lyahmahrseh |
| camera | la máquina/cámara<br>fotográfica | lah mahkeenah/<br>kahmahrah<br>fohtohgrahfeekah |
| camp | acampar | ahkahmpahr |
| camp shop | la tienda del<br>camping | lah tyehndah dehl<br>kahmpeen |
| camp site | el camping | ehl kahmpeen |
| camper van | el autocaravana | ehl ahootohkahrah-<br>bahnah |
| campfire | la fogata | lah fohgahtah |
| camping guide | la guía de camping | lah gheeah deh<br>kahmpeen |
| camping permit | el permiso de<br>acampar | ehl pehrmeesoh deh<br>ahkahmpahr |
| canal boat | el barco de<br>excursión | ehl bahrkoh deh<br>ehxkoorsyohn |
| cancel | cancelar | kahnsehlahr |
| candies | las golosinas | lahs gohlohseenahs |
| candle | la vela | lah behlah |
| candy | el caramelo | ehl kahrahmehloh |
| canoe | la canoa | lah kahnohah |
| canoeing | el piragüismo | ehl peerahgweesmoh |
| cap (hat) | el gorro | ehl gohrroh |
| car | el carro/auto/coche | ehl kahrroh/ahootoh/<br>kohcheh |
| car deck | la bodega para<br>carros/autos/coches | lah bohdehgah pahrah<br>kahrrohs/ahootohs/<br>kohchehs |
| car documents | los papeles del<br>carro/auto | lohs pahpehlehs dehl<br>kahrroh/ahootoh |
| car hood | el capó | ehl kahpoh |
| car registration | el permiso de<br>circulación | ehl pehrmeesoh<br>deh seerkoolahsyohn |
| car trouble | la avería | lah ahbehreeah |
| carafe | la jarra | lah hahrrah |
| cardigan | el chaleco | ehl chahlehkoh |
| careful | con cuidado | kohn kweedahdoh |
| carrot | la zanahoria | lah sahnahohryah |
| carton | el cartón | ehl kahrtohn |
| cartridge | el carrete de<br>cassette | ehl kahrrehteh deh<br>kahseht |
| cascade | la cascada | lah kahskahdah |
| cashier | la caja | lah kahhah |

| | | |
|---|---|---|
| casino | el casino | *ehl kahseenoh* |
| cassette | el cassette | *ehl kahseht* |
| castle | el castillo | *ehl kahsteelyoh* |
| cat | el gato | *ehl gahtoh* |
| catalogue | el catálogo | *ehl kahtahlohgoh* |
| cathedral | la catedral | *lah kahtehdrahl* |
| cauliflower | la coliflor | *lah kohleeflohr* |
| cave | la gruta | *lah grootah* |
| CD | el compact disc | *ehl kohmpahkt deesk* |
| celebrate | celebrar una fiesta | *sehlehbrahr oonah fyehstah* |
| cemetery | el cementerio | *ehl sehmehntehryoh* |
| center (in the) | en el centro/medio | *ehn ehl sehntroh/ mehdyoh* |
| center | el centro | *ehl sehntroh* |
| centimeter | centímetro(s) | *sehnteemehtroh(s)* |
| central heating | la calefacción central | *lah kahlehfaksyohn sehntrahl* |
| chair | la silla | *lah seelyah* |
| chambermaid | la camarera | *lah kahmahrehrah* |
| chamois | la gamuza | *lah gahmoosah* |
| champagne | el champán/el cava | *ehl chahmpahn/ehl kahbah* |
| change (from paying) | el vuelto | *ehl bwehltoh* |
| change (train/plane etc.) | hacer trasbordo | *ahsehr trahsbohrdoh* |
| change (verb) | cambiar | *kahmbyahr* |
| change the baby's diaper | cambiar los pañales | *kahmbyahr lohs pahnyahlehs* |
| change the oil | cambiar el aceite | *kahmbyahr ehl ahseyteh* |
| chapel | la capilla | *lah kahpeelyah* |
| charter flight | el vuelo chárter | *ehl bwehloh chahrtehr* |
| check | el cheque | *ehl chehkeh* |
| check (verb) | controlar | *kohntrohlahr* |
| checkers | jugar a las damas | *hoogahr ah lahs dahmahs* |
| check in | facturar | *fahktoorahr* |
| checked luggage | el depósito de equipajes | *ehl dehpohseetoh deh ehkeepahhehs* |
| cheers | salud | *sahloodh* |
| cheese (tasty, mild) | el queso (añejo, blando) | *ehl kehsoh (ahnyehhoh, blahndoh)* |
| chef | el jefe/chef | *ehl hehfeh/chehf* |
| cherries | las cerezas | *lahs sehrehsahs* |
| chess (play) | jugar al ajedrez | *hoogahr ahl ahehdres* |
| chewing gum | el chicle | *ehl cheekleh* |
| chicken | el pollo | *ehl pohlyoh* |
| chicory | las endivias | *lahs ehndeebyahs* |
| child | el hijo, el niño | *ehl eehoh, ehl neenyoh* |
| child seat | el asiento para niños | *ehl ahsyehntoh pahrah neenyohs* |
| child's seat | la silla para niños | *lah seelyah pahrah neenyohs* |
| chilled | refrigerado | *rehfreehehrahdoh* |
| chin | la barbilla | *lah bahrbeelyah* |
| chocolate | el chocolate | *ehl chohkohlahteh* |
| choose | elegir/escoger | *ehlehheer/ehskohhehr* |

| | | |
|---|---|---|
| chop | la chuleta | *la choolehtah* |
| chopped meat | la carne picada | *lah kahrneh peekahdah* |
| christian/given name | el nombre | *ehl nohmbreh* |
| church | la iglesia | *lah eeglehsyah* |
| church service | el servicio religioso | *ehl sehrbeesyoh rehlee<u>h</u>yohsoh* |
| cigar | el puro | *ehl pooroh* |
| cigarette | el cigarro | *ehl seegahrroh* |
| cigarette paper | el papel de fumar | *ehl pahpehl deh foomahr* |
| circle | el círculo | *ehl seerkooloh* |
| circus | el circo | *ehl seerkoh* |
| city map | el plano | *ehl plahnoh* |
| classic/classical | clásica | *klahseekah* |
| clean (adj.) | limpio | *leempyoh* |
| clean (verb) | limpiar | *leempyahr* |
| clear (adj.) | claro | *klahroh* |
| clearance | la liquidación | *lah leekeedahsyohn* |
| closed | cerrado | *sehrrahdoh* |
| closed off | (la carretera) cerrada | *(lah kahrrehtehrah) sehrrahdah* |
| clothes | la ropa | *lah rohpah* |
| clothes hanger | la percha | *lah pehrchah* |
| clothes pin | la pinza/el broche para la ropa | *lah peensah/ehl brohcheh pahrah lah rohpah* |
| coat | el abrigo | *ehl ahbreegoh* |
| cockroach | la cucaracha | *lah kookahrahchah* |
| cod | el bacalao (fresco) | *ehl bahkahlahoh (frehskoh)* |
| coffee | el café | *ehl kahfeh* |
| coffee creamer | la crema para el café | *lah krehmah pahrah ehl kahfeh* |
| coffee filter | el filtro de café | *ehl feeltroh deh kahfeh* |
| cognac | el coñac | *ehl kohnyakh* |
| cold | frío | *freeoh* |
| cold (n) | el resfrío | *ehl rehsfreeoh* |
| cold cuts | los fiambres | *lohs fyahmbrehs* |
| collarbone | la clavícula | *lah klahbeekoolah* |
| colleague | el/la colega | *ehl/lah kohlehgah* |
| collision | el choque | *ehl chohkeh* |
| cologne | el agua de tocador | *ehl ahgwah deh tohkahdohr* |
| color | el color | *ehl kohlohr* |
| color TV | el televisor de color | *ehl tehlehbeesohr deh kohlohr* |
| colored pencils | los lápices de colores | *lohs lahpeesehs deh kohlohrehs* |
| coloring book | el libro para colorear | *ehl leebroh pahrah kohlohrehahr* |
| comb | el peine | *ehl peeeneh* |
| come | venir | *behneer* |
| compartment | el compartimiento | *ehl kohmpahrteemyehntoh* |
| complaint (medical) | la molestia | *lah mohlehstyah* |
| complaint | la queja | *lah kehhah* |
| complaints book | el libro de quejas | *ehl leebroh deh kehhahs* |

**Word list**

**15**

| completely | del todo | dehl tohdoh |
| compliment | el cumplido | ehl koompleedoh |
| compulsory | obligatorio | ohbleegahtohryoh |
| concert | el concierto | ehl kohnsyehrtoh |
| concert hall | la sala de conciertos | lah sahlah deh kohnsyehrtohs |
| concussion | la conmoción cerebral | lah kohnmohsyohn sehrehbrahl |
| condiments | los condimentos | lohs kohndeemehntohs |
| condom | el condón | ehl kohndohn |
| congratulate | felicitar | fehleeseetahr |
| connection | el enlace | ehl ehnlahseh |
| constipation | el estreñimiento | ehl ehstrehnyeemyehntoh |
| consulate | el consulado | ehl kohnsoolahdoh |
| consultation | la consulta | lah kohnsooltah |
| contact lens | la lentilla/el lente de contacto | lah lehnteelyah/ehl lehnteh deh kohntahktoh |
| contact lens solution | el líquido para las lentillas | ehl leekeedoh pahrah lahs lehnteelyahs |
| contagious | contagioso | kohntahhyohsoh |
| contest | el concurso | ehl kohnkoorsoh |
| contraceptive | el anticonceptivo | ehl ahnteekohn-sehpteeboh |
| contraceptive pill | la píldora anticonceptiva | lah peeldohrah ahnteekohnsehpteebah |
| convent | el convento | ehl kohnbehntoh |
| cook (verb) | cocinar | kohseenahr |
| cook | el cocinero | ehl kohseenehroh |
| copper | el cobre | ehl kohbreh |
| copy | la copia | lah kohpyah |
| corkscrew | el sacacorchos | ehl sahkahkohrchohs |
| corn flour | la maicena | lah maheesehnah |
| corner | el rincón | ehl reenkohn |
| correct | correcto | kohrrehktoh |
| correspond | cartearse | kahrtehahrseh |
| corridor | el pasillo | ehl pahseelyoh |
| costume | el traje | ehl trahheh |
| cot | la cuna | lah koonah |
| cotton | el algodón | ehl ahlgohdohn |
| cotton (antiseptic) | el algodón | ehl ahlgohdohn |
| cough | la tos | lah tohs |
| cough syrup | el jarabe para la tos | ehl hahrahbeh pahrah lah tohs |
| counter | el mostrador | ehl mohstrahdohr |
| country | el país | ehl pahees |
| country code | el indicativo del país | ehl eendeekahteeboh dehl pahees |
| country(side) | el campo | ehl kahmpoh |
| course (of treatment) | la cura | lah koorah |
| cousin (f) | la prima | lah preemah |
| cousin (m) | el primo | ehl preemoh |
| crab | el cangrejo | ehl kahngrehhoh |
| cracker | la galleta | lah gahlyehtah |
| cream | la crema, la nata | lah krehmah, lah nahtah |
| credit card | la tarjeta de crédito | lah tahr_ehtah deh krehdeetoh |

| croissant | el croissant | ehl krwahsahn |
| cross the road | cruzar la calle | kroosahr lah kahlyeh |
| cross-country run | la pista de esquí de fondo | lah peestah deh ehskee deh fohndoh |
| cross-country skiing | el esquí de fondo | ehl ehskee deh fohndoh |
| cross-country skis | los esquís de fondo | lohs ehskees deh fohndoh |
| crossing (journey) | la travesía | lah trahbehseeah |
| cry (verb) | llorar | lyohrahr |
| cubic meter(s) | metro(s) cúbico(s) | mehtroh(s) koobeekoh(s) |
| cucumber | el pepino | ehl pehpeenoh |
| cuddly toy | el animal de peluche | ehl ahneemahl deh pehloocheh |
| cuff links | los gemelos/ las mancuernas | lohs hehmehlohs/ lahs mahnkwehrnahs |
| culottes | la falda-pantalón | lah fahldah pahntahlohn |
| cup | la taza | lah tahsah |
| curly | rizado | reesahdoh |
| current | la corriente | lah kohrryehnteh |
| cushion | el cojín | ehl cohheen |
| custard | las natillas/el flan | lahs nahteelyahs/ ehl flahn |
| customary | habitual | ahbeetwahl |
| customs | la aduana | lah ahdwahna |
| customs check | el control de aduanas | ehl kohntrohl deh ahdwahnahs |
| cut (verb) | cortar | kohrtahr |
| cutlery | los cubiertos | lohs koobyehrtohs |
| cycling | andar en bicicleta | ahndahr ehn beeseeklehtah |

## D

| dairy products | los productos lácteos | lohs prohdooktohs lahktehohs |
| damaged | dañado, estropeado | dahnyahdoh, ehstrohpehahdoh |
| dance | bailar | bahylahr |
| dandruff | la caspa | lah kahspah |
| danger | el peligro | ehl pehleegroh |
| dangerous | peligroso | pehleegrohsoh |
| dark | oscuro | ohskooroh |
| date | la cita | lah seetah |
| daughter | la hija | lah eehah |
| day | el día, las 24 horas | ehl deeah, lahs beheenteekwahtroh ohrahs |
| day before yesterday | anteayer | ahntehahyehr |
| dead | muerto | mwehrtoh |
| decaffeinated | sin cafeína | seen kahfeheenah |
| December | diciembre | deesyehmbreh |
| deck chair | el sillón de playa | ehl seelyohn deh plahyah |
| declare(customs) | declarar | dehklahrahr |
| deep | hondo | ohndoh |
| deep sea diving | el buceo | ehl boosehoh |

| degrees | los grados | *lohs grahdohs* |
|---|---|---|
| delay | el retraso | *ehl rehtrahsoh* |
| delicious | delicioso | *dehleesyohsoh* |
| dentist | el dentista | *ehl dehnteestah* |
| dentures | la dentadura postiza | *lah dehntahdoorah pohsteesah* |
| deodorant | el desodorante | *ehl dehsohdohrahnteh* |
| department (in store) | la sección | *lah sehksyohn* |
| department stores | los grandes almacenes | *lohs grahndehs ahlmahsehnehs* |
| departure | la partida | *lah pahrteedah* |
| departure time | la hora de salida | *lah ohrah deh sahleedah* |
| depilatory cream | la crema depilatoria | *lah krehmah dehpeelahtohryah* |
| deposit (in) | en consigna | *ehn kohnseegnah* |
| deposit | la fianza | *lah fyahnsah* |
| dessert | el postre | *ehl pohstreh* |
| destination | el destino, el punto final | *ehl dehsteenoh, ehl poontoh feenahl* |
| detergent | el detergente | *ehl dehtehrhehnteh* |
| develop (photos) | revelar | *rehbehlahr* |
| diabetic | el diabético | *ehl dyahbehteekoh* |
| dial (verb) | marcar | *mahrkahr* |
| diamond | el diamante | *ehl deeahmahnteh* |
| diaper | el pañal | *ehl pahnyahl* |
| diarrhea | la diarrea | *lah deeahrrehah* |
| dictionary | el diccionario | *ehl deeksyohnahryoh* |
| diesel | el gasóleo/gasoil | *ehl gahsohlehoh/gahsoheel* |
| diet | la dieta | *lah dyehtah* |
| difficulty | la dificultad | *lah deefeekooltahdh* |
| dining room | el comedor | *ehl kohmehdohr* |
| dining/buffet car | el coche restaurante | *ehl kohcheh rehstahoorahnteh* |
| dinner (to have) | cenar | *sehnahr* |
| dinner | la cena, la comida | *lah sehnah, lah kohmeedah* |
| dinner jacket | el smoking | *ehl ehsmohkeen* |
| direction | la dirección | *lah deerehksyohn* |
| directly | directo | *deerehktoh* |
| dirty | sucio | *soosyoh* |
| disabled person | el minusválido | *ehl meenoosbahleedoh* |
| disappearance | la desaparición | *lah dehsahpahreesyohn* |
| disco | la discoteca | *lah deeskohtehkah* |
| discount | el descuento | *ehl dehskwehntoh* |
| dish | el plato | *ehl plahtoh* |
| dish of the day | el plato del día | *ehl plahtoh dehl deeah* |
| disinfectant | el desinfectante | *ehl dehseenfehktahnteh* |
| distance | la distancia | *lah deestahnsyah* |
| distilled water | el agua destilada | *ehl ahgwah dehsteelahdah* |
| disturb | molestar | *mohlehstahr* |
| disturbance | el fallo | *ehl fahlyoh* |
| dive (verb) | bucear | *boosehahr* |

| | | |
|---|---|---|
| diving | el buceo | *ehl boosehoh* |
| diving board | el trampolín | *ehl trahmpohleen* |
| diving gear | el equipo de buzo | *ehl ehkeepoh deh boosoh* |
| divorced | divorciado | *deebohrsyahdoh* |
| Do-it-yourself-shop | la tienda de artículos de bricolaje | *lah tyehndah deh ahrteekoolohs deh breekohlaheh* |
| dizzy | mareado | *mahrehahdoh* |
| do (verb) | hacer | *ahsehr* |
| doctor | el médico | *ehl mehdeekoh* |
| dog | el perro | *ehl pehrroh* |
| doll | la muñeca | *lah moonyehkah* |
| domestic | nacionales | *nahseeohnahlehs* |
| done | hecho | *ehchoh* |
| door | la puerta | *lah pwehrtah* |
| double | doble | *dohbleh* |
| down | abajo | *ahbahhoh* |
| draft (to be a) | haber corriente | *ahbehr kohrryehnteh* |
| dream | soñar | *sohnyahr* |
| dress | el vestido | *ehl behsteedoh* |
| dressing gown | la bata | *lah bahtah* |
| drink (verb) | beber | *behbehr* |
| drinking water | el agua potable | *ehl ahgwah pohtahbleh* |
| drive (verb) | ir en coche | *eer ehn kohcheh* |
| driver | el chófer | *ehl chohfehr* |
| driving license | el permiso de conducir | *ehl pehrmeesoh deh kohndooseer* |
| drought | la sequía | *lah sehkeeah* |
| drugstore | la farmacia | *lah fahrmahsyah* |
| dry (verb) | secar | *sehkahr* |
| dry | seco | *sehkoh* |
| dry clean | lavar en seco | *lahbahr ehn sehkoh* |
| dry cleaner's | la tintorería | *lah teentohrehreeah* |
| dry shampoo | el champú seco | *ehl chahmpoo sehkoh* |
| during | durante | *doorahnteh* |
| during the day | de día | *deh deeah* |

# E

| | | |
|---|---|---|
| ear | la oreja | *lah ohrehhah* |
| ear, nose and throat (ENT) specialist | el médico de oídos | *ehl mehdeekoh deh oheedohs* |
| earache | el dolor de oído | *ehl dohlohr deh oheedoh* |
| eardrops | las gotas para los oídos | *lahs gohtahs pahrah lohs oheedohs* |
| early | temprano | *tehmprahnoh* |
| earrings | los pendientes/aretes | *lohs pehndyehntehs/ahrehtehs* |
| earth | la tierra | *lah tyehrrah* |
| earthenware | la cerámica | *lah sehrahmeekah* |
| east | el este | *ehl ehsteh* |
| easy | fácil | *fahseel* |
| eat | comer | *kohmehr* |
| eczema | el eczema | *ehl ehksehmah* |
| eel | la anguila | *lah ahngueelah* |
| egg | el huevo/blanquillo | *ehl wehboh/blahnkeelyoh* |

**Word list**

**15**

125

| eggplant | la berenjena | lah behrehnhehnah |
| electric | eléctrico | ehlehktreekoh |
| electricity | la corriente | lah kohrryehnteh |
| elevator | el ascensor/elevador | ehl ahsehnsohr ehlehbahdohr |
| embassy | la embajada | lah ehmbahhahdah |
| emergency brake | el freno de emergencia | ehl frehnoh deh ehmehrhehnsyah |
| emergency cone (car) | el triángulo reflectante | ehl treeahngooloh rehflehktahnteh |
| emergency exit | la salida de emergencia | lah sahleedah deh ehmehrhehnsyah |
| emergency number | el número de urgencias | ehl noomehroh deh oorhehnsyahs |
| emergency phone | el teléfono de emergencia | ehl tehlehfohnoh deh ehmehrhehnsyah |
| emery board | la lima (para uñas) | lah leemah (pahrah oonyahs) |
| empty | vacío | bahseeoh |
| English | inglés | eenglehs |
| enjoy | disfrutar | deesfrootahr |
| entertainment guide | la guía de los espectáculos | lah gheeah deh lohs ehspehktahkoolohs |
| entrance (driveway) | la entrada | lah ehntrahdah |
| envelope | el sobre | ehl sohbreh |
| escort | el/la acompañante | ehl/lah ahkohmpahnyahnteh |
| evening | la tarde | lah tahrdeh |
| evening wear | el traje de etiqueta | ehl trahheh deh ehteekehtah |
| event | el acontecimiento | ehl akohntehseemyehntoh |
| event (social) | la función | lah foonsyohn |
| everything | todo | tohdoh |
| everywhere | en todas partes | ehn tohdahs pahrtehs |
| examine | reconocer/ examinar | rehkohnohsehr/ ehksahmeenahr |
| excavation | las excavaciones | lahs ehxkahbahsyohnehs |
| excellent | excelente, estupendo | ehxsehlehnteh, ehstoopehndoh |
| exchange (verb) | cambiar | kahmbyahr |
| exchange office | la oficina de cambio | lah ohfeeseenah deh kahmbyoh |
| exchange rate | la cotización, el tipo de cambio | lah kohteesahsyohn, ehl teepoh deh kahmbyoh |
| excursion | la excursión organizada | lah ehxkoorsyohn ohrgahneesahdah |
| exhibition | la exposición | lah ehxpohseesyohn |
| exit | la salida | lah sahleedah |
| expenses | los gastos | lohs gahstohs |
| expensive | caro | kahroh |
| explain | explicar | ehxpleekahr |
| express train | el tren rápido | ehl trehn rahpeedoh |
| external | tópico, externo | tohpeekoh, ehxtehrnoh |
| eye | el ojo | ehl ohhoh |
| eye drops | las gotas para los ojos | lahs gohtahs pahrah lohs ohhohs |

| eye shadow | la sombra de ojos | lah sohmbrah deh ohhohs |
| eye specialist | el oculista | ehl ohkooleestah |
| eyeliner | el lápiz de ojos | ehl lahpees deh ohhohs |

## F

| face | la cara | lah kahrah |
| factory | la fábrica | lah fahbreekah |
| fair | la feria | lah fehryah |
| fall | caer(se) | kahehr(seh) |
| family | la familia | lah fahmeelyah |
| famous | famoso | fahmohsoh |
| far away | lejos | lehhohs |
| farm | la granja | lah grahnhah |
| farmer | el campesino | ehl kahmpehseenoh |
| farmer's wife | la campesina | lah kahmpehseenah |
| fashion | la moda | lah mohdah |
| fast | rápido | rahpeedoh |
| father | el padre | ehl pahdreh |
| fault (blame) | la culpa | lah koolpah |
| fax (verb) | enviar un fax | ehnbyahr oon fahx |
| February | febrero | fehbrehroh |
| feel (verb) | sentir | sehnteer |
| feel like | tener ganas | tehnehr gahnahs |
| fence | la verja/cerca | lah behrhah/sehrkah |
| ferry | el transbordador | ehl trahnsbohrdahdohr |
| fever | la fiebre | lah fyehbreh |
| fill (tooth) | empastar | ehmpahstahr |
| fill out | rellenar | rehlyehnahr |
| filling | el empaste | ehl ehmpahsteh |
| film (camera) | el rollo | ehl rohlyoh |
| film (movie) | la película | lah pehleekoolah |
| filter | el filtro | ehl feeltroh |
| find (verb) | encontrar | ehnkohntrahr |
| fine | la multa | lah mooltah |
| finger | el dedo | ehl dehdoh |
| fire | el fuego | ehl fwehgoh |
| fire (house etc.) | el incendio | ehl eensehndyoh |
| fire department | los bomberos | lohs bohmbehrohs |
| fire escape | la escalera de incendios | lah ehskahlehrah deh eensehndyohs |
| fire extinguisher | el extintor | ehl ehxteentohr |
| first | primero | preemehroh |
| first aid | los primeros auxilios | lohs preemehrohs ahooxeelyohs |
| first class | la primera clase | lah preemehrah klahseh |
| fish (verb) | pescar | pehskahr |
| fish | el pescado | ehl pehskahdoh |
| fishing rod | la caña de pescar | lah kanyah deh pehskahr |
| fitness club | el gimnasio | ehl heemnahsyoh |
| fitness training | la gimnasia | lah heemnahsyah |
| fitting room | el probador | ehl prohbahdohr |
| fix puncture | arreglar el pinchazo | ahrrehglahr ehl peenchahsoh |

| flag | la bandera | lah bahndehrah |
| flamenco | el flamenco | ehl flahmehnkoh |
| flash cube | el cuboflash | ehl koobohflahsh |
| flash gun/bulb | el flash | ehl flahsh |
| flight | el vuelo | ehl bwehloh |
| flight number | el número de vuelo | ehl noomehroh deh bwehloh |
| flood | la inundación | lah eenoondasyohn |
| floor | el piso | ehl peesoh |
| flour | la harina | lah ahreenah |
| flu | la gripe | lah greepeh |
| fly (insect) | la mosca | lah mohskah |
| fly (verb) | volar | bohlahr |
| fog | la niebla | lah nyehblah |
| foggy (be) | haber niebla | ahbehr nyehblah |
| folkloristic | folclórico | fohlklohreekoh |
| follow | seguir | sehgueer |
| food | el alimento | ehl ahleemehntoh |
| food poisoning | la intoxicación alimenticia | lah eentohxeekahsyohn ahleemehnteesyah |
| foodstuffs | los víveres | lohs beebehrehs |
| foot | el pie | ehl pyeh |
| for hire | se alquila | seh ahlkeelah |
| forbidden | prohibido | proheebeedoh |
| forehead | la frente | lah frehnteh |
| foreign | extranjero | ehxtrahnhehroh |
| forget | olvidar | ohlbeedahr |
| fork | el tenedor | ehl tehnehdohr |
| form | el formulario | ehl fohrmoolahryoh |
| fort | la fortificación | lah fohrteefeekahsyohn |
| forward (send) | enviar | ehnbyahr |
| fountain | la fuente | lah fwehnteh |
| four-star gas | súper | soopehr |
| frame | la montura | lah mohntoorah |
| free | libre | leebreh |
| free of charge | gratuito | grahtweetoh |
| free time | el tiempo libre | ehl tyehmpoh leebreh |
| freeze | helar | ehlahr |
| French | francés | frahnsehs |
| French bread | la barra de pan | lah bahrrah deh pahn |
| French fries | las patatas/papas fritas | lahs pahtahtahs/ pahpahs freetahs |
| fresh | fresco | frehskoh |
| Friday | el viernes | ehl byehrnehs |
| fried | frito | freetoh |
| fried egg | el huevo al plato | ehl wehboh ahl plahtoh |
| friend | el amigo | ehl ahmeegoh |
| friendly | cordial, amable | kohrdyahl, ahmahbleh |
| frightened | miedoso | myehdohsoh |
| front (at the) | adelante | ahdehlahnteh |
| frozen goods | los productos congelados | los prohdooktohs kohnhehlahdohs |
| fruit | la fruta | lah frootah |
| fruit juice | el jugo de frutas | ehl hoogoh deh frootahs |
| frying pan | la sartén | lah sahrtehn |

**Word list**

5

| | | |
|---|---|---|
| full | lleno | *lyehnoh* |
| fun | la diversión | *lah deebehrsyohn* |

## G

| | | |
|---|---|---|
| gallery | la galería de arte | *lah gahlehreeah deh ahrteh* |
| game | el juego | *el <u>h</u>wehgoh* |
| garage (for repairs) | el taller mecánico | *ehl tahlyehr mehkahneekoh* |
| garbage bag | la bolsa de basura | *lah bohlsah deh bahsoorah* |
| garden | el jardín | *ehl <u>h</u>ahrdeen* |
| gas | la gasolina/bencina/nafta | *lah gahsohleenah/behnseenah/naftah* |
| gas station | la gasolinera/estación de servicio | *lah gahsohleenehrah ehstahsyohn deh sehrbeesyoh* |
| gastroenteritis | la gastroenteritis | *lah gahstrohehnteh-reetees* |
| gauze | la gasa esterilizada | *lah gahsah ehstehreeleesahdah* |
| gear (bicycle) | el cambio | *ehl kahmbyoh* |
| gel (hair) | el gel | *ehl <u>h</u>ehl* |
| German | alemán | *ahlehmahn* |
| get married | casarse | *kahsahrseh* |
| get off | bajarse | *bah<u>h</u>ahrse* |
| gift | el regalo | *ehl rehgahloh* |
| gilt | dorado | *dohrahdoh* |
| ginger | el jengibre | *ehl <u>h</u>ehn<u>h</u>eebreh* |
| girl | la chica | *lah cheekah* |
| girlfriend | la amiga | *lah ahmeegah* |
| giro card | la tarjeta de la caja postal | *lah tahr<u>h</u>ehtah deh lah kah<u>h</u>ah pohstahl* |
| giro check | el cheque postal | *ehl chehkeh pohstahl* |
| glacier | el glaciar | *ehl glahsyahr* |
| glass (tumbler) | el vaso | *ehl bahsoh* |
| glass (wine -) | la copa | *lah kohpah* |
| glasses | las gafas/los lentes | *lahs gahfahs/lohs lehntes* |
| glider | el vuelo sin motor | *ehl bwehloh seen mohtohr* |
| glove | el guante | *ehl gwahnteh* |
| glue | la cola/el pegamento | *lah kohlah/ehl pehgahmehntoh* |
| gnat | el mosquito | *ehl mohskeetoh* |
| go (verb) | ir | *eer* |
| go back, come back | volver | *bohlbehr* |
| go backwards | ir para atrás | *eer pahrah ahtrahs* |
| go out | salir | *sahleer* |
| goat's cheese | el queso de cabra | *ehl kehsoh deh kahbrah* |
| gold | el oro | *ehl ohroh* |
| golf | el golf | *ehl gohlf* |
| golf course | el campo de golf | *ehl kahmpoh deh gohlf* |
| good afternoon | buenas tardes (after noon) | *bwehnahs tahrdehs* |
| good evening | buenas tardes | *bwehnahs tahrdehs* |
| good morning | buenos días (before noon) | *bwehnohs deeahs* |

| good night | buenas noches | bwehnahs nohchehs |
| good-bye | adiós/la despedida | ahdeeohs/ |
| | | lah dehspehdeedah |
| grade crossing | el paso a nivel | ehl pahsoh ah neebehl |
| gram | el gramo | ehl grahmoh |
| grandchild | el nieto | ehl nyehtoh |
| grandfather | el abuelo | ehl ahbwehloh |
| grandmother | la abuela | lah ahbwehlah |
| grape juice | el jugo de uvas | ehl hoogoh deh oobahs |
| grapefruit | el pomelo/la toronja | ehl pohmehloh/ |
| | | lah tohrohnhah |
| grapes | las uvas | lahs oobahs |
| grave | la tumba | lah toombah |
| gray (hair) | canoso | kahnohsoh |
| gray | gris | grees |
| grease | la grasa | lah grahsah |
| green | verde | behrdeh |
| green card | la tarjeta verde | lah tahrhehtah behrdeh |
| greet | saludar | sahloodahr |
| grill (verb) | asar a la parrilla | ahsahr ah lah |
| | | pahrreelyah |
| grilled | tostado | tohstahdoh |
| grocer's | la tienda de | lah tyehndah deh |
| | comestibles | kohmehsteeblehs |
| | el almacén | ehl ahlmahcehn |
| ground | la tierra | lah tyehrrah |
| group | el grupo | ehl groopoh |
| guest house | la pensión | lah pehnsyohn |
| guide (book) | la guía | lah geeah |
| guide (person) | el/la guía | ehl/lah geeah |
| guided tour | la visita guiada | lah beeseetah |
| | | geeahdah |
| gynecologist | el ginecólogo | ehl heenehkohlohgoh |

## H

| hair | el pelo | ehl pehloh |
| hairbrush | el cepillo para el | ehl sehpeelyoh parah |
| | pelo | ehl pehloh |
| hairdresser | la peluquería | lah pehlookehreeah |
| (ladies', men's) | (de señoras, | (deh sehnyohrahs, |
| | caballeros) | kahbahlyehrohs) |
| hairpins | las horquillas | lahs ohrkeelyahs |
| hairspray | la laca para el pelo | lah lahkah pahrah ehl |
| | | pehloh |
| half | medio, media, la | mehdyoh, mehdyah, |
| | mitad | lah meetahdh |
| half full | lleno hasta la mitad | lyehnoh ahstah lah |
| | | meetahdh |
| half kilo | el medio kilo | ehl mehdyoh keeloh |
| hammer | el martillo | ehl mahrteelyoh |
| hand | la mano | lah mahnoh |
| hand brake | el freno de mano | ehl frehnoh deh |
| | | mahnoh |
| handbag | el bolso de mano | ehl bohlsoh deh |
| | | mahnoh |
| handkerchief | el pañuelo | ehl pahnywehloh |
| handmade | hecho a mano | ehchoh ah mahnoh |

| | | |
|---|---|---|
| happy | contento | *kohntehntoh* |
| harbor | el puerto | *ehl pwehrtoh* |
| hard | duro | *dooroh* |
| haste | la prisa | *lah preesah* |
| hat | el sombrero | *ehl sohmbrehroh* |
| hay fever | la fiebre del heno | *lah fyehbreh dehl ehnoh* |
| hazelnut | la avellana | *lah ahbehlyahnah* |
| head | la cabeza | *lah kahbehsah* |
| headache | el dolor de cabeza | *ehl dohlohr deh kahbehsah* |
| health | la salud | *lah sahloodh* |
| health food shop | la tienda naturista | *lah tyehndah nahtooreestah* |
| hear | entender/oír | *ehntehndehr/oheer* |
| hearing aid | el audífono | *ehl ahoodeefohnoh* |
| heart | el corazón | *ehl kohrahsohn* |
| heart patient | el enfermo cardíaco | *ehl ehnfehrmoh kahrdeeahkoh* |
| heat | el calor | *ehl kahlohr* |
| heater | la calefacción | *lah kahlehfahksyohn* |
| heavy | pesado | *pehsahdoh* |
| heel | el talón | *ehl tahlohn* |
| heel (on shoe) | el tacón | *ehl tahkohn* |
| hello | hola | *ohlah* |
| helmet | el casco | *ehl kahskoh* |
| help (verb) | ayudar | *ahyoodahr* |
| help | la ayuda | *lah ahyoodah* |
| helping/portion | la ración | *lah rahsyohn* |
| herbal tea | la infusión | *lah eenfoosyohn* |
| here | aquí | *ahkee* |
| herring | el arenque | *ehl ahrehnkeh* |
| high | alto | *ahltoh* |
| high tide | la marea alta | *lah mahrehah ahltah* |
| highchair | la silla para niños | *lah seelyah pahrah neenyohs* |
| highway | la autovía, la autopista | *lah ahootohbeeah, lah ahootohpeestah* |
| hiking | el excursionismo | *ehl ehxkoorsyohneesmoh* |
| hip | la cadera | *lah kahdehrah* |
| hire | alquilar | *ahlkeelahr* |
| hitchhike | hacer autostop | *ahsehr ahootohstohp* |
| hobby | el hobby | *ehl hohbee* |
| hold-up/robbery | el asalto | *ehl ahsahltoh* |
| holiday (public) | el día de fiesta | *ehl deeah deh fyehstah* |
| holiday rental | el chalet | *ehl chahleh* |
| holiday park | la urbanización | *lah oorbahneesahsyohn* |
| holidays | las vacaciones | *lahs bahkahsyohnehs* |
| home (at) | en casa | *ehn kahsah* |
| homesickness | la nostalgia | *lah nohstahlhyah* |
| honest | sincero | *seensehroh* |
| honey | la miel | *lah myehl* |
| horizontal | horizontal | *ohreesohntahl* |
| horrible | horrible | *ohrreebleh* |
| horse | el caballo | *ehl kahbahlyoh* |
| hospital | el hospital | *ehl ohspeetahl* |
| hospitality | la hospitalidad | *lah ohspeetahleedahdh* |

**Word list**

**15**

| | | |
|---|---|---|
| hot | cálido/caluroso | *kahleedoh/ kahloorohsoh* |
| hot (spicy) | picante | *peekahnteh* |
| hotel | el hotel | *ehl ohtehl* |
| hot-water bottle | la bolsa de agua caliente | *lah bohlsah deh ahgwah kahlyehnteh* |
| hour | la hora | *lah ohrah* |
| house | la casa | *lah kahsah* |
| household items | los artículos del hogar | *lohs ahrteekoolohs dehl ohgahr* |
| houses of parliament | la cámara de diputados | *lah kahmahrah deh deepootahdohs* |
| housewife | el ama de casa | *ehl ahmah deh kahsah* |
| how far? | ¿a qué distancia? | *ah keh deestahnsyah?* |
| how long? | ¿cuánto tiempo? | *kwahntoh tyehmpoh?* |
| how much? | ¿cuánto? | *kwahntoh?* |
| how? | ¿cómo? | *kohmoh?* |
| hunger | el hambre/el apetito | *ehl ahmbreh/ehl ahpehteetoh* |
| hurricane | el huracán | *ehl oorahkahn* |
| hurry | la prisa | *lah preesah* |
| husband | el marido | *ehl mahreedoh* |
| hut | el camarote | *ehl kahmahrohteh* |
| hyperventilation | la hiperventilación | *lah eepehr-behnteelahsyohn* |

**I**

| | | |
|---|---|---|
| ice cream | el helado | *ehl ehlahdoh* |
| ice cubes | los cubitos de hielo | *lohs koobeetohs deh yehloh* |
| ice skating | el patinaje sobre hielo | *ehl pahteenahheh sohbreh yehloh* |
| idea | la idea | *lah eedehah* |
| identification card | el carnet de identidad | *ehl kahrneh deh eedehnteedahd* |
| identify | identificar | *eedehnteefeekahr* |
| ignition key | la llave de contacto | *lah lyahbeh deh kohntahktoh* |
| ill | enfermo | *ehnfehrmoh* |
| illness | la enfermedad | *lah ehnfehrmehdahd* |
| imagine | imaginarse | *eemahheenahrseh* |
| immediately | inmediatamente | *eenmehdyahtah-mehnteh* |
| import duty | los derechos de aduana | *lohs dehrehchohs deh ahdwahnah* |
| impossible | imposible | *eempohseebleh* |
| in | en | *ehn* |
| in the evening | por la tarde | *pohr lah tahrdeh* |
| in the morning | por la mañana | *pohr lah mahnyahnah* |
| included | incluido | *eenklooeedoh* |
| indicate | señalar | *sehnyahlahr* |
| indicator | el intermitente | *ehl eentehrmeeteehnteh* |
| inexpensive | barato | *bahrahtoh* |
| infection (viral -, bacterial -) | la infección (vírica/viral, bacteriana) | *lah eenfehksyohn (beereekah, beerahl bahktehryahnah)* |
| inflammation | la inflamación | *lah eenflahmahsyohn* |

| | | |
|---|---|---|
| information | la información | *lah eenfohrmahsyohn* |
| information office | la oficina de | *lah ohfeeseenah* |
| | información | *deh eenfohrmahsyohn* |
| injection | la inyección | *lah eenyehksyohn* |
| injured | herido | *erhreedoh* |
| inner ear | el oído | *ehl oheedoh* |
| inner tube | la cámara | *lah kahmahrah* |
| innocent | inocente | *eenohsehnteh* |
| insect | el insecto | *ehl eensehktoh* |
| insect bite | la picadura de | *lah peekahdoorah deh* |
| | insecto | *eensehktoh* |
| insect repellent | el aceite para los | *ehl ahsehyteh pahrah* |
| | mosquitos | *lohs mohskeetohs* |
| inside | adentro | *ahdehntroh* |
| insole | la plantilla | *lah plahnteelyah* |
| instructions | las instrucciones | *lahs eenstrooksyohnehs* |
| insurance | el seguro | *ehl sehgooroh* |
| intermission | la pausa | *lah pahoosah* |
| international | internacional | *eentehrnahsyohnahl* |
| interpreter | el intérprete | *ehl eentehrprehteh* |
| intersection/crossing | el cruce | *ehl krooseh* |
| introduce oneself | presentarse | *prehsehntahrseh* |
| invite (verb) | invitar | *eenbeetahr* |
| iodine | el yodo | *ehl yohdoh* |
| iron (metal) | el hierro | *ehl yehrroh* |
| iron (verb) | planchar | *plahnchahr* |
| iron | la plancha | *lah plahnchah* |
| ironing board | la tabla de planchar | *lah tahblah deh* |
| | | *plahnchahr* |
| island | la isla | *lah eeslah* |
| it's a pleasure | de nada | *deh nahdah* |
| Italian | italiano | *eetahlyahnoh* |
| itch | la picazón | *lah peekahsohn* |

## J

| | | |
|---|---|---|
| jack | el gato | *ehl gahtoh* |
| jacket | la chaqueta/el saco | *lah chahkehtah/* |
| | | *ehl sahkoh* |
| jam | la mermelada | *lah mehrmehlahdah* |
| January | enero | *ehnehroh* |
| jaw | la mandíbula | *lah mahndeeboolah* |
| jellyfish | la medusa | *lah mehdoosah* |
| jeweler | la joyería | *lah <u>h</u>oyehreeah* |
| jewels | las alhajas | *lahs ahla<u>h</u>hahs* |
| jog (verb) | hacer footing | *ahsehr footeen* |
| joke | la broma | *lah brohmah* |
| journey | el viaje | *ehl byah<u>h</u>eh* |
| juice | el jugo | *ehl <u>h</u>oogoh* |
| July | julio | *<u>h</u>oolyoh* |
| jumper cables | el cable de arranque | *ehl kahbleh deh* |
| | | *ahrrahnkeh* |
| June | junio | *<u>h</u>oonyoh* |

## K

| | | |
|---|---|---|
| key | la llave | *lah lyahbeh* |
| kilo | el kilo | *ehl keeloh* |
| kilometer | kilómetro(s) | *keelohmehtroh(s)* |

**Word list**

**15**

133

| | | |
|---|---|---|
| king | el rey | *ehl rehee* |
| kiss (verb) | besar | *behsahr* |
| kiss | el beso | *ehl behsoh* |
| kitchen | la cocina | *lah kohseenah* |
| knee | la rodilla | *lah rohdeelyah* |
| knee socks | las medias cortas | *lahs mehdyahs kohrtahs* |
| knife | el cuchillo | *ehl koocheelyoh* |
| know | saber | *sahbehr* |

## L

| | | |
|---|---|---|
| lace | el encaje | *ehl ehnkah<u>h</u>eh* |
| ladies' room | el baño para señoras | *ehl bahnyoh pahrah sehnyohrahs* |
| lake | el lago | *ehl lahgoh* |
| lamp | la lámpara | *lah lahmpahrah* |
| land (verb) | aterrizar | *ahtehrreesahr* |
| lane | el carril | *ehl kahrreel* |
| language | el idioma | *ehl eedyohmah* |
| large | grande | *grahndeh* |
| last | pasado, último | *pahsahdoh, oolteemoh* |
| last night | anoche | *ahnohcheh* |
| late | tarde | *tahrdeh* |
| later | luego | *lwehgoh* |
| latest (at the) | a más tardar | *ah mahs tahrdahr* |
| laugh | reír | *reheer* |
| launderette | la lavandería (automática) | *lah lahbahndehreeah (ahootohmahteekah)* |
| law | el derecho | *ehl dehrehchoh* |
| lawyer | el abogado | *ehl ahbohgahdoh* |
| laxative | el laxante | *ehl lahxahnteh* |
| leak | la fuga, gotera | *lah foogah, gohtehrah* |
| leather | la piel, el cuero | *lah pyehl, ehl kwehroh* |
| leather goods | los artículos de piel | *lohs ahrteekoolohs deh pyehl* |
| leave (verb) | partir, salir | *pahrteer, sahleer* |
| leek | el puerro, porro | *ehl pwehrroh, pohroh* |
| left (on the) | a la izquierda | *ah lah eeskyehrdah* |
| left | izquierda | *eeskyehrdah* |
| leg | la pierna | *lah pyehrnah* |
| lemon | el limón | *ehl leemohn* |
| lemonade | la limonada | *lah leemohnahdah* |
| lend | prestar | *prehstahr* |
| lens | el objetivo | *ehl ohb<u>h</u>ehteeboh* |
| lentils | las lentejas | *lahs lehnteh<u>h</u>ahs* |
| less | menos | *mehnohs* |
| lesson | la clase | *lah klahseh* |
| letter | la carta | *lah kahrtah* |
| lettuce | la lechuga | *lah lehchoogah* |
| library | la biblioteca | *lah beeblyohtehkah* |
| lie | mentir | *mehnteer* |
| lie down | estar tumbado | *ehstahr toombahdoh* |
| lift (hitchhike) | el viaje (en autostop) | *ehl byah<u>h</u>eh (ehn ahootohstohp)* |
| lift (ski) | el telesquí, el telesilla | *ehl tehlehskee, ehl tehlehseelyah* |
| light (for cigarette) | el fuego | *ehl fwehgoh* |
| light (not dark) | claro | *klahroh* |

| | | |
|---|---|---|
| light (not heavy) | ligero | *leehehroh* |
| lighter | el mechero | *ehl mehchehroh* |
| | encendedor | *ehnsehndehdohr* |
| lighthouse | el faro | *ehl fahroh* |
| lightning | el rayo | *ehl rahyoh* |
| like (verb) | gustar | *goostahr* |
| line | la línea | *lah leenehah* |
| linen | el hilo, el lino | *ehl eeloh, ehl leenoh* |
| lipstick | el lápiz de labios | *ehl lahpees deh lahbyohs* |
| liqueur | el licor | *ehl leekohr* |
| liquor store | la bodega, la tienda | *lah bohdehgah, lah* |
| | de vinos y licores | *tyehndah deh beenohs* |
| | | *ee leekohrehs* |
| liquorice | el regaliz | *ehl rehgahlees* |
| listen | escuchar | *ehskoochahr* |
| liter | el litro | *ehl leetroh* |
| literature | la literatura | *lah leetehrahtoorah* |
| little | poco | *pohkoh* |
| live (verb) | vivir | *beebeer* |
| live together | vivir con otra | *beebeer kohn ohtrah* |
| | persona | *pehrsohnah* |
| lobster | la langosta | *lah lahngohstah* |
| local | local | *lohkahl* |
| lock | la cerradura | *lah sehrrahdoorah* |
| long | largo | *lahrgoh* |
| long distance call | interurbano | *eentehroorbahnoh* |
| look (verb) | mirar | *meerahr* |
| look for | buscar | *booskahr* |
| look up (person) | buscar | *booskahr* |
| lose | perder | *pehrdehr* |
| loss | la pérdida | *lah pehrdeedah* |
| lost (to get) | perderse, | *pehrdehrseh,* |
| | extraviarse | *ehxtrahbyahrseh* |
| lost | extraviado, perdido | *ehxtrahbyahdoh,* |
| | | *pehrdeedoh* |
| lost item | extravío | *ehxtrahbeeoh* |
| lost and found office | los objetos perdidos | *lohs ohbhehtohs* |
| | | *pehrdeedohs* |
| lotion | la loción | *lah lohsyohn* |
| loud | alto | *ahltoh* |
| love (be in - with) | estar enamorado de | *ehstahr* |
| | | *ehnahmohrahdoh deh* |
| love (verb) | querer | *kehrehr* |
| love | el amor | *ehl ahmohr* |
| low | bajo | *bahhoh* |
| low tide | la marea baja | *lah mahrehah bahhah* |
| luck | la suerte | *lah swehrteh* |
| luggage | el equipaje | *ehl ehkeepahheh* |
| luggage locker | la consigna | *lah kohnseegnah* |
| | automática | *ahootohmahteekah* |
| lunch | el almuerzo, la | *ehl ahlmwehrsoh,* |
| | comida | *lah kohmeedah* |
| lungs | los pulmones | *lohs poolmohnehs* |

## M

| | | |
|---|---|---|
| macaroni | los macarrones | *lohs mahkahrrohnehs* |
| madam/Mrs | señora | *sehnyohrah* |

| | | |
|---|---|---|
| magazine | la revista | lah rehbeestah |
| magnificent | magnífico | mahgneefeekoh |
| mail | el correo | ehl kohrrehoh |
| mailman | el cartero | ehl kahrtehroh |
| main post office | la oficina central de Correos | ah ohfeeseenah sehntrahl deh kohrrehohs |
| main road | la carretera principal | lah kahrrehtehrah preenseepahl |
| make an appointment | pedir hora/cita | pehdeer ohrah/seetah |
| make love | acostarse/hacer el amor | ahkohstahrseh/ahsehr ehl ahmohr |
| makeshift | provisional(mente) | prohbeesyohnahl (mehnteh) |
| man | el hombre | ehl ohmbreh |
| manager | el encargado | ehl ehnkahrgahdoh |
| mandarin (fruit) | la mandarina | lah mahndahreenah |
| manicure | la manicura | lah mahneekoorah |
| map | el mapa | ehl mahpah |
| marble | el mármol | ehl mahrmohl |
| March | marzo | mahrsoh |
| margarine | la margarina | lah mahrgahreenah |
| marina | el puerto deportivo | ehl pwehrtoh dehpohrteeboh |
| market | el mercado | ehl mehrkahdoh |
| marriage | el matrimonio | ehl mahtreemohnyoh |
| married | casado | kahsahdoh |
| mass | la misa | lah meesah |
| massage | el masaje | ehl mahsah<u>h</u>eh |
| mat | mate | mahteh |
| matches | las cerillas | lahs sehreelyahs |
| | los fosforos | lohs fohsfohrohs |
| May | mayo | mahyoh |
| maybe | quizá | keesah |
| mayonnaise | la mayonesa | lah mahyohnehsah |
| mayor | el alcalde | ehl ahlkahldeh |
| meal | la comida | lah kohmeedah |
| mean (verb) | significar | seegneefeekahr |
| meat | la carne | lah kahrneh |
| medical insurance | el seguro de enfermedad | ehl sehgooroh deh ehnfehrmehdahd |
| medication | el medicamento | ehl mehdeekahmehntoh |
| medicine | el medicamento, la medicina | ehl mehdeekahmehntoh, lah mehdeeseenah |
| meet | conocer | kohnohsehr |
| melon | el melón | ehl mehlohn |
| membership | el ser socio | ehl sehr sohsyoh |
| menstruate | tener la regla | tehnehr lah rehglah |
| menstruation | la menstruación | lah mehnstrooahsyohn |
| menu | el menú, la carta | ehl mehnoo, lah kahrtah |
| menu of the day | el menú del día | ehl mehnoo dehl deeah |
| message | el recado/mensaje | ehl rehkahdoh/ mehnsah<u>h</u>eh |
| metal | el metal | ehl mehtahl |
| meter (taxi) | el taxímetro | ehl tahxeemehtroh |

| meter | metro(s) | *mehtroh(s)* |
|---|---|---|
| migraine | la jaqueca | *lah hahkehkah* |
| mild (tobacco) | rubio | *roobyoh* |
| milk | la leche | *lah lehcheh* |
| millimeter(s) | milímetro(s) | *meeleemehtroh(s)* |
| mineral water | el agua mineral | *ehl ahgwah meenehrahl* |
| minute | el minuto | *ehl meenootoh* |
| mirror | el espejo | *ehl ehspehoh* |
| miss (person) | echar de menos | *ehchahr deh mehnohs* |
| missing (be) | faltar | *fahltahr* |
| mistake | el error, la equivocación | *ehl ehrrohr, lah ehkeebohkahsyohn* |
| mistaken (be) | equivocarse | *ehkeebohkahrseh* |
| misunderstanding | el malentendido | *ehl mahlehntehndeedoh* |
| mixture | el jarabe, la poción | *ehl hahrahbeh, lah pohsyohn* |
| mocha | el moca | *ehl mohkah* |
| modern art | el arte moderno | *ehl ahrteh mohdehrnoh* |
| molar | la muela | *lah mwehlah* |
| moment | el momento | *ehl mohmehntoh* |
| Monday | el lunes | *ehl loonehs* |
| money | el dinero | *ehl deenehroh* |
| month | el mes | *ehl mehs* |
| moped | el ciclomotor | *ehl seeklohmohtohr* |
| morning-after pill | la píldora para el día después | *lah peeldohrah pahrah ehl deeah dehspwehs* |
| mosque | la mezquita | *lah mehskeetah* |
| motel | el motel | *ehl mohtehl* |
| mother | la madre | *lah mahdreh* |
| | la mamá | *lah mahmah* |
| motor cross | el motocrós | *ehl mohtohkrohs* |
| motorbike | la moto | *lah mohtoh* |
| motorboat | la lancha motor | *lah lahnchah mohtohr* |
| movie | la película | *lah pehleekoolah* |
| mountain | la montaña | *lah mohntahnyah* |
| mountain hut | el refugio | *ehl rehfoohyoh* |
| mountaineering | el montañismo | *ehl mohntahnyeesmoh* |
| mountaineering shoes | las botas de alpinismo | *lahs bohtahs deh ahlpeeneesmoh* |
| mouse | el ratón | *ehl rahtohn* |
| mouth | la boca | *lah bohkah* |
| movie camera | la filmadora | *lah feelmahdohrah* |
| much/many | mucho | *moochoh* |
| multi-story garage | el estacionamiento | *ehl ehstahsyohnah-myehntoh* |
| muscle | el músculo | *ehl mooskooloh* |
| muscle spasms | los calambres (en los músculos) | *lohs kahlahmbrehs (ehn lohs mooskoolohs)* |
| museum | el museo | *ehl moosehoh* |
| mushrooms | los champiñones | *lohs chahmpeenyohnehs* |
| music | la música | *lah mooseekah* |
| musical show | la comedia musical | *lah kohmehdyah mooseekahl* |
| mussels | los mejillones | *lohs meheelyohnehs* |
| mustard | la mostaza | *lah mohstahsah* |

# N

| | | |
|---|---|---|
| nail (on hand) | la uña | *lah oonyah* |
| nail | el clavo | *ehl klahboh* |
| nail polish | el esmalte (para uñas) | *ehl ehsmahlteh(pahrah oonyahs)* |
| nail polish remover | el quitaesmalte | *ehl keetahehsmahlteh* |
| nail scissors | las tijeras de uñas | *lahs tee<u>h</u>ehrahs pahrah oonyahs* |
| naked | desnudo | *dehsnoodoh* |
| napkin | la servilleta | *lah sehrbeelyehtah* |
| nationality | la nacionalidad | *lah nahsyohnahlee-dahdh* |
| nature | la naturaleza | *lah nahtoorahlehsah* |
| naturism | el naturismo | *ehl nahtooreesmoh* |
| nauseous | con náuseas | *kohn nahoosehahs* |
| near | junto a | *<u>h</u>oontoh ah* |
| nearby | cerca | *sehrkah* |
| necessary | necesario | *nehsehsahryoh* |
| neck | la nuca/el cuello | *lah nookah/ehl kwehlyoh* |
| necklace | la cadena/el collar | *lah kahdehnah/ ehl kohlyar* |
| needle | la aguja | *lah ahoo<u>h</u>ah* |
| negative | el negativo | *ehl nehgahteeboh* |
| neighbors | los vecinos | *lohs behseenohs* |
| nephew | el sobrino | *ehl sohbreenoh* |
| Netherlands | los Países Bajos | *lohs paheesehs bah<u>h</u>ohs* |
| never | jamás/nunca | *<u>h</u>ahmahs/noonkah* |
| new | nuevo | *nwehboh* |
| news | las noticias | *lahs nohteesyahs* |
| news stand | el quiosco | *ehl kyohskoh* |
| newspaper | el periódico | *ehl pehryohdeekoh* |
| next | próximo, que viene | *prohxeemoh, keh byehneh* |
| next to | al lado de | *ahl lahdoh deh* |
| nice (friendly) | amable | *ahmahbleh* |
| nice (to look at) | bonito, lindo | *bohneetoh, leendoh* |
| nice | bien, agradable | *byehn, ahgrahdahbleh* |
| niece | la sobrina | *lah sohbreenah* |
| night (at) | por la noche | *pohr lah nohcheh* |
| night | la noche | *lah nohcheh* |
| night duty | la guardia nocturna | *lah gwahrdyah nohktoornah* |
| nightclub | el cabaré | *ehl kahbahreh* |
| nightlife | la vida nocturna | *lah beedah nohktoornah* |
| nipple | la tetina/el chupón | *lah tehteenah/ ehl choopohn* |
| no | no | *noh* |
| no passing | la prohibición de adelantar | *lah proheebeesyohn deh ahdehlahntahr* |
| noise | el ruido | *ehl rooeedoh* |
| nonstop | sin escalas | *seen ehskahlahs* |
| no one | nadie | *nahdyeh* |
| normal | normal, corriente | *nohrmahl, kohrryehnteh* |
| north | el norte | *ehl nohrteh* |
| nose | la nariz | *lah nahrees* |

| | | |
|---|---|---|
| nose bleed | la hemorragia nasal | lah ehmohrrah<u>h</u>yah nahsahl |
| nose drops | las gotas para la nariz | lahs gohtahs pahrah lah nahrees |
| notepaper | el papel de escribir | ehl pahpehl deh ehskreebeer |
| nothing | nada | nahdah |
| November | noviembre | nohbyehmbreh |
| nowhere | en ninguna parte | ehn neengoonah pahrteh |
| nudist beach | la playa nudista | lah plahyah noodeestah |
| number | el número | ehl noomehroh |
| number plate | la matrícula | lah mahtreekoolah |
| nurse | la enfermera | lah ehnfehrmehrah |
| nutmeg | la nuez moscada | lah nwehs mohskahdah |
| nuts | los frutos secos/ las nueces | lohs frootohs sehkohs/ lahs nwehsehs |

# O

| | | |
|---|---|---|
| October | octubre | ohktoobreh |
| of course | claro | klahroh |
| off | podrido | pohdreedoh |
| offer | ofrecer | ohfrehsehr |
| office | la oficina | lah ohfeeseenah |
| oil | el aceite | ehl ahseyteh |
| oil level | el nivel del aceite | ehl neebehl deh ahseyteh |
| ointment | la pomada, el ungüento | lah pohmahdah, ehl oongwehntoh |
| ointment for burns | la pomada contra las quemaduras | lah pohmahdah kohntrah lahs kehmahdoorahs |
| okay | de acuerdo | deh ahkwehrdoh |
| old | viejo | byeh<u>h</u>oh |
| old part of town | el casco antiguo | ehl kahskoh ahnteegwoh |
| olive oil | el aceite de oliva | ehl ahseyteh deh ohleebah |
| olives | las aceitunas | lahs ahseytoonahs |
| omelette | la tortilla | lah tohrteelyah |
| on | sobre | sohbreh |
| on board | a bordo | ah bohrdoh |
| oncoming car | el vehículo que viene | ehl beheekooloh keh byehneh |
| one hundred grams | los cien gramos | lohs syehn grahmohs |
| one-way traffic | la dirección única | lah deerehksyohn ooneekah |
| onion | la cebolla | lah sehbohlyah |
| open (adj.) | abierto | ahbyehrtoh |
| open (verb) | abrir | ahbreer |
| opera | la ópera | lah ohpehrah |
| operate | operar | ohpehrahr |
| operator (telephone) | la operadora | lah ohpehrahdohrah |
| operetta | la opereta, la zarzuela | lah ohpehrehtah, lah sahrswehlah |

**Word list**

**15**

| | | |
|---|---|---|
| opposite | al frente, enfrente de | ahl frehnteh, ehnfrehnteh deh |
| optician | la óptica | lah ohpteekah |
| orange | la naranja | lah nahrahn<u>h</u>ah |
| orange (adj.) | naranja | nahrahn<u>h</u>ah |
| orange juice | el jugo de naranja | ehl hoogoh deh nahrahn<u>h</u>ah |
| orchestra (theater) | la platea | lah plahtehah |
| order (in -,) tidy | en orden, ordenado | ehn ohrdehn, ohrdehnahdoh |
| order (verb) | pedir | pehdeer |
| order | el pedido | ehl pehdeedoh |
| other | otro | ohtroh |
| other side | el otro lado | ehl ohtroh lahdoh |
| outside | afuera | ahfwehrah |
| overpass | el viaducto | ehl beeahdooktoh |
| overtake | adelantar/rebasar | ahdehlahntahr/ rehbahsahr |
| oysters | las ostras | lahs ohstrahs |

## P

| | | |
|---|---|---|
| page | la página | lah pah<u>h</u>eenah |
| pain | el dolor | ehl dohlohr |
| painkiller | el analgésico | ehl ahnahl<u>h</u>ehseekoh |
| paint (verb) | pintar | peentahr |
| paint | la pintura | lah peentoorah |
| painting (art) | el cuadro | ehl kwahdroh |
| pajamas | el pijama | ehl pee<u>h</u>ahmah |
| palace | el palacio | ehl pahlahsyoh |
| pancake | la crepe/ el panqueque | lah krehp/ ehl pahnkehkeh |
| pane | el cristal | ehl kreestahl |
| pants (briefs) | las bragas | lahs brahgahs |
| panty liner | el protegeslip | ehl prohteh<u>h</u>ehsleep |
| paper | el papel | ehl pahpehl |
| paraffin oil | el querosén | ehl kehrohsehn |
| parasol | el quitasol | ehl keetahsohl |
| parcel | el paquete | ehl pahkehteh |
| pardon | perdone | pehrdohneh |
| parents | los padres | lohs pahdrehs |
| park | el parque | ehl pahrkeh |
| park (verb) | estacionarse | ehstahsyohnahrseh |
| parking space | el lugar para estacionar | ehl loogahr pahrah ehstahsyohnahr |
| parsley | el perejil | ehl pehreh<u>h</u>eel |
| partition | la secreción | lah sehkrehsyohn |
| partner | la pareja | lah pahreh<u>h</u>ah |
| party | la fiesta | lah fyehstah |
| passable (road) | practicable | prahkteekahbleh |
| passenger | el pasajero | ehl pahsah<u>h</u>ehroh |
| passport | el pasaporte | ehl pahsahpohrteh |
| passport photo | la foto de carnet | lah fohtoh deh kahrneh |
| patient | el paciente | ehl pahsyehnteh |
| pavement | la acera/la banqueta | lah ahsehrah/ lah bahnkehtah |
| pay (verb) | pagar | pahgahr |
| pay the bill | pagar la cuenta | pahgahr lah kwehntah |

| | | |
|---|---|---|
| peach | el durazno | *ehl doorahsnoh* |
| peanuts | los cacahuetes | *lohs kahkahwehtehs* |
| | maníes | *mahnyes* |
| pear | la pera | *lah pehrah* |
| peas | los chícharos | *lohs cheechahrohs* |
| | las arvejas | *lahs ahrbeh<u>h</u>as* |
| pedal | el pedal | *ehl pehdahl* |
| pedestrian crossing | el paso de peatones | *ehl pahsoh deh pehahtohnehs* |
| pedicure | la pedicura | *lah pehdeekoorah* |
| pen | la pluma | *lah ploomah* |
| pencil (hard/soft) | el lápiz (duro/blando) | *ehl lahpees (dooroh /blahndoh)* |
| penis | el pene | *ehl pehneh* |
| pepper | el pimiento/chile | *ehl peemyehntoh cheeleh* |
| performance | la función de teatro /música | *lah foonsyohn deh tehahtroh/mooseekah* |
| perfume | el perfume | *ehl pehrfoomeh* |
| perm (verb) | hacer una permanente | *ahsehr oonah pehrmahnehnteh* |
| perm | la permanente | *lah pehrmahnehnteh* |
| permit | el permiso | *ehl pehrmeesoh* |
| person | la persona | *lah pehrsohnah* |
| personal | personal | *pehrsohnahl* |
| pets | los animales domésticos | *lohs ahneemahles dohmehsteekohs* |
| pharmacy | la farmacia | *lah fahrmahsyah* |
| phone (by) | por teléfono | *pohr tehlehfohnoh* |
| phone (tele-) | el teléfono | *ehl tehlehfohnoh* |
| phone (verb) | llamar por teléfono | *lyahmahr pohr tehlehfohnoh* |
| phone booth | la caseta/cabina telefónica | *lah kahsehtah/ kahbeenah tehlehfohneekah* |
| phone directory | la guía de teléfonos | *lah geeah deh tehlehfohnohs* |
| phone number | el número de teléfono | *ehl noomehroh deh tehlehfohnoh* |
| photo | la foto | *lah fohtoh* |
| photocopier | la fotocopiadora | *lah fohtohkohpyahdohrah* |
| photocopy (verb) | fotocopiar | *fohtohkohpyahr* |
| photocopy | la fotocopia | *lah fohtohkohpyah* |
| pick up (fetch person) | (ir a) buscar, pasar a buscar | *(eer ah) booskahr, pahsahr ah booskahr* |
| picnic | el picnic | *ehl peekneek* |
| piece of clothing | la prenda | *lah prehndah* |
| pier | el muelle | *ehl mwehlyeh* |
| pigeon | la paloma | *lah pahlohmah* |
| pill (contraceptive) | la píldora (anticonceptiva) | *lah peeldohrah (ahnteekohnsehpteebah)* |
| pillow | la almohada | *lah ahlmohahdah* |
| pillowcase | la funda de almohada | *lah foondah deh ahlmohahdah* |
| pin | el alfiler | *ehl ahlfeelehr* |
| pineapple | la piña | *lah peenyah* |
| pipe | la pipa | *lah peepah* |

**Word list**

**15**

| pipe tobacco | el tabaco de pipa | ehl tahbahkoh deh peepah |
| pity | lástima | lahsteemah |
| place of entertainment | el sitio para salir | ehl seetyoh pahrah sahleer |
| place of interest | el punto de interés | ehl poontoh deh eentehrehs |
| plan/map | el plano | ehl plahnoh |
| plant | la planta | lah plahntah |
| plastic | el plástico | ehl plahsteekoh |
| plastic bag | la bolsita | lah bohlseetah |
| plate | el plato | ehl plahtoh |
| platform | la vía, el andén | lah beeah, ehl ahndehn |
| play (theater) | la obra de teatro | lah ohbrah deh tehahtroh |
| play (verb) | jugar | hoogahr |
| playground | el parque infantil | ehl pahrkeh eenfahnteel |
| playing cards | los naipes | lohs naheepehs |
| pleasant | agradable | ahgrahdahbleh |
| please | por favor | pohr fahbohr |
| pleasure | el placer | ehl plahsehr |
| plum | la ciruela | lah seerwehlah |
| pocketknife | la navaja | lah nahbahhah |
| point (verb) | indicar | eendeekahr |
| poison | el veneno | ehl behnehnoh |
| police | la policía | lah pohleeseeah |
| police station | la comisaría | la kohmeesahreeah |
| policeman | el guardia | ehl gwahrdyah |
| pond | el estanque | ehl ehstahnkeh |
| pony | el poney | ehl pohnehy |
| pop concert | el concierto pop | ehl kohnsyehrtoh pohp |
| population | la población | lah pohblahsyohn |
| pork | la carne de cerdo/ puerco/chanco | lah kahrneh deh sehrdoh/pwehrkoh/ chahnchoh |
| port wine | el oporto | ehl ohpohrtoh |
| porter | el portero | ehl pohrtehroh |
| post (zip) code | el código postal | ehl cohdeegoh pohstahl |
| post office | la oficina de Correos | lah ohfeeseenah deh cohrrehohs |
| postage | el franqueo | ehl frahnkehoh |
| postbox | el buzón | ehl boosohn |
| postcard | la (tarjeta) postal | lah (tahrhehtah) pohstahl |
| potato | la patata/papa | lah pahtahtah/pahpah |
| potato chips | las patatas fritas | lahs pahtahtahs freetahs |
| poultry | las aves | lahs ahbehs |
| powdered milk | la leche en polvo | lah lehcheh ehn pohlboh |
| power outlet | la toma de corriente | lah tohmah deh kohrryehnteh |
| prawns | las gambas | lahs gahmbahs |
| | los camarones | lohs kahmahrohnehs |
| precious | querido | kehreedoh |

| | | |
|---|---|---|
| prefer | preferir | prehfehreer |
| preference | la preferencia | lah prehfehrehnsyah |
| pregnant | embarazada | ehmbahrahsahdah |
| present | presente | prehsehnteh |
| present (gift) | el regalo | ehl rehgahloh |
| press (verb) | apretar | ahprehtahr |
| pressure | la tensión/ | lah tehnsyohn/ |
| | la presión | lah prehsyohn |
| price | el precio | ehl prehsyoh |
| price list | la lista de precios | lah leestah deh prehsyohs |
| print (verb) | copiar | kohpyahr |
| print | la copia | lah kohpyah |
| probably | probablemente | prohbahblehmehnteh |
| problem | el problema | ehl prohblehmah |
| profession | la profesión | lah prohfehsyohn |
| program | el programa | ehl prohgrahmah |
| pronounce | pronunciar | prohnoonsyahr |
| propane camping gas | el gas propano | ehl gahs prohpahnoh |
| pull | sacar/jalar | sahkahr/halahr |
| pull a muscle | distender un músculo | deestehndehr oon mooskooloh |
| pure | puro | pooroh |
| purple | violeta | beeohlehtah |
| purse | el monedero | ehl mohnehdehroh |
| push | empujar | ehmpoohahr |
| puzzle | el rompecabezas | ehl rohmpehkahbehsahs |

## Q

| | | |
|---|---|---|
| quarter | la cuarta parte | lah kwahrtah pahrteh |
| quarter of an hour | el cuarto de hora | ehl kwahrtoh deh ohrah |
| queen | la reina | lah reheenah |
| question | la pregunta | lah prehgoontah |
| quick | rápido | rahpeedoh |
| quiet | tranquilo | trahnkeeloh |

## R

| | | |
|---|---|---|
| radio | la radio | lah rahdyoh |
| railways | los ferrocarriles | lohs fehrrohkahrreelehs |
| rain (verb) | llover | lyohbehr |
| rain | la lluvia | lah lyoobyah |
| raincoat | el impermeable | ehl eempehrmehahbleh |
| raisins | las uvas pasas | lahs oobahs pahsahs |
| rape | la violación | lah beeohlahsyohn |
| rapids | el rápido | ehl rahpeedoh |
| rash (skin) | la erupción cutánea | lah ehroopsyohn kootahnehah |
| raspberries | las frambuesas | lahs frahmbwehsahs |
| raw | crudo | kroodoh |
| raw ham | el jamón crudo (serrano) | ehl hahmohn kroodoh sehrrahnoh |
| raw vegetables | las verduras crudas | lahs behrdoorahs kroodahs |
| razor blades | las hojas de afeitar | lahs ohahs deh ahfeheetahr |
| read (verb) | leer | lehehr |
| ready | listo | leestoh |

Word list

15

143

| really | en realidad | ehn rehahleedahdh |
|---|---|---|
| receipt | el recibo | ehl rehseeboh |
| recipe | la receta | lah rehsehtah |
| reclining chair | la reposera | lah rehpohsehrah |
| recommend | recomendar | rehkohmehndahr |
| rectangle | el rectángulo | ehl rehktahngooloh |
| red | rojo | rohhoh |
| red wine | el vino tinto | ehl beenoh teentoh |
| refrigerator | el refrigerador | ehl rehfreehehrahdohr |
| regards | recuerdos | rehkwehrdohs |
| region | la región | lah rehhyohn |
| registered | certificado | sehrteefeekahdoh |
| relatives | los parientes | lohs pahryehntehs |
| reliable | fiable/seguro | fyahbleh/sehgooroh |
| religion | la religión | lah rehleehyohn |
| rent out | alquilar | ahlkeelahr |
| repair (verb) | arreglar | ahrrehglahr |
| repairs | el arreglo | ehl ahrrehgloh |
| repeat | repetir | rehpehteer |
| report | el atestado | ehl ahtehstahdoh |
| | la declaración | lah dehklahrahsyohn |
| resent | tomar a mal | tohmahr ah mahl |
| reserve (verb) | reservar | rehsehrbahr |
| reserved | reservado | rehsehrbahdah |
| responsible | responsable | rehspohnsahbleh |
| rest (verb) | descansar | dehskahnsahr |
| restaurant | el restaurante | ehl rehstahoorahnteh |
| retired | jubilado | hoobeeladoh |
| retirement | la jubilación | lah hoobeelahsyohn |
| return (ticket) | el boleto de ida y vuelta | ehl bohlehtoh deh eedah ee bwehltah |
| reverse (vehicle) | dar marcha atrás | dahr mahrchah ahtrahs |
| rheumatism | el reuma | ehl rehoomah |
| rice | el arroz | ehl ahrrohs |
| ridiculous | tontería(s) | tohntehreeah(s) |
| riding (horseback) | montar a caballo | mohntahr ah kahbahlyoh |
| riding school | el picadero | ehl peekahdehroh |
| right | derecha | dehrehchah |
| right (on the) | a la derecha | ah lah dehrehchah |
| right of way | la preferencia | lah prehfehrehnsyah |
| ripe | maduro | mahdooroh |
| risk | el riesgo | ehl ryehsgoh |
| river | el río | ehl reeoh |
| road | el camino | ehl kahmeenoh |
| roadway | la calzada | lah kahlsahdah |
| roasted | asado | ahsahdoh |
| rock | la roca | lah rohkah |
| rolling tobacco | el tabaco para liar | ehl tahbahkoh pahrah leeahr |
| roof rack | la baca | lah bahkah |
| room | la habitación | lah ahbeetahsyohn |
| room number | el número de la habitación | ehl noomehroh deh lah ahbeetahsyohn |
| room service | el servicio en la habitación | ehl sehrbeesyoh ehn lah ahbeetahsyohn |
| rope | la cuerda | lah kwehrdah |
| rosé | el vino rosado | ehl beenoh rohsahdoh |

| | | |
|---|---|---|
| rotary | la rotonda | *lah rohtohndah* |
| route | la ruta | *lah rootah* |
| rowing boat | el bote de remos | *ehl bohteh deh rehmohs* |
| rubber | la goma | *lah gohmah* |
| rubber band | la goma elástica/ liga | *lah gohmah ehlahsteekah/leegah* |
| rucksack | la mochila | *lah mohcheelah* |
| rude | descortés/ maleducado | *dehskohrtehs/ mahlehdookahdoh* |
| ruins | las ruinas | *lahs rweenahs* |
| run into | encontrar | *ehnkohntrahr* |

## S

| | | |
|---|---|---|
| sad | triste | *treesteh* |
| safari | el safari | *ehl sahfahree* |
| safe | la caja fuerte | *lah ka<u>h</u>hah fwehrteh* |
| safe/secure | seguro | *sehgooroh* |
| safety pin | el imperdible/ alfiler de seguridad | *ehl eempehrdeebleh/ ahlfeelehr deh sehgooreedad* |
| sail | la vela | *lah behlah* |
| sailing boat | el velero | *ehl behlehroh* |
| salad | la ensalada | *lah ehnsahlahdah* |
| salad oil | el aceite | *ehl ahsehyteh* |
| salami | el salame | *ehl sahlahmeh* |
| sale | las rebajas, la liquidación | *lahs rebah<u>h</u>ahs, lah leekeedahsyohn* |
| salt | la sal | *lah sahl* |
| same | mismo | *meesmoh* |
| same | lo mismo | *loh meesmoh* |
| sandwich | el sandwich | *ehl sandwich* |
| sandy beach | la playa de arena | *lah plahyah deh ahrehnah* |
| sanitary napkin | la compresa/ toalla sanitaria | *lah kohmprehsah/tohah- lyah sahneetahreeah* |
| sardines | las sardinas | *lahs sahrdeenahs* |
| satisfied | contento | *kohntehntoh* |
| Saturday | el sábado | *ehl sahbahdoh* |
| sauce | la salsa | *lah sahlsah* |
| saucepan | la cacerola | *lah kahsehrohlah* |
| sauna | la sauna | *lah sahoonah* |
| sausage | el embutido/ la salchicha | *ehl ehmbooteedoh/ lah sahlcheechah* |
| savory | salado | *sahlahdoh* |
| say (verb) | decir | *dehseer* |
| scarf | la bufanda (woollen) | *lah boofahndah* |
| scarf | el pañuelo | *ehl pahnywehloh* |
| scenic walk | la visita a la ciudad (a pie) | *lah beeseetah ah lah syoodahdh (ah pyeh)* |
| school | la escuela | *lah ehskwehlah* |
| scissors | las tijeras | *lahs tee<u>h</u>ehrahs* |
| scooter | la vespa | *lah behspah* |
| scorpion | el escorpión | *ehl ehskohrpyohn* |
| scotch tape | la cinta adhesiva | *lah seentah ahdehseebah* |

**Word list**

**15**

145

| | | |
|---|---|---|
| scrambled eggs | los huevos revueltos | *lohs wehbohs rehbwehltohs* |
| screw | el tornillo | *ehl tohrneelyoh* |
| screwdriver | el destornillador | *ehl dehstohrneelyahdohr* |
| sculpture | la escultura | *lah ehskooltoorah* |
| sea | el mar | *ehl mahr* |
| seasick | mareado | *mahrehahdoh* |
| seat | el asiento, la butaca | *ehl ahsyehntoh, lah bootahkah* |
| second (adj.) | segundo | *sehgoondoh* |
| second | el segundo | *ehl sehgoondoh* |
| second-hand | de segunda mano | *deh sehgoondah mahnoh* |
| sedative | el calmante | *ehl kahlmahnteh* |
| see (person) | visitar | *beeseetahr* |
| see | mirar | *meerahr* |
| self-timer | el disparador automático | *ehl deespahrahdohr ahootohmahteekoh* |
| semi-skimmed | semidesnatado | *sehmeedehsnahtahdoh* |
| | semidescremado | *sehmeedehskrehmahdoh* |
| send | enviar | *ehnbyahr* |
| sentence | la frase | *lah frahseh* |
| September | septiembre | *sehptyehmbreh* |
| serious | grave | *grahbeh* |
| service | el servicio | *ehl sehrbeesyoh* |
| service station | la gasolinera/ estación de servicio | *lah gahsohleenehrah ehstahsyohn deh sehrbeesyoh* |
| set (verb) | marcar | *mahrkahr* |
| sewing thread | el hilo de coser | *ehl eeloh deh kohsehr* |
| shade | la sombra | *lah sohmbrah* |
| shallow | poco profundo | *pohkoh prohfoondoh* |
| shampoo | el champú | *ehl chahmpoo* |
| shark | el tiburón | *ehl teeboorohn* |
| shave (verb) | afeitar | *ahfeheetahr* |
| shaver | la afeitadora eléctrica | *lah ahfeheytahdohrah ehlehktreekah* |
| shaving brush | la brocha de afeitar | *lah brohchah deh ahfeheetahr* |
| shaving cream | la crema de afeitar | *lah krehmah deh ahfeheetahr* |
| shaving soap | el jabón de afeitar | *ehl <u>h</u>ahbohn deh ahfeheetahr* |
| sheet | la sábana | *lah sahbahnah* |
| sherry | el jerez | *ehl <u>h</u>ehrehht* |
| shirt | la camisa | *lah kahmeesah* |
| shoe | el zapato | *ehl thahpahtoh* |
| shoe polish | la crema de zapatos | *lah krehmah deh sahpahtohs* |
| shoe shop | la zapatería | *lah sahpahtehreeah* |
| shoelaces | los cordones/ las agujetas | *lohs kohrdohnehs/ lahs ahgoo<u>h</u>ehtahs* |
| shoemaker | el zapatero | *ehl sahpahtehroh* |
| shop (verb) | hacer la compra | *ahsehr lah kohmprah* |
| shop | la tienda | *lah tyehndah* |
| shop assistant | la vendedora | *lah behndehdohrah* |

| | | |
|---|---|---|
| shop window | el escaparate | ehl ehskahpahrahteh |
| shopping center | el centro comercial | ehl sehntroh kohmehrsyahl |
| short | corto | kohrtoh |
| short circuit | el cortocircuito | ehl kohrtohseer-kweetoh |
| shoulder | el hombro | ehl ohmbroh |
| show | el espectáculo | ehl ehspehktahkooloh |
| shower | la ducha | lah doochah |
| shutter | el obturador | ehl ohbtoorahdohr |
| sieve | el tamiz/la coladera | ehl tahmees/lah kohlahdehrah |
| sign (verb) | firmar | feermahr |
| sign | el cartel | ehl kahrtehl |
| signature | la firma | lah feermah |
| signposted walk | la excursión señalizada | lah ehxkooresyohn sehnyahleesahdah |
| silence | el silencio | ehl seelehnsyoh |
| silliness | tontería(s) | tohntehreeah(s) |
| silver | la plata | lah plahtah |
| silver-plated | plateado | plahtehahdoh |
| simple | sencillo | sehnseelyoh |
| single (unmarried) | soltero | sohltehroh |
| single | individual | eendeebeedwahl |
| single ticket | el boleto de ida | ehl bohlehtoh deh eedah |
| sir | señor | sehnyohr |
| sister | la hermana | lah ehrmahnah |
| sit | estar sentado | ehstahr sehntahdoh |
| size (shoes) | el número | ehl noomehroh |
| size | la talla | lah tahlyah |
| ski boots | las botas de esquí | lahs bohtahs deh ehskee |
| ski goggles | las gafas de esquí | lahs gahfahs deh ehskee |
| ski instructor | el profesor de esquí | ehl prohfehsohr deh ehskee |
| ski lessons/class | la clase de esquiar | lah klahseh deh ehskeeahr |
| ski lift | el telesquí | ehl tehlehskee |
| ski pants | los pantalones de esquiar | lohs pahntahlohnehs deh ehskeeahr |
| ski pass | el bono (de remontes/esquí) | ehl bohnoh (deh rehmohntehs/ehskee) |
| ski slope | la pista de esquí (alpino) | lah peestah deh ehskee (ahlpeenoh) |
| ski stick | el bastón de esquí | ehl bahstohn deh ehskee |
| ski suit | el traje de esquiar | ehl trahheh deh ehskeeahr |
| ski wax | la cera para esquí | lah sehrah pahrah ehskee |
| ski/skiing | esquiar, el esquí | ehskeeahr, ehl ehskee |
| skin | la piel | lah pyehl |
| skirt | la falda | lah fahldah |
| skis | los esquís | lohs ehskees |
| sleep (verb) | dormir | dohrmeer |
| sleep well | que descanse | keh dehskahnseh |
| sleeping car | el coche cama | ehl kohcheh kahmah |
| sleeping pills | los somníferos | lohs sohmneefehrohs |

| slide | la diapositiva | lah deeahpohseeteebah |
| slip (women's) | la combinación | lah kohmbeenahsyohn |
| slow | despacio | dehspahsyoh |
| slow train | el tren local/autovía | ehl trehn lohkahl ahootohbeeah |
| small | pequeño | pehkehnyoh |
| small change | el cambio, el dinero suelto | ehl kahmbyoh, ehl deenehroh swehltoh |
| smell unpleasant (verb) | oler mal | ohlehr mahl |
| smoke | el humo | ehl oomoh |
| smoke (verb) | fumar | foomahr |
| smoked | ahumado | ahoomahdoh |
| smoking compartment | el departamento de fumadores | ehl dehpahrtahmehntoh deh foomahdohrehs |
| snake | la serpiente | lah sehrpyehnteh |
| snorkel | el esnórquel | ehl ehsnohrkehl |
| snow (verb) | nevar | nehbahr |
| snow | la nieve | lah nyehbeh |
| snow chains | la cadena antideslizante | lah kahdehnah ahnteedehsleesahnte |
| soap | el jabón | ehl _hahbohn |
| soap box | la jabonera | lah _hahbohnehrah |
| soap powder | el jabón en polvo | ehl _hahbohn ehn pohlboh |
| soccer | el fútbol | ehl footbohl |
| soccer match | el partido de fútbol | ehl pahrteedoh deh footbohl |
| socket | el enchufe | ehl ehnchoofeh |
| socks | los calcetines | lohs kahlsehteenehs |
| soft drink | el refresco | ehl rehfrehskoh |
| sole (fish) | el lenguado | ehl lehngwahdoh |
| sole | la suela | lah swehlah |
| someone | alguien | ahlguyehn |
| sometimes | a veces | ah behsehs |
| somewhere | en alguna parte | ehn ahlgoonah pahrteh |
| son | el hijo | ehl eehoh |
| soon | pronto | prohntoh |
| sorbet | el sorbete | ehl sohrbehteh |
| sore | la úlcera | lah oolsehrah |
| sore throat | el dolor de garganta | ehl dohlohr deh gahrgahntah |
| sorry | perdón | pehrdohn |
| sort/type | la clase | lah klahseh |
| soup | la sopa | lah sohpah |
| sour | agrio | ahgreeoh |
| sour cream | la nata/crema ácida | lah nahtah/krehmah ahseedah |
| source | la fuente | lah fwehnteh |
| south | el sur | ehl soor |
| souvenir | el recuerdo de viaje | ehl rehkwehrdoh deh byah_heh |
| spaghetti | los espaguetis | lohs ehspahgehtees |
| Spanish | español | ehspahnyohl |
| spare | la reserva | lah rehsehrbah |
| spare part | la pieza de recambio | lah pyehsah deh rehkahmbyoh |
| spare tire | el neumático de reserva | ehl nehoomahteekoh deh rehsehrbah |

| spare wheel | la rueda de auxilio | *lah rwehdah deh ahookseeleeoh* |
| speak | hablar | *ahblahr* |
| special | especial | *ehspehsyahl* |
| specialist | el especialista | *ehl ehspesyahleestah* |
| specialty | la especialidad | *lah ehspehsyahleedahd* |
| speed limit | la velocidad máxima | *lah behlohseedahd mahxeemah* |
| spell (verb) | deletrear | *dehlehtrehahr* |
| spicy | picante | *peekahnteh* |
| splinter | la astilla | *lah ahsteelyah* |
| spoon | la cuchara | *lah koochahrah* |
| spoonful | la cucharada | *lah koochahrahdah* |
| sport (play) | hacer deporte | *ahsehr dehpohrteh* |
| sport | el deporte | *ehl dehpohrteh* |
| sports center | la sala de deportes | *lah sahlah deh dehpohrtehs* |
| spot/place | el sitio | *ehl seetyoh* |
| sprain (verb) | torcerse | *tohrsehrseh* |
| spring | la primavera | *lah preemahbehrah* |
| square | el cuadrado | *ehl kwahdrahdoh* |
| square (town) | la plaza/el zócalo | *lah plahsah/ehl sohkahloh* |
| square meter(s) | metro(s) cuadrado(s) | *mehtroh(s) kwahdrahdoh(s)* |
| squash (veg.) | el squash | *ehl skwahsh* |
| stadium | el estadio | *ehl ehstahdyoh* |
| stain | la mancha | *lah mahnchah* |
| stain remover | el quitamanchas | *ehl keetahmahnchahs* |
| stairs | las escaleras | *lahs ehskahlehrahs* |
| stamp | la estampilla/ el timbre | *lah ehstahmpeelyah/ ehl teembreh* |
| start (car) | arrancar | *ahrrahnkahr* |
| station | la estación | *lah ehstahsyohn* |
| statue | la estatua | *lah ehstahtooah* |
| stay (lodge) | alojarse | *ahlohhahrseh* |
| stay (verb) | quedarse | *kehdahrseh* |
| stay | la estancia | *lah ehstahnsyah* |
| steal (verb) | robar | *rohbahr* |
| steel, stainless | el acero, inoxidable | *ehl ahsehroh, eenohxeedahbleh* |
| stench | el mal olor | *ehl mahl ohlohr* |
| sting (verb) | picar | *peekahr* |
| stitch (med.) | el punto | *ehl poontoh* |
| stitch (verb) | suturar | *sootoorahr* |
| stock | el caldo | *ehl kahldoh* |
| stockings | las medias | *lahs mehdyahs* |
| stomach | el estómago, el vientre | *ehl ehstohmahgoh, ehl byehntreh* |
| stomach ache | el dolor de vientre/ estómago | *ehl dohlohr deh byehntreh/ ehstohmahgoh* |
| stomach cramps | los retortijones | *lohs rehtohrteehohnehs* |
| stools | las heces | *lahs ehsehs* |
| stop (verb) | parar | *pahrahr* |
| stop | la parada | *lah pahrahdah* |
| stopover | la escala | *lah ehskahlah* |

| | | |
|---|---|---|
| storm | la tormenta | *lah tohrmehntah* |
| straight | liso | *leesoh* |
| straight ahead | derecho | *dehrehchoh* |
| straw | la pajita/el popote | *lah pah<u>h</u>eetah/ ehl pohpohteh* |
| strawberries | las fresas/frutillas | *lahs frehsahs/ frooteelyahs* |
| street | la calle | *lah kahlyeh* |
| street side | el lado de la calle | *ehl lahdoh deh lah kahlyeh* |
| strike | la huelga | *lah wehlgah* |
| stroller (baby) | el cochecito | *ehl kohchehseetoh* |
| strong (tobacco) | negro | *nehgroh* |
| study (verb) | estudiar | *ehstoodyahr* |
| stuffing | el relleno | *ehl rehlyehnoh* |
| subscriber's number | el número de abonado | *ehl noomehroh deh ahbohnahdoh* |
| subtitled | subtitulada | *soobteetoolahdah* |
| subway | el metro/tren subterráneo | *ehl mehtroh/trehn soobtehrrahnehoh* |
| subway station | la estación de metro | *lah ehstahthyohn deh mehtroh* |
| succeed | salir bien | *sahleer byehn* |
| sugar | el azúcar | *ehl ahsookahr* |
| sugar lumps | los terrones de azúcar | *lohs tehrrohnehs deh ahsookahr* |
| suit | el traje | *ehl trah<u>h</u>eh* |
| suitcase | la maleta/valija | *lah mahlehtah/ bahlee<u>h</u>ah* |
| summer | el verano | *ehl behrahnoh* |
| summertime | la hora de verano | *lah ohrah deh behrahnoh* |
| sun | el sol | *ehl sohl* |
| sun hat | el sombrero de playa | *ehl sohmbrehroh deh plahyah* |
| sunbathe | tomar el sol | *tohmahr ehl sohl* |
| Sunday | el domingo | *ehl dohmeengoh* |
| sunglasses | las gafas/los lentes de sol | *lahs gahfahs/lohs lehntehs de sohl* |
| sunrise | la salida del sol | *lah sahleedah dehl sohl* |
| sunset | la puesta del sol | *lah pwehstah dehl sohl* |
| sunstroke | la insolación | *lah eensohlahthyohn* |
| suntan lotion | la crema solar | *lah krehmah sohlahr* |
| suntan oil | el aceite bronceador | *ehl ahsehyteh brohnthehahdohr* |
| supermarket | el supermercado | *ehl soopehrmehrkahdoh* |
| surcharge | el suplemento | *ehl sooplehmehntoh* |
| surf | el surf | *ehl soorf* |
| surf board | la tabla de surf | *lah tahblah deh soorf* |
| surgery | el consultorio | *ehl kohnsooltohryoh* |
| surname | el apellido | *ehl ahpehlyeedoh* |
| surprise | la sorpresa | *lah sohrprehsah* |
| swallow (verb) | tragar | *trahgahr* |
| swamp | el terreno pantanoso | *ehl tehrrehnoh pahntahnohsoh* |
| sweat | el sudor | *ehl soodohr* |
| sweater | el jersey/pulóver | *ehl <u>h</u>ehrsehee/ poolohbehr* |

| | | |
|---|---|---|
| sweet | dulce | doolseh |
| swee tcorn | el maíz | ehl mahees |
| sweetener | la sacarina | lah sahkahreenah |
| swim (verb) | nadar | nahdahr |
| swimming pool | la piscina/pileta | lah peesseenah/ peelehtah |
| swimming trunks | el bañador/ la malla/ el traje de baño | ehl bahnyahdohr/ lah mahlyah/ ehl trahheh deh bahnyoh |
| swindle | la estafa | lah ehstahfah |
| switch | el interruptor | ehl eentehrrooptohr |
| synagogue | la sinagoga | lah seenahgohgah |
| syrup | la melaza | lah mehlahsah |

# T

| | | |
|---|---|---|
| table | la mesa | lah mehsah |
| table tennis | el pingpong | ehl peenpohn |
| tablet | la tableta | lah tahblehtah |
| take (photograph) | sacar | sahkahr |
| take (time) | durar, tardar | doorahr, tahrdahr |
| take (verb) | emplear, usar, tomar | ehmplehahr, oosahr, tohmahr |
| take pictures | fotografiar, sacar fotos | fohtohgrahfyahr, sahkahr fohtohs |
| taken | ocupado | ohkoopahdoh |
| talcum powder | el talco | ehl tahlkoh |
| talk (verb) | hablar | ahblahr |
| tampons | los tampones | lohs tahmpohnehs |
| tap | la llave/canilla | lah lyahbeh/kahneelyah |
| tap water | el agua de la llave/ canilla | ehl ahgwah deh lah lyahbeh/kahneelyah |
| tart (pastry) | la tarta | lah tahrtah |
| taste (verb) | probar | prohbahr |
| tax free shop | la tienda libre de impuestos | lah tyehndah leebreh deh eempwehstohs |
| taxi | el taxi | ehl tahxee |
| taxi stand | la parada de taxis | lah pahrahdah deh tahxees |
| tea | el té | ehl teh |
| teapot | la tetera | lah tehtehrah |
| teaspoon | la cuchara de té | lah koochahrah deh teh |
| telegram | el telegrama | ehl tehlehgrahmah |
| telephoto lens | el teleobjetivo | ehl tehlehohbhehteeboh |
| television | la televisión | lah tehlehbeesyohn |
| telex | el télex | ehl tehlehx |
| temperature | la temperatura | lah tehmpehrahtoorah |
| temporary filling | el empaste provisional | ehl ehmpahsteh prohbeesyohnahl |
| tender | tierno | tyehrnoh |
| tennis | el tenis | ehl tehnees |
| tennis ball | la pelota de tenis | lah pehlohtah deh tehnees |
| tennis court | la pista de tenis | lah peestah deh tehnees |
| tennis racket | la raqueta de tenis | lah rahkehtah deh tehnees |
| tennis shoes | las zapatillas de tenis | lahs sahpahteelyahs deh tehnees |

**Word list**

**15**

151

| tent | la tienda/carpa | *lah tyehndah/kahrpah* |
|------|-----------------|------------------------|
| tent peg | la estaca | *lah ehstahkah* |
| terrace | la terraza | *lah tehrrahsah* |
| terrible | terrible | *tehrreebleh* |
| thank (verb) | agradecer | *ahgrahdehsehr* |
| thank you | gracias | *grahsyahs* |
| thaw | deshelar | *dehsehlahr* |
| the day after tomorrow | pasado mañana | *pahsahdoh mahnyahnah* |
| theatre | el teatro | *ehl tehahtroh* |
| theft | el robo | *ehl rohboh* |
| there | allí | *ahlyee* |
| thermal bath | el baño termal | *ehl bahnyoh tehrmahl* |
| thermometer | el termómetro | *ehl tehrmohmehtroh* |
| thick | grueso/gordo | *grwehsoh/gohrdoh* |
| thief | el ladrón | *ehl lahdrohn* |
| thigh | el muslo | *ehl moosloh* |
| thin | fino, flaco | *feenoh, flahkoh* |
| things | las cosas | *lahs kohsahs* |
| think | pensar | *pehnsahr* |
| third | la tercera parte | *lah tehrsehrah pahrteh* |
| thirsty, to be | la sed | *lah sehdh* |
| this afternoon | esta tarde | *ehstah tahrdeh* |
| this evening | esta noche | *ehstah nohcheh* |
| this morning | esta mañana | *ehstah mahnyahnah* |
| thread | el hilo | *ehl eeloh* |
| throat | la garganta | *lah gahrgahntah* |
| throat lozenges | las pastillas para la garganta | *lahs pahsteelyahs pahrah lah gahrgahntah* |
| throw up | vomitar | *bohmeetahr* |
| thunderstorm | la tormenta eléctrica | *lah tohrmehntah ehlehktreekah* |
| Thursday | el jueves | *ehl ẖwehbehs* |
| ticket (admission) | la entrada | *lah ehntrahdah* |
| ticket (travel) | el boleto | *ehl bohlehtoh* |
| ticket office | la taquilla | *lah tahkeelyah* |
| tickets | los boletos | *lohs bohlehtohs* |
| tidy (verb) | recoger | *rehkoẖehr* |
| tie | la corbata | *lah kohrbahtah* |
| tights | el panty/las medias | *ehl pahntee/lahs mehdyahs* |
| time (occasion) | la vez | *lah behs* |
| time | el tiempo | *ehl tyehmpoh* |
| timetable | el horario | *ehl ohrahryoh* |
| tin can | la lata | *lah lahtah* |
| tip (money) | la propina | *lah prohpeenah* |
| tire (bicycle) | la cubierta | *lah koobyehrtah* |
| tire lever | el desmontador de neumáticos | *ehl dehsmohntahdohr deh nehoomahteekohs* |
| tire pressure | la presión de los neumáticos | *lah prehsyohn deh lohs nehoomahteekohs* |
| tissues | los pañuelitos de papel | *lohs pahnywehleetohs de pahpehl* |
| toast | el pan tostado, las tostadas | *ehl pahn tohstahdoh, lahs tohstahdahs* |
| tobacco | el tabaco | *ehl tahbahkoh* |
| toboggan | el trineo | *ehl treenehoh* |

| | | |
|---|---|---|
| today | hoy | *ohee* |
| toe | el dedo del pie | *ehl dehdoh dehl pyeh* |
| together | juntos | *hoontohs* |
| toilet | el water/el baño/ | *ehl bahtehr/ehl bahnyoh* |
| | el lávabo | *ehl lahbahboh* |
| toilet paper | el papel higiénico | *ehl pahpehl* |
| | | *ee<u>h</u>yehneekoh* |
| toiletries | los artículos de | *lohs ahrteekoolohs* |
| | tocador | *deh tohkahdohr* |
| tomato | el tomate | *ehl tohmahteh* |
| tomato purée | el tomate triturado | *ehl tohmahteh* |
| | | *treetoorahdoh* |
| tomato sauce | el ketchup | *ehl kehchoop* |
| tomorrow | mañana | *mahnyahnah* |
| tongue | la lengua | *lah lehngwah* |
| tonic water | el agua tónica | *ehl agwah tohneekah* |
| tonight | esta noche | *ehstah nohcheh* |
| too much | demasiado | *dehmahsyahdoh* |
| tools | las herramientas | *lahs ehrrahmyehntahs* |
| tooth | el diente | *ehl dyehnteh* |
| toothache | el dolor de muelas | *ehl dohlohr deh* |
| | | *mwehlahs* |
| toothbrush | el cepillo de dientes | *ehl sehpeelyoh deh* |
| | | *dyehntehs* |
| toothpaste | el dentífrico | *ehl dehnteefreekoh* |
| toothpick | el palillo | *ehl pahleelyoh* |
| top up | rellenar | *rehlyehnahr* |
| total | el total | *ehl tohtahl* |
| tough | duro | *dooroh* |
| tour | la excursión, | *lah ehxkoorsyohn, ehl* |
| | el paseo | *pahsehoh* |
| tour guide | el guía | *ehl geeah* |
| tourist card | la tarjeta de turista | *lah tahr<u>h</u>ehtah deh* |
| | | *tooreestah* |
| tourist class | la clase turista | *lah klahseh tooreestah* |
| Tourist Information | la oficina de | *lah ohfeeseenah deh* |
| office | (información y) | *(eenfohrmahsyohn ee)* |
| | turismo | *tooreesmoh* |
| tourist menu | el menú turístico | *ehl mehnoo* |
| | | *tooreesteekoh* |
| tow | remolcar | *rehmohlkahr* |
| tow cable | el cable de | *ehl kahbleh deh* |
| | remolque | *rehmohlkeh* |
| towel | la toalla | *lah tohahlyah* |
| tower | la torre | *lah tohrreh* |
| town hall | el ayuntamiento | *ehl ahyoontahmyehntoh* |
| town/city | la ciudad | *lah syoodahdh* |
| toys | los juguetes | *lohs hooguehtehs* |
| traffic | el tráfico | *ehl trahfeekoh* |
| traffic light | el semáforo | *ehl sehmahfohroh* |
| trailer | la caravana | *lah kahrahbahnah* |
| | casa rodante | *kahsah rohdahnteh* |
| trailer tent | el remolque tienda | *ehl rehmohlkeh* |
| | | *tyehndah* |
| train | el tren | *ehl trehn* |
| train ticket | el boleto de tren | *ehl bohlehtoh deh trehn* |
| train timetable | la guía de trenes | *lah geeah deh trehnehs* |

| translate | traducir | trahdooseer |
| travel (verb) | viajar | byahhahr |
| travel agent | la agencia de viajes | lah ahhehnsyah deh byahhehs |
| travel guide | la guía | lah geeah |
| traveler | el pasajero | ehl pahsahhehroh |
| traveler's check | el cheque de viajero | ehl chehkeh deh byahhehroh |
| treatment | el tratamiento | ehl trahtahmyehntoh |
| triangle | el triángulo | ehl treeahngooloh |
| trim | cortar las puntas | kohrtahr lahs poontahs |
| trip | el paseo, la excursión | ehl pahsehoh,lah ehxkoorsyohn |
| trouble | la molestia | lah mohlehstyah |
| trousers (long, short) | los pantalones (cortos, largos) | lohs pahntahlohnehs (kohrtohs,lahrgohs) |
| trout | la trucha | lah troochah |
| truck | el camión | ehl kahmyohn |
| trustworthy | digno de confianza | deegnoh deh kohnfyahnsah |
| try on (clothes) | probarse | prohbahrseh |
| T-shirt | la camiseta | lah kahmeesehtah |
| tube | el tubo | ehl tooboh |
| Tuesday | el martes | ehl mahrtehs |
| tumble drier | la secadora | lah sehkahdohrah |
| tuna | el atún | ehl ahtoon |
| tunnel | el túnel | ehl toonehl |
| turn | la vez | lah behs |
| TV | la televisión | lah tehlehbeesyohn |
| tv and radio guide | la guía de radio y televisión | lah gheeah deh rahdyoh ee tehlehbeesyohn |
| tweezers | los alicates | lohs ahleekahtehs |

## U

| ugly | feo | fehoh |
| umbrella | el paraguas | ehl pahrahgwahs |
| under | abajo, debajo de | ahbahhoh, dehbahhoh deh |
| underpants | los calzoncillos | lohs kahlsohnseelyohs |
| understand | entender | ehntehndehr |
| underwear | la ropa interior | lah rohpah eentehryohr |
| undress (verb) | desvestirse | dehsbehsteerseh |
| unemployed | sin trabajo | seen trahbahjoh |
| uneven | desigual | dehseegwahl |
| university | la universidad | lah ooneebehrseedahd |
| unleaded | sin plomo | seen plohmoh |
| urgent | urgente | oorhehnteh |
| urine | la orina | lah ohreenah |
| usually | por lo general | pohr loh hehnehrahl |

## V

| vacate | desalojar | dehsahlohhahr |
| vaccinate | vacunarse | bahkoonahrseh |
| vagina | la vagina | lah bahheenah |
| vaginal infection | la infección vaginal | lah eenfehksyohn bahheenal |

| valid | válido | bahleedoh |
| valley | el valle | ehl bahlyeh |
| valuable | costoso | kohstohsoh |
| van | la furgoneta | lah foorgohnehtah |
| vanilla | la vainilla | lah baheeneelyah |
| vase | el florero | ehl flohrehroh |
| vaseline | la vaselina | lah bahsehleenah |
| veal | la carne de ternera | lah kahrneh deh tehrnehrah |
| vegetable soup | la sopa de verduras | lah sohpah deh behrdoorahs |
| vegetables | la verdura | lah behrdoorah |
| vegetarian | vegetariano | beh<u>h</u>ehtahryahnoh |
| vein | la vena | lah vehnah |
| vending machine | la máquina automática | lah mahkeenah ahootohmahteekah |
| venereal disease | la enfermedad venérea | lah ehnfehrmehdah behnehrehah |
| via | pasando por | pahsahndoh pohr |
| video recorder | el video | ehl beedehoh |
| video tape | la cinta de vídeo | lah seentah deh beedehoh |
| view | la vista | lah beestah |
| village | el pueblo | ehl pwehbloh |
| visa | la visa | lah beesah |
| visit (verb) | visitar | beeseetahr |
| visit | la visita | lah beeseetah |
| vitamin tablets | las tabletas de vitaminas | lahs tahblehtahs deh beetahmeenahs |
| vitamins | la vitamina | lah beetahmeenah |
| volcano | el volcán | ehl bohlkahn |
| volleyball (play) | jugar al vóleibol | <u>h</u>oogahr ahl bohleheebohl |
| vomit (verb) | vomitar | bohmeetahr |

# W

| wait (verb) | esperar | ehspehrahr |
| waiter | el mesero/mozo | ehl mehsehroh/mohsoh |
| waiting room | la sala de espera | lah sahlah deh ehspehrah |
| wake up (verb) | despertar | dehspehrtahr |
| walk | el paseo | ehl pahsehoh |
| walk (take a) | salir a caminar | sahleer ah kahmeenahr |
| walk (verb) | caminar | kahmeenahr |
| wallet | la cartera | lah kahrtehrah |
| wardrobe | el guardarropa | ehl gwahrdahrrohpah |
| warm | caliente | kahlyehnteh |
| warn | avisar, llamar | ahbeesahr, lyahmahr |
| warning | el aviso | ehl ahbeesoh |
| wash (verb) | lavar | lahbahr |
| washing (dirty) | la ropa sucia | lah rohpah soosyah |
| washing line | la cuerda de colgar la ropa | lah kwehrdah deh kohlgahr lah rohpah |
| washing machine | la lavadora | lah lahbahdohrah |
| wasp | la avispa | lah ahbeespah |
| watch | el reloj | ehl rehlohh |
| water | el agua | ehl ahgwah |

Word list

15

155

| water ski | el esquí acuático | *ehl ehskee ahkwahteekoh* |
| waterproof | impermeable | *eempehrmehahbleh* |
| wave-pool | la piscina con oleaje | *lah peesseenah kohn ohlehahheh* |
| way (means) | el remedio | *ehl rehmehdyoh* |
| way (on the) | en el camino | *ehn ehl kahmeenoh* |
| way | el lado | *ehl lahdoh* |
| we | nosotros | *nohsohtrohs* |
| weak | débil | *dehbeel* |
| weather | el tiempo | *ehl tyehmpoh* |
| weather forecast | el pronóstico del tiempo | *ehl prohnohsteekoh dehl tyehmpoh* |
| wedding | la boda | *lah bohdah* |
| Wednesday | el miércoles | *ehl myehrkohlehs* |
| week | la semana | *lah sehmahnah* |
| weekend | el fin de semana | *ehl feen deh sehmahnah* |
| weekend duty | la guardia de fin de semana | *lah gwahrdyah deh feen deh sehmahnah* |
| weekly ticket | el abono semanal | *ehl ahbohnoh sehmahnahl* |
| welcome | bienvenido | *byehnbehneedoh* |
| well | bien, bueno | *byehn, bwehnoh* |
| west | el oeste | *ehl ohehsteh* |
| wet | mojado | *mohahdoh* |
| wet (weather) | lluvioso | *lyoobyohsoh* |
| wetsuit | el traje de surf | *ehl trahheh deh soorf* |
| what? | ¿qué? | *keh?* |
| wheel | la rueda | *lah rwehdah* |
| wheelchair | la silla de ruedas | *lah seelyah deh rwehdahs* |
| when? | ¿cuándo? | *kwahndoh?* |
| where? | ¿dónde? | *dohndeh?* |
| which? | ¿cuál? | *kwahl?* |
| whipped cream | el chantilly | *ehl chahnteelyee* |
| whipping cream | la nata/crema para batir | *lah nahtah/krehmah pahrah bahteer* |
| white | blanco | *blahnkoh* |
| who? | ¿quién? | *kyehn?* |
| whole wheat | integral | *eentehgrahl* |
| whole wheat bread | el pan integral | *ehl pahn eentehgrahl* |
| why? | ¿por qué? | *pohr keh?* |
| wide-angle lens | el objetivo gran angular | *ehl obhehteeboh grahn ahngoolahr* |
| widow | la viuda | *lah byoodah* |
| widower | el viudo | *ehl byoodoh* |
| wife | la esposa | *lah ehspohsah* |
| wind | el viento | *ehl byehntoh* |
| windbreak | la protección contra el viento | *lah prohtehksyohn kohntrah ehl byehntoh* |
| windmill | el molino | *ehl mohleenoh* |
| window | la ventanilla, la ventana | *lah behntahneelyah, lah behntahnah* |
| windshield wiper | el limpiaparabrisas | *ehl leempyahpahrah-breesahs* |

| | | |
|---|---|---|
| wine | el vino | *ehl beenoh* |
| wine list | la carta de vinos | *lah kahrtah deh beenohs* |
| winter | el invierno | *ehl eenbyehrnoh* |
| witness | el testigo | *ehl tehsteegoh* |
| woman | la mujer | *lah moo<u>h</u>ehr* |
| wood | la madera | *lah mahdehrah* |
| wool | la lana | *lah lahnah* |
| word | la palabra | *lah pahlahbrah* |
| work | el trabajo | *ehl trahbah<u>h</u>oh* |
| working day | el día laborable | *ehl deeah lahbohrahbleh* |
| worn/used | gastado | *gahstahdoh* |
| worried | inquieto | *eenkyehtoh* |
| wound | la herida | *lah ehreedah* |
| wrap (verb) | envolver | *ehnbohlbehr* |
| wrench (openended) | la llave (de boca) | *lah lyahbeh (deh bohkah)* |
| wrench | la llave de tuercas | *lah lyahbeh deh twehrkahs* |
| wrist | la muñeca | *lah moonyehkah* |
| write | escribir | *ehskreebeer* |
| write down | anotar | *ahnohtahr* |
| writing pad | el bloc (cuadriculado, a rayas) | *ehl blohk(kwahdreekoolahdoh, ah rahyahs)* |
| writing paper | el papel de escribir | *ehl pahpehl deh ehskreebeer* |
| written | por carta | *pohr kahrtah* |
| wrong | mal, equivocado | *mahl, ehkeebohkahdoh* |

## Y

| | | |
|---|---|---|
| yacht | el yate | *ehl yahteh* |
| year | el año | *ehl anyoh* |
| yellow | amarillo | *ahmahreelyoh* |
| yes | sí | *see* |
| yes, please | con (mucho) gusto/ sí, por favor | *kohn (moochoh) goostoh/see, pohr fahbohr* |
| yesterday | ayer | *ahyehr* |
| yogurt | el yogur | *ehl yohgoor* |
| you (formal) | usted | *oostehdh* |
| you too | igualmente | *eegwahlmehnteh* |
| youth hostel | el albergue juvenil | *ehl ahlbehrgueh <u>h</u>oobehneel* |

## Z

| | | |
|---|---|---|
| zip | la cremallera | *lah krehmahlyehrah* |
| | el cierre | *ehl syehrreh* |
| zip code | el código postal | *ehl cohdeegoh pohstahl* |
| zoo | el parque zoológico | *ehl pahrkeh sohohloh<u>h</u>eekoh* |
| zucchini | el calabacín | *ehl kahlahbahseen* |

# **B**asic grammar

## **1** The article

Spanish nouns and adjectives are divided into 2 categories: masculine and feminine. The definite article (the) is **el** or **la**. Most masculine words end in **o** and most feminine words end in **a**.

**el** is used before masculine nouns, as in **el tren** (the train)
**la** is used before feminine nouns, as in **la playa** (the beach)
**el** is also used before feminine nouns beginning with the vowel **a**, as in **el agua** (water).

Other examples are:

| | | | |
|---|---|---|---|
| **el techo** | the roof | **la casa** | the house |
| **el hambre** | hunger | **el alma** | the soul |

The plural of **el** is **los**; the plural of **la** is **las**.

In the case of the indefinite article (**a, an**):

**un** is used before masculine nouns, as in **un libro** (a book).

**una** is used before feminine nouns, as in **una mesa** (a table).

The plural is constructed by adding s, as in **unos camiones** (some trucks), **unas tazas** (some cups).

Other examples are:

| | | | |
|---|---|---|---|
| **un padre** | a father | **una madre** | a mother |
| **un hombre** | a man | **una mujer** | a woman |
| **unos hombres** | men | **unas mujeres** | women |

## **2** The plural

The plural of Spanish nouns and adjectives ends in **s**. Examples are:

| singular | plural |
|---|---|
| **el avión** (the plane) | **los aviones** |
| **la manzana** (the apple) | **las manzanas** |

## **3** Personal pronouns

| | |
|---|---|
| I | **yo** |
| You | **Usted/tu** |
| He/she/it | **él/ella** |
| We | **nosotros/nosotras** |
| You | **Ustedes** |
| They | **ellos/ellas** |

It is **always** prefeerable to use **Usted** (you formal) rather than **tu** (informal). **Usted** (sg) and **ustedes** (pl) take the third person of the verb:

e.g. **Usted sabe/Ustedes saben**     you know

## 4 Possessive pronouns

|  | masculine/feminine | plural |
|---|---|---|
| my | **mi** | **mis** |
| your | **tu** | **tus** |
| his/her/its | **su** | **sus** |
| our | **nuestro/nuestra** | **nuestros/nuestras** |
| your | **su** | **sus** |
| their | **su** | **sus** |

They agree with the object they modify, e.g. our house = **nuestra casa**.

## 5 Verbs

Note: pronouns are only used with verbs when absolutely necessary or to emphasise.

| **hablar** | to speak |
|---|---|
| **hablo** | I speak |
| **hablas** | you speak |
| **habla** | he/she/you speak |
| **hablamos** | we speak |
| **hablan** | they/you speak |

Here are some useful verbs:

| **ser** | **estar** (to be) |
|---|---|
| **soy** | **estoy** |
| **eres** | **estás** |
| **es** | **está** |
| **somos** | **estamos** |
| **son** | **están** |

Note: **estar** is used with places and also means a temporary state, e.g. **el hotel está en la plaza**, (the hotel is in the square), **la niña está cansada** (the little girl is tired).

| **tener** (to have) | **hacer** (to do/make) |
|---|---|
| **tengo** | **hago** |
| **tienes** | **haces** |
| **tiene** | **hace** |
| **tenemos** | **hacemos** |
| **tienen** | **hacen** |

| **ir** (to go) | **ver** (to see) |
|---|---|
| **voy** | **veo** |
| **vas** | **ves** |
| **va** | **ve** |
| **vamos** | **vemos** |
| **van** | **ven** |

Negatives are formed by putting no before the verb:
e.g. **no entiendo**, I do not understand; **no oigo**, I cannot hear.

## 6 Basic prepositions

**a** = to, e.g. **voy a Madrid, voy al mercado**.
**en**= in or at, e.g. **estoy en la tienda, estoy en casa**.